# Women, Democracy, and Globalization in North America

## A Comparative Study

Jane Bayes
Patricia Begné
Laura Gonzalez
Lois Harder
Mary Hawkesworth
Laura Macdonald

PERSPECTIVES IN COMPARATIVE POLITICS

Published by Palgrave Macmillan

*The Struggle Against Corruption: A Comparative Study*
Edited by Roberta Ann Johnson

*Women, Democracy, and Globalization in North America: A Comparative Study*
By Jane Bayes, Patricia Begné, Laura Gonzalez, Lois Harder, Mary Hawkesworth, and Laura Macdonald

*Politics and Ethnicity: A Comparative Study*
By Joseph Rudolph

*Immigration Policy and the Politics of Immigration: A Comparative Study*
By Martin Schain

*Politics, Policy, and Health Care: A Comparative Study*
By Paul Godt

*In memory of*
*Rita Mae Kelly*

WOMEN, DEMOCRACY, AND GLOBALIZATION IN NORTH AMERICA
© Jane Bayes, Patricia Begné, Laura Gonzalez, Lois Harder,
Mary Hawkesworth, Laura Macdonald, 2006.

First published in 2006 by
PALGRAVE MACMILLAN™
175 Fifth Avenue, New York, N.Y. 10010 and
Houndmills, Basingstoke, Hampshire, England RG21 6XS
Companies and representatives throughout the world.

PALGRAVE MACMILLAN is the global academic imprint of the Palgrave
Macmillan division of St. Martin's Press, LLC and of Palgrave Macmillan Ltd.
Macmillan® is a registered trademark in the United States, United Kingdom
and other countries. Palgrave is a registered trademark in the European
Union and other countries.

ISBN 1–4039–7088–2
ISBN 1–4039–7089–0 (pbk.)

Library of Congress Cataloging-in-Publication Data

Women, democracy, and globalization in North America :
A Comparative Study / Jane Bayes . . . [et al.].
      p. cm.
   Includes bibliographical references and index.
   ISBN 1–4039–7088–2—ISBN 1–4039–7089–0 (pbk.)
    1. Women and democracy—North America. 2. Women in politics—
North America. 3. Women's rights—North America. 4. Women in
development—North America. 5. Globalization—Social aspects.
   I. Bayes, Jane H., 1939–

HQ1236.5.N7W66 2006
320'.082'097—dc22                                          2005048700

A catalogue record for this book is available from the British Library.

Design by Newgen Imaging Systems (P) Ltd., Chennai, India.

First edition: January 2006

10  9  8  7  6  5  4  3  2  1

Printed in the United States of America.

# CONTENTS

# LIST OF TABLES AND

## FIGURES

### Tables

### Figures

# ACKNOWLEDGMENTS

A book by six authors from three nations is highly unusual in contemporary academic publishing. In tracing the genesis of this transnational collaboration, all trails lead to one scholar, Rita Mae Kelly, who at various stages in her career befriended and mentored all of the authors of this book. A versatile and inspiring feminist scholar and a talented administrator, Rita Mae Kelly helped shape the field of women and politics research prior to her untimely death in 2001. We dedicate this book to Rita, in loving memory of all that she has been to us and to so many others.

With the assistance of distinguished Japanese political scientist Kinhide Mushakoji, Rita Mae Kelly recruited an international team of anthropologists, economists, psychologists, political scientists, and sociologists to launch a research initiative on Gender, Globalization, and Democratization under the auspices of the International Social Science Council (ISSC), a UNESCO funded nonprofit organization, whose mission is to develop interdisciplinary and transnational research networks to address contemporary policy issues of critical importance. The earliest discussions of this collaborative project occurred at the 1997 International Political Science Association meetings in Korea.

Following these early discussions, Rita Mae Kelly, Jane Bayes, Patricia Begné, and Janine Brodie developed a grant proposal, "Gender and Governance: An Integrated North American Studies Curriculum," to support the exchange of students and scholars, to integrate curricula at universities in the three countries, and to develop new courses and course materials on gender and globalization and on women's political participation in Mexico, Canada, and the United States. This book is the culmination of a five-year North American Mobility Program (NAMP) grant on Gender, Globalization, and Democracy from the Fund for the Improvement of Post Secondary Education in the United States in cooperation with separate grants from the governments of Mexico and Canada. The grants provided for research, curriculum development, and the exchange of students between seven universities in North America including the Universidad de Guanajuato, Instituto Tecnológico y de Estudios Superiores de Occidente (ITESO) in Guadelajara, Carleton University in Ottawa, University of Alberta in Edmonton, the University of Texas at Dallas, California State University Northridge, and Rutgers University-New

Brunswick. Each of the authors served as a director of the program at her respective university and met at least once a year with other directors to share research, curriculum ideas, and issues pertaining to the administration of a transnational grant.

This book is a product of our many exchanges over the five years with one another and with others closely involved in the program; in particular, Olga Aikin (ITESO), and Janine Brodie (University of Alberta), as well as Breny Mendoza (California State University, Northridge), Sheila Piñeres and Jennifer S. Holmes, both of the University of Texas at Dallas, and Adriana Cortés Jiménez of Irapuato, Mexico.

Numerous people have been helpful in supporting the collaborative work of the NAMP project. Sylvia Crowder at the U.S. Department of Education has provided invaluable guidance and counsel throughout the grant, but especially after the untimely death of our project director, Rita Mae Kelly, in 2001. We are also grateful to the Department of Human Resources and Development Canada and the Secretaría de Educación Pública of Mexico for their support and guidance. Our special thanks go to Alexandra Cole of California State University, Northridge, and Simon Fass of the University of Texas at Dallas who served as evaluators of the program.

Each of the authors also owes a debt of gratitude to the many administrators on our respective campuses whose work made this project possible. They include, but are not limited to, Isabel Valdez at ITESO, Martin Pantoja at the University of Guanajuato, Scott Perez, John Charles, and Mary Baxton at California State University Northridge, Joanne Givand at Rutgers University, Laura Chrabolowsky at Carleton University, and Tara Mish at the University of Alberta.

Each author has benefited from the editorial comments and the unique perspectives of her coauthors. Special thanks are due to Laura Macdonald for her assistance in translating chapter 2, and to Jane Bayes and Mary Hawkesworth for preparing the final version of the manuscript for publication. The authors also thank Joseph Bayes and Kyle Bayes for their help in formatting the figures.

For sustaining us and enriching our lives throughout the research and writing process, we extend our heartfelt thanks to our families.

Jane Bayes
Patricia Begné
Laura Gonzalez
Lois Harder
Mary Hawkesworth
Laura Macdonald

April 2005

*Women, Democracy, and Globalization in North America* by Jane Bayes, Patricia Begné, Laura Gonzalez, Lois Harder, Mary Hawkesworth, and Laura Macdonald is a remarkable demonstration of the power of the comparative method employed by authors who choose a topic of great importance and timeliness, who do not flinch before the task of rendering the complex palpable and clear, and who know how to organize.

All books in this series, Perspectives in Comparative Politics, are designed to be scholarly, topic-oriented studies of a particular problem, accessible to upper-division students as well as to graduate students and professors. They begin with an introductory chapter, covering the relevant literature and laying out the problem, and end with a concluding chapter, summarizing what has been learned about the problems in the three or more nations covered, and elucidating the important comparative lessons learned. This book follows that format. It offers parallel consideration of its topic in three nations: Mexico, Canada, and the United States.

What makes this book different, however, is the nature of the topic chosen and the remarkable teamwork of its six authors. Working together in a series of workshops, they have recognized the manifold nature of the question at hand. Discussing the role of women in politics in North America not only means discussing the role women have played in the struggle for a meaningful democracy, in general, but also the efforts women have made—and must continue to make—to ensure that they themselves will someday have a full and equal part in that democracy. Furthermore, the obstacles to be overcome in achieving gender equality have changed dramatically in the past several decades with the advance of globalization. The nature of the problems faced today are thus profoundly different from what they were a few decades ago, and different in every nation.

Finding a way to deal with such complex realities in a straightforward and easily comprehensible way is a challenge before which many would have faltered. But these authors have had long experience in writing, individually and sometimes in combination, about these problems. Furthermore, they are all strong teachers. They know the audience they are seeking to reach, and they know how to do it. And perhaps most important of all, they have had and have used the skills necessary to draw from each other, to make diversity of expertise and approach a strong advantage, while at the same time smoothly blending each author's contribution into a cohesive whole. The result is little short of a tour de force.

Of course it is always important to consider how women's political activity has changed and multiplied, in general terms. But by linking these developments to the themes of democracy, the shifting meanings of gender, and globalization, these authors go far beyond the mere recounting of the history of the role of women in politics in these three states. They have produced a volume that advances and deepens our understanding of what it means to be a woman and a political actor in today's world. I am very pleased indeed to have this book join the series Perspectives in Comparative Politics.

—Kay Lawson

# PART 1

## *Introduction*

# CHAPTER 1

## Introduction

### JANE BAYES AND MARY HAWKESWORTH

The story of North America is often told in terms of conquest, colonization, exploitation, and extermination of indigenous peoples, territorial wars, revolutionary wars, and finally nation building as Canada, Mexico, and the United States declared their independence, drafted constitutions, and undertook the project of self-governance. How did women figure in these political and economic transformations? What roles have they played in the creation and survival of the three distinctive nations of North America? How have they contributed to the practices of democracy in these states? How are their economic, political, and familial responsibilities being transformed in the current period of globalization?

This book explores these issues. Written jointly by scholars from Canada, Mexico, and the United States, the book seeks to illuminate various dimensions of women's political and economic contributions to the development and consolidation of their nations. By placing women's lives at the center of analysis, the book raises important questions about the nature and extent of democracy in these three states. It also explores gendered effects of globalization, that is, how changing economic, political, cultural, and technological developments affect men and women in particular nations differently.

## Globalization

The nature and meaning of globalization have been subjects of intensive debate among scholars (Hardt and Negri 2000; Held et al. 1999; Hirst and Thompson 1999). Perhaps the broadest definition construes globalization as "the spatial extension of social relations across the globe" (James 2004, 29). Scholars suggest that the ancient Roman Empire, which spanned 800 years, fifteenth- and sixteenth-century European colonialism, and nineteenth- and twentieth-century capitalist imperialism are various manifestations of globalization understood in this way, because in each instance a particular social, economic, and political order tried to control the known world.

Other scholars suggest that globalization is linked to the emergence of an understanding of the world as a sphere or globe and the "age of discovery" in which European explorers set out to map and claim territories on the far side of the world (Robertson 1992). Within this frame, globalization is typically traced to the fifteenth century and the efforts of the Spanish, French, British, Portuguese, Dutch, Swedish, and Germans to conquer and colonize North, Central, and South America, Africa, the Middle East, and South and East Asia. In addition to the acquisition of territory, this form of globalization is linked to the extraction of natural resources and the exploitation of indigenous peoples by European powers, which contributed to the accumulation of vast wealth and which set the stage for the emergence of capitalism, a mode of economic production and exchange that privileges profit making as its primary objective.

Still others have linked globalization to "modernity," to "Enlightenment" beliefs about the relationship between reason and progress, and to the emergence of new forms of individualism and arguments for self-governance associated with the American and French revolutions in the late eighteenth century (Giddens 1990). Breaking with feudal religious, economic, and political traditions, proponents of "modernity" advocated the application of human reason to the resolution of human problems and to the promotion of progress across all domains of human endeavor (Bayes and Tohidi 2001; 17–60). Associated with the development of experimental science and technological innovation, with industrialization and the development of global trade networks, and with the celebration of the "civilizing effects" of democratization, "modernity" has also been linked with a "foundational ethnocentrism," a deep and abiding form of racism which masks its intricate ties to the slave trade and colonial exploitation (Gilroy 1992).

Yet other scholars advance a conception of globalization tied to much more recent history, restricting its application to developments that are traced to the last three decades of the twentieth century. In this view, globalization refers to ongoing and often interrelated economic, political, cultural, and technological transformations that are reshaping the contemporary world. Chief among these is the "death of distance" occasioned by technological developments in communications—telephone, television, Internet, and transportation (Cairncross 1997). Others emphasize the "network society," referring to the changed nature of production, distribution, and communication (Castells 1996). In the economic sphere, some suggest that this phase of globalization began with the demise of the Bretton Woods Agreement in 1971 and the creation of a new global financial architecture, one that brought with it new networked and flexible ways of organizing production to replace the post–World War II Keynesian institutional regulatory structures and the "Fordist" assembly-line production methods of the 1945–1970 era (Young 2001). Still others suggest that the collapse of the Soviet Union and the end of the Cold War in 1989–1991 mark the beginning of an expansion of capitalist economic systems around the world, an expansion led by the United States that has produced growing inequality within and between nations (Johnson 2004; Todd 2002). In the political domain, globalization is manifest in the spread of competitive elections and "democratization," decentralization of power within nation–states, neoliberal policies of privatization and deregulation, the growing power of transnational actors (often in conjunction with U.S. hegemony), and the emergence of global civil society. Fast-breaking developments in the spheres of information and communication technology provide the infrastructure essential to these economic and political transformations and create opportunities for new modes of production, finance, transnational mobilization, and cultural transformation.

## Globalization, Democracy, and Women

Several scholars have investigated the "globalization of democracy," understood in terms of the spread of competitive elections and liberal democratic institutions throughout the world (Diamond 1993; Huntington 1991). Samuel Huntington identifies three waves of democratization: the first beginning in 1828 with the expansion of white male suffrage in the United States; a second wave that emerged after World War II and continued until 1962; and a third wave beginning in 1974 and extending to the present. Claims concerning the most recent wave of democratization often rest on data collected by Freedom House, a nongovernmental organization that has attempted to index democratization since 1972, ranking countries according to the political and civil rights they afford their citizens. According to their count, 44 of the 100 nations existing in 1973 could be considered "independent, democratic, and free." That number had increased to 65 by the end of 1990, 75 by the end of 1991, and 89 of 130 countries at the end of 2004 (Freedom House 2005).

Feminist scholars, who analyze democratic practices from the standpoint of women, have noted that the conception of democracy circulating within globalization studies is particularly "thin" (Kelly et al. 2001). Focusing on competitive electoral practices, the rule of law, and the development of civil society, these discussions of democratization do not engage the fact that even in the most advanced democracies, women, the majority of the world's population, have been, and continue to be, excluded from full participation in governance. While women have made progress in many countries in gaining the vote and some of the privileges of citizenship, they remain at great remove from equal power in democratic decision making. Gender and racial hierarchies within these societies, produced and reinforced by ideologies, religions, family structures, and long-standing economic and political institutions (both public and private), perpetuate ongoing practices of marginalization and exclusion. In recognition of the profound effects of racial and gender stratification, feminist scholars have suggested that democratic ideals of equality, inclusion, and popular decision making remain elusive. In the words of Carole Pateman (1989, 210): "For feminists, democracy has never existed; women have never been and still are not admitted as full and equal members and citizens in any country known as a democracy."

The complex processes associated with globalization during the past three decades are, however, reshaping power relations in multiple ways. Changes in technology that facilitate rapid communications and instant finance, changes in the global forms of production linked to the "feminization" of labor forces in the manufacturing, agricultural and service sectors, improved forms of transportation that facilitate mass migration and sexual trafficking, changes in trade that transform processes of production and consumption, and changes in the policy priorities of states—all have an impact on race and gender hierarchies within and across states. These changes influence the prospects for building "thicker" forms of democracy, while also posing challenges to the possibility of inclusive democracy within nation-states. Transnational feminist activists are pressing for "thicker" democracies, combining grassroots mobilizations with the leverage of international institutions to advance "gender mainstreaming," which enables women to participate fully and equally in all aspects of governance. Yet these feminist initiatives to enhance democratic participation are facing powerful challenges from male-dominated state institutions, political parties, and international financial institutions pressing neoliberal policy priorities and unregulated market practices. These practices heighten gender-based inequalities in education, employment, and health care, while exacerbating the feminization of poverty.

Feminist scholars who investigate the changing dynamics of globalization and democratization have developed new analytical tools to help illuminate how gender operates as a site of power and to explicate the mechanisms within traditional scholarship that "naturalize" and "normalize" gender hierarchies, rendering raced and gendered power relations invisible. Drawing upon the conception of an "analytic category" developed by Imre Lakatos (1970), feminist scholars have deployed gender as an analytical tool. In contrast to popular understandings of gender as cultural constructions of masculinity and femininity, gender as an analytic category functions as a heuristic device that illuminates areas for inquiry, frames questions for investigation, identifies puzzles in need of exploration, and provides concepts, definitions, and hypotheses to guide research (Hawkesworth 1997).

In an important and influential essay, Joan Scott (1986, 1067) defined gender as a concept involving two interrelated but analytically distinct parts: "Gender is a constitutive element of social relationships based on perceived differences between the sexes, and gender is a primary way of signifying relationships of power." In explicating gender as a constitutive element of social relationships, Scott emphasized that gender operates in multiple fields, including culturally available symbols, normative concepts, social institutions and organizations, and subjective identities (pp. 1067–1068). Attuned to the structuring power of gender in these various domains, feminist scholars investigate in concrete circumstances how inequalities between men and women are produced, reproduced, contested, and transformed over time. According to Scott (p. 1070), gender is a useful category of analysis precisely because it "provides a way to decode meaning" and to illuminate how gender hierarchies are created, preserved, and changed through the complex interaction of norms, symbols, interpersonal relations, social practices, and religious, economic, and political institutions.

Sandra Harding has also advanced an account of gender as an analytic category. "In virtually every culture, gender difference is a pivotal way in which humans identify themselves as persons, organize social relations, and symbolize meaningful natural and social events and processes" (1986, 18). Thus Harding argues that gender must be understood as "an analytic category within which humans think about and organize their social activity rather than as a natural consequence of sex difference, or even merely as a social variable assigned to individual people in different ways from culture to culture" (p. 17). Recognizing that gender appears only in culturally specific forms, Harding, like Scott, emphasized that gender as an analytic category illuminates crucial cultural processes in need of further investigation.

> Gendered social life is produced through three distinct processes: it is the result of assigning dualistic gender metaphors to various perceived dichotomies that rarely have anything to do with sex differences (gender symbolism); it is the consequence of appealing to these gender dualisms to organize social activity, dividing necessary social activities between different groups of humans (gender structure); it is a form of socially constructed individual identity only imperfectly correlated with either the reality or the perception of sex differences (individual gender). (pp. 17–18)

In this book, we will be using gender as an analytic category in order to investigate changing dimensions of gender symbolism, gender structure, and gender power in the three nations of North America as globalization progresses from early modes of conquest and settlement through the development of capitalist and increasingly interconnected economies. We will also explore women's continuing struggles for democratic inclusion in these states, which claim the name of democracy but which realize the promise of democracy only imperfectly.

Contradicting the optimistic predictions of "neoliberals" and "neo-Kantian cosmopolitans" that economic globalization will necessarily promote global democracy, this book uses the complex gender transformations associated with globalization as a way of raising critical questions concerning the empirical effects of globalization on democracy within three nations in North America. Reiterating arguments first developed by modernization theorists, neoliberal and cosmopolitan advocates of globalization insist that the liberalization of markets, deregulation by states, and unrestricted flows of capital, goods, services, and (to a lesser extent) labor, will promote democracy. Using gender as the analytical lens through which to examine globalization, this book investigates a number of processes associated with globalization that diminish rather than enhance the prospects for democracy. Analyses of the changing condition of women under globalization illuminate growing inequalities among women within particular nation-states, as well as growing inequalities between women in the North and women in the global South, thereby raising critical questions concerning the relationship between globalization and democracy. If current globalization processes are generating increased inequality within and between countries, can "thin" democracies fulfill their promise of equal citizenship?

A second set of concerns focuses on the changing role of the state under globalization. Since the eighteenth century, citizens, social activists, and revolutionaries have engaged the state in order to expand the rights and immunities afforded to citizens. If, as some scholars suggest, globalization is undermining state authority, diminishing the sovereignty of nation-states and state democratic institutions, how can globalization be leading to greater "democratization" of the world? If, on the other hand, the erosion of certain dimensions of state sovereignty coincides with the increasingly invasive regulation of other aspects of citizens' lives (e.g., regulation of poor women's labor and sexuality), does globalization contribute to democracy? One might alternatively ask, democracy for whom? If neoliberal states and states responding to structural adjustment policies imposed by international financial institutions are growing more responsive to multinational corporations than to citizens, how exactly is globalization contributing to transparent and accountable democratic practices?

A final set of concerns arises from attention to the differential effects of globalization on states that are differently positioned within the global economy. Are nations that have advocated and promoted neoliberal policies, like the United States, crafting globalization in ways that heighten the power, privilege, and wealth of a particular sector of the human population? Are states that have cultivated a stronger social-welfare tradition, like Canada, able to protect their citizens from some of the worst consequences of globalization in ways that other states cannot or will not? How do the rigid constraints of structural adjustment imposed on developing nations like Mexico compromise the state's ability to determine its own future via democratic practices? What does the unequal dispersion of power within the global economic and political system portend for democratization?

This book explores these complex issues through the comparative analysis of women's political and economic struggles in the three countries of North America: Mexico, a nation with a long history of colonization and a much more recent emergence of competitive democratic elections; Canada, a relatively wealthy, moderately social democratic nation; and the United States, one of the wealthiest nations in the world and one of the strongest proponents of neoliberalism.

## Why Mexico, Canada, and the United States?

Within political science, most comparative studies attempt to compare countries that are somewhat alike in terms of size, political power, economic power, history, or geography. In certain respects, this book deviates from that pattern. What, then, can be learned from comparing a country like Canada, which has a population of 32 million people (the size of the state of California), a gross domestic product (GDP) of C$957 billion, and a per capita income of C$29,700, with a behemoth like the United States, which has a population of 293 million people, a GDP of almost C$11 trillion, and a per capita income of C$37,800? By the same token, why compare a relatively poor country like Mexico, with a population of 104.9 million, a GDP of C$942.2 billion, and a per capita income of C$9,000, a country in which 40 percent of the population lives in poverty—with two of the most developed and affluent nations in the world?

The importance of geography and history are obvious answers. All three countries compose the region known as North America (although in the past, Mexico's identity has hovered between North America and Central America). Canada and Mexico both have long borders with the United States, stretching across the continent. Conquest, colonization, exploitation, and the extermination of indigenous peoples characterize the histories of all three nations, although in quite different ways. Spain first conquered and colonized what is now Mexico and much of the western United States, extracting large quantities of gold and silver, while institutionalizing Spanish law and the influence of the Catholic Church. The British and French colonized Canada, extracting fish, timber, and minerals. The 13 original states of the United States were initially colonies of the British and important sites for the production and trade of sugar, rice, cotton, and rum, for the importation and reproduction of slaves, and for the early development of manufacturing. Both the United States and Mexico have had revolutionary wars of independence against the colonial powers, while Canada evolved as a British Commonwealth, although Quebec preserved strong cultural connections with France.

Canada is a bilingual country that celebrates multiculturalism. Mexico retains Spanish as its official language, although certain indigenous communities preserve their traditional languages, and the nation celebrates its "mestiza" identity. Despite its heritage as a "nation of immigrants," the United States continues to promote assimilation, with several of the most linguistically diverse states passing "English-only" legislation. The central cleavage in Canada has been related to the founding settler heritage groups, with Francophone Quebec defending its distinctive identity from the dominance of Canada's Anglophone majority. In the United States, race continues to be a signal axis of difference, while in Mexico, class cleavages continue to play a critical role in politics. Even as this brief survey of differences suggests, comparison of social, economic, and political differences among neighboring states in North America can afford insights into the intricate relations between historical legacies, strategies for nation building, institutional practices, policy outcomes, and the production, reproduction, and transformation of political identities.

The importance of geography and economic integration in an age of globalization is a second reason for comparing the three countries. The three nations are heavily interdependent economically, although that interdependence is marked by major asymmetries in wealth and power. Over the past 200 years, Mexico has had nearly half its territory conquered and annexed by the United States. Mexican labor and knowledge of ranching, agriculture, and mining were extremely important to the development of the western United States. Mexican labor has continued to be vital to the United States economy. In 1942, the U.S. government created the Bracero Program, which brought male Mexican workers to the United States to work in mines, on farms, and on railroads for a contractual period of 18 months, providing vital labor while many U.S. men were fighting overseas. The Bracero Program that continued after World War II recruited nearly 5 million Mexican men by the time it ended in 1964 (Alba 1982, 43–44). In 1965, the Border Industrial Program replaced the Bracero Program. Initially, the Border Industrial Program involved building twin plants on either side of the border. Raw materials and equipment were imported to Mexico tariff-free to be assembled by cheap Mexican labor and exported for final assembly in the "twin plant" across the border in the United States. U.S. manufacturers used this program to avoid tariffs, take advantage of cheap Mexican labor, and thereby increase their profit margins.

Although Mexico implemented an import-substitution policy in the 1960s and 1970s to avoid becoming further intertwined with its powerful neighbor to the north, the nation's growing debt, which triggered the Mexican peso crisis and devaluation of the peso in 1982, heightened Mexico's dependence on international financial institutions, which were largely controlled by the United States. Responding to pressure to open the Mexican economy to foreign direct investment, the Mexican de la Madrid government abandoned its import–substitution development policy in favor of a greater reliance on trade; and in 1986, Mexico joined the General Agreement on Tariffs and Trade (GATT). Economic integration was advanced even further with the North American Free Trade Agreement (NAFTA) of 1994.

Since the implementation of NAFTA, Mexico has become increasingly reliant on trade with the United States: 89 percent of all Mexico's exports are now sent to the United States. The Border Industrial Program expanded into the *Maquiladora* Program, which has increased foreign direct investment in *maquiladora* plants, not only along the border, but also throughout the interior of Mexico. Foreign direct investment has increased three times between 1993 and 2000, with the fastest growing and most important investments in the manufacturing sector. Between 1994 and 2004, foreign direct investment in Mexico increased from US$3.87 billion to US$13.43 billion a year. By 2000, the United States had 11,630 subsidiary companies established in Mexico, accounting for 60.4 percent of all direct foreign investment (Ministry of Finance 2000).

The U.S. economy has simultaneously become more integrated with the Canadian economy, although the two economies have always been closely linked. The Canada–U.S. Free Trade Agreement (CUFTA) in 1989 constituted the first move toward further economic integration. In 1994 the

NAFTA between Mexico, Canada, and the United States deepened and expanded the economic ties among all three states. Canada's economy has been dubbed a "staples" economy, in that its economic infrastructure and policies historically capitalized on providing the United States with "staples," such as timber, minerals, gas, and other natural resources, relying on the U.S. branch plants to supply manufactured goods. To this day, Canada's manufacturing sector remains heavily integrated with U.S. firms. Canada and the United States remain each other's largest trade partners. As Laura Macdonald notes in chapter 3 of this book, "nearly $1.9 billion in goods and services cross the Canada–U.S. border *every day*, making this the largest bilateral trade relationship in the world." In 2001, 64 percent of all imports to Canada came from the United States; and 87 percent of Canada's exports were sent to the United States. Increasing levels of foreign direct investment also help to illuminate corporate transnational integration. Canadian investment in the United States grew by 157 percent between 1990 and 2000, increasing from C$60 billion to C$154 billion. During the same period, U.S. investment in Canada grew by 121 percent (Standing Committee on Foreign Affairs 2002, 58–61).

Exploring the comparative effects of economic integration upon women in the three nations helps provide some answers to questions concerning the effects of globalization upon democratic practices. As the following chapters demonstrate, globalization's impact on women varies within and across regions, and differs significantly on the basis of race, ethnicity, nationality, class, sexuality, religion, and a host of other variables. Political and economic transformations within and across the three countries of North America instantiate many dimensions of global change currently occurring around the world. Comparing the effects of globalization in Canada, Mexico, and the United States, then, helps to illuminate the effects of globalization upon social-welfare states (Canada), liberal democratic or neoliberal states (the United States), and developing countries (Mexico).

Feminist scholars find another important reason for comparing ongoing social, economic, and political transformations in Mexico, Canada, and the United States. Comparative studies of women and politics have identified a variety of models of women's political mobilization and developed hypotheses concerning the efficacy of these alternative strategies for women's empowerment. Systematic comparison of women's political struggles for inclusion in the three nation-states can shed light on the advantages and disadvantages of a range of feminist tactics to empower women.

Throughout the better part of human history, the state has served as a mechanism of women's oppression, passing laws that bar women from the rights of citizens and laws that give men power to dictate the conditions of women's lives. In many parts of the contemporary world, states continue to represent some "men's interests" at women's expense, denying women equal representation, reproductive freedom, education, health care, and equitable treatment. Many feminist organizations, which have mobilized against oppressive state practices and rampant political corruption, continue to see the state as part of the political problem. Demanding transparency, accountability, and gender balance in good governance, women's rights advocates have advanced a vision of inclusive, democratic practices designed to meet the needs of all members of a political society.

Given such a history of oppositional politics, however, many women's organizations are cynical about the prospects for change in the present neoliberal political climate. Yet feminist activists are keenly aware that the state is still enormously powerful, possessing the authority to grant or revoke rights, to determine budgets that allocate public funds equitably or inequitably, to devise innovative or conservative public policy. Deciding when to work with government insiders to promote change, when to seek recourse to international institutions to try to leverage outside influence, and when to resort to political protest remains a huge question for women's rights activists—a question decided on a case by case basis in particular political contexts.

"Outsider tactics" may emphasize autonomous mobilizations of women at the grass roots, who seek to devise collective strategies to solve pressing social issues, while eschewing the corruption and elitism, which they associate with government at local and national levels. A second version of outsider tactics emphasizes partial engagement with the state, whether in the form of organized efforts to lobby legislators and policy makers, or to use international organizations like the UN Commission on the Status of Women to pressure governments to comply with international conventions and agreements.

Alternatively, efforts to "engender good governance" by increasing the number of women in elective and appointive offices has been another strategy to make states more responsive to women's concerns. Research on women officeholders suggests that women are more likely than their male counterparts to include policies for women and families among their top legislative priorities. In contrast to neoliberal concerns with privatization, women are more supportive of government intervention to meet the most basic human needs. Women candidates often run for office on anticorruption platforms, incorporating feminist concerns with transparency and accountability. By supporting women candidates for office and helping to secure their election, women's organizations can gain access to decision makers, a critical step in efforts to create a policy agenda for women. Both elected women officials and NGO activists emphasize that the combination of "insider/outsider" tactics can be enormously helpful for the achievement of feminist policy objectives. Women's groups working outside of government to press for radical change can give women in office leverage essential to legislative success. By mobilizing voters around particular women's issues, grassroots activists can also develop a powerful tool to hold their elective representatives to account.

A third "insider" strategy for women's political empowerment emphasizes the adoption of dramatic means to increase the number of women in elective offices by creating "quotas," which establish numerical targets for women candidates on political parties' nominating slates, or "reservation" policies, which set aside a number of seats in an elective body specifically for women. Norway was the first nation in which political parties voluntarily set quotas, stipulating that "no gender should have more than 60 percent of the slots on a party's nominating slate." Adopted in the 1980s, Norway quickly catapulted to the top rank of nations in terms of the representation of women in parliament, the cabinet, and the office of prime minister. In 1990, India established a reservation policy that set aside 33 percent of the seats in village councils for women. Since then, women who were first elected to reserved seats have successfully run for non-reserved seats with the result that more than 40 percent of local elected officials in India are women, twice the national average around the globe. Learning from these impressive accomplishments, feminists mobilized to press for quotas and reservation policies. By 2004, feminist activists had accrued impressive victories: more than 30 nations have introduced gender quotas for elections to national parliaments either by constitutional amendment or through electoral law; and major political parties in more than 50 nations have altered their party electoral practices to require that a minimum number of candidates on party electoral lists (often 30 percent) be women (Dahlerup and Freidenvall 2003).

"State feminism" is the name given to the strategy of women's rights activists who pursue insider tactics in an effort to use the state to promote women's interests and policies that redress gender subordination (Stetson and Mazur 1995). While some versions of state feminism rely upon electoral mechanisms to increase the power of women within the state, other versions emphasize the role of "femocrats" working within state agencies to produce egalitarian and women-friendly policies (Eisenstein 1996; Chappell 2002).

Comparison of women's political mobilizations in Mexico, Canada, and the United States helps to clarify when, and under what conditions, these various strategies of empowerment are chosen and the factors that contribute to their success or failure. The Mexican case studies in this book, for example, make visible the consequences of a long history of colonialism (Spain) and neocolonialism (United States) on women's political participation. They also illustrate attempts by the dominant political party to co-opt women's organizations and women's issues, and the struggle of women to mobilize autonomously for their own priorities. Conversely, the Mexican case studies also make clear how quickly progress can be made in the electoral representation of women, once the ruling parties set their mind to it and commit themselves to quotas. Colonialism and neocolonialism have structured the economy and the political system in ways that have made Mexico in need of "development" assistance. For this reason, Mexico is far more susceptible to external pressure from international organizations, such as the World Bank, the International Monetary Fund, and the United Nations, than is Canada or the United States. Ironically, however, this form of "dependency" has created opportunities that some women's rights activists in Mexico have seized, using the political spaces created by four UN World Conferences on Women to press for progressive changes for women. Through such innovative tactics, women in Mexico have secured constitutional guarantees for equality that women in the United States have failed to achieve.

The Canadian case studies powerfully demonstrate the possibilities of state feminism, ranging from the critical intervention of the Royal Commission on the Status of Women through the development of state "machinery" for women, including a Minister Responsible for Women's Issues, the Secretary of State for Women Program, and Status of Women Canada. Creating a "women's state," these institutions helped fund feminist initiatives across Canada, while also working within the government to change laws and policies to promote gender equality. Assessing the impressive policy accomplishments of state feminism in Canada, two recent studies have ranked Canada as one of the top two nations in the world with respect to gender justice (Chappell 2002; Weldon 2002). Despite a record of promoting women-friendly policies, the elective institutions of governance have not been markedly open to power sharing with women. Women in Canada have been stalled at 20 percent of the seats in the federal Parliament and in the provincial assemblies for nearly a decade. The Canadian case studies also make clear how changes in the dominant party in governance and changes in political philosophy can redound to women's detriment, suggesting that women's political empowerment is fragile and in danger of reversal. In contrast to the Mexican case, the Canadian government under Liberal Prime Minister Jean Chretien co-opted the momentum generated by the UN World Conference on Women in Beijing in 1995, using the feminist commitments to "gender mainstreaming" as a rationale to cut the funding and undercut the initiatives of the state machinery for women. Frustrated by setbacks within the nation, many Canadian feminists have shifted their attention to the international arena and contestations over globalization.

Despite their efforts to infiltrate the state and use existing institutions to advance an agenda for women, women's rights activists in the United States have been consistently marginalized by the major parties and governmental institutions. For this reason, feminists have relied on social movement and interest group "outsider" strategies, achieving far less success in changing legislation or in securing constitutional guarantees of equality than women in Canada, and making far slower progress in increasing their presence in elective offices than women in Mexico. In contrast to Mexico and Canada, the United States has not enshrined a guarantee of equality in the Constitution. Nor has it ratified the Convention to Eliminate All Forms of Discrimination Against Women (CEDAW), or the Convention on Human Rights, or any of the international conventions designed to redress gender-, race-, and class-based inequities. The United States has been particularly resistant to international pressure to improve the status and power of women in the United States. Although the United States sent an official delegation to the Beijing conference, the government has done virtually nothing to implement the Beijing Platform for Action. The report submitted by the United States for the Beijing Plus Five review, emphasized foreign policy initiatives, that is, how the United States was "advancing women's rights" in other nations. The "President's Interagency Task Force on Women," which compiled the report for the Beijing Plus Five review, was headed by a career professional from the State Department and composed of women who worked in a range of U.S. government agencies. Rather than using the review process as an opportunity for pressuring the government to address the Platform issues, they simply summarized long-standing policies as "evidence" of how well-off U.S. women are.

Comparative analysis of these three national cases on one continent, then, has a great deal to teach about the intricacies of globalization and the complexity of efforts to achieve and maintain inclusive democratic practices within contemporary nation-states. This book is divided into three parts. The first part is this introduction. Part 2 discusses women and the struggle for democracy in each of the three countries. The third part discusses what globalization has meant for each of the three nations and how globalization has impacted women within and across these national boundaries.

## Part II: Women and the Struggle for Democracy

The term "democracy" originated in ancient Greek linguistic and political practices and means "rule by the people." From the earliest experiments in Athens in the fourth-century BCE, however, the development of democratic practices have also been classed and gendered. In classical Athenian democracy, a small group of property-owning men declared themselves citizens of the political community and accorded themselves full rights of participation in decision making. But they premised their collective deliberations upon exclusionary practices. All women were excluded from rights of participation, as were non-property owning men, and men who had been captured in war, who became a slave caste within this "democratic system."

With the formation of three distinctive states in North America, constitution making coincided with the granting of special rights of participation to particular groups of men. Indeed, the proclamation of the "rights of man" led to a loss of rights for many women in these new nations. Indigenous women who held positions of power and respect within their communities lost power, status, and rights of self-determination under colonization. Settler women who owned properties also lost rights of political participation as constitutions stipulated "maleness" as well as property as conditions for political citizenship. Officially excluded from the institutions of governance, women in Canada, Mexico, and the United States struggled to create new arenas for citizenship and to win full rights of political participation. In doing this, they expanded the notion of democratic practices well beyond the activities of voting and office holding. The chapters focusing on political formations in these three nations trace these historic struggles.

During the last three decades of the twentieth century, women's political activism has grown significantly at national and transnational levels. As the average percentage of women in national legislatures hovered at 13 percent throughout the 1990s, more than 80 political parties in 35 nations including Mexico created "quotas" or reservation policies as mechanisms to increase the number of women in elective offices. As a result of this important intervention, Mexico now has a higher percentage of women in the federal Congress (23 percent) than Canada has in its federal Parliament (20 percent) and the United States has in its federal Congress (14 percent). Yet the number of women in elective offices alone cannot convey a thorough assessment of women's political activism in these three nations. Chapters 2, 3, and 4 explore the diverse political engagements of women in these three nations, examining the areas in which they have made significant gains, as well as those in which they have lost ground. These chapters also investigate a range of contemporary issues around which women are mobilizing in Mexico, Canada, and the United States.

## *Mexico*

In chapter 2, Patricia Begné provides an account of women's role in Mexican society and politics with particular attention to the impact of significant changes in the law upon women's lives, livelihoods, and rights. Prior to Spanish colonization, women's roles focused primarily on food production and preparation, weaving, sewing, marketing, and childbearing. Within some indigenous communities, women also participated as combatants and helpers in the conduct of war. Although a marked division of labor existed between men and women in many indigenous cultures, occupational segregation did not necessarily coincide with gender subordination. Women were highly respected because of their distinctive contributions to the survival of their people and their cultures.

The Spanish Conquest dramatically transformed the status of indigenous women. Imposing their system of law, including family law, on the colonial territories, the Spanish introduced new modes of political and gender hierarchy. The Spanish conquistadors sexually exploited indigenous women, killed or enslaved some men and women, and expropriated the labor of others.

From the period of conquest until 1814, the Spanish viceroy ruled Mexico. During this period, educated and religious women from Spain came to the New World, joining their countrymen in the project of colonization. The presence of Spanish women created new forms of hierarchy among women, rooted in national origin and ancestry. They also helped to disseminate new norms for womanhood, embodying an ideal of an educated woman, who could study Latin, read literature, become an artist, poet, or teacher, while always remaining under the patriarchal protection of men, whether those men were their fathers, husbands, brothers, or priests. The fate prescribed for indigenous women in this new hierarchy of women was far less noble. Most were reduced to the status of servants or prostitutes.

In 1821, Mexico declared its independence from Spain, and in 1857 established a new Constitution, but the various roles of women did not change significantly during the nineteenth century. Mexico's first years of independence were marred by conflict, border disputes, rebellions in Texas, the Texas War for Independence (1835–1836) and repeated attempts by the U.S. government to buy or annex half of the territory of Mexico, which finally culminated in a war and the Treaty of Guadalupe Hidalgo ceding the lands that were later to become Arizona, California, New Mexico, Nevada, and Utah to the United States. In Mexico, the nation's struggle to secure its own borders against outside aggression left little space for autonomous mobilization by women. Mexican women, like their male counterparts, devoted their energies to nation building and survival under extremely difficult circumstances.

Gender relations in Mexico began to change during the Mexican Revolution of 1910. During this revolutionary period, Patricia Begné notes that women of all classes became involved in a host of public activities as teachers, journalists, propagandists, messengers, transporters of arms, and spies. Building upon the opening of new political spaces in the revolution, women, especially middle-class women, assumed leadership roles in newly created organizations, including government bureaucracies, where they worked to realize their revolutionary ideals. In the Revolution, working-class women also took on new roles as camp followers, nurses, cooks, and even combatants. All these activities established a new set of possibilities for the relations between men and women in Mexico. The workers movement in Mexico during the early twentieth century was also extremely important in changing gender roles.

Despite guarantees of sexual equality in the Constitution of 1857 and the Family Relations Law of 1917, women were not able to hold office or vote. Married women were prohibited from working outside of the home without the permission of their husbands. The Civil Code of 1928, which became effective in 1932, allowed women to work without their husband's permission but stipulated that women were responsible for the education and welfare of children, while no comparable responsibility was imposed on men. After struggling for half a century, Mexican women finally secured the suffrage in municipal elections in 1947 and in federal elections in 1953.

Patricia Begné provides an overview of women's efforts to achieve full participation in all aspects of Mexican political life since their enfranchisement, noting the particular challenges posed by seven decades of one-party political dominance by the *Partido Revolucionario Institucional* (PRI or Institutional Revolutionary Party). She traces efforts of the PRI to co-opt women's organizations and interests for party purposes and she also demonstrates how women have tried to create autonomous organizations to withstand such co-optation and the role of international organizations in moving the Mexican government to implement important reforms that benefit women.

## Canada

In chapter 3, Lois Harder explores the elusive nature of women's power over the course of Canadian history, as demarcations between private and public life were introduced and rigidified. Challenging unilinear narratives of progress, she traces gains and losses, advances and setbacks experienced by women as they have struggled to attain full inclusion in the Canadian polity. She also calls attention to social forces that have "erased" public recognition of women's historic contributions to nation building in Canada.

Providing an overview of women's history in the northernmost territories of North America, Lois Harder explores the relatively egalitarian gender orders of the Aboriginal people, which were disrupted and later transformed by European settlement. Despite the critical roles played by native women as guides, interpreters, provisioners, and wives of the early fur traders, increasing numbers of European settlers, shifts in power from French colonization to British colonization, and changes from a fur-trapping economy to an agricultural economy contributed to major losses of power and status for women in indigenous communities. Indeed, in contrast to egalitarian and matrilineal gender orders in many of the native communities, subsequent "Indian Acts" passed by the government of Canada entrenched sex discrimination, stripping native women, but not native men, of tribal rights and "status" rights, if they married someone other than an "Indian."

British conquest of formerly French colonies also radically restructured gender relations, especially in Quebec. In contrast to the property rights, economic power, and political power wielded by French settler women, British occupation created a power vacuum within the colony, which was later filled by a complex division of secular and sacred domains. These accorded direct political power to British administrators and left the Catholic Church in control of education, health, welfare, family codes, and morality. Drawing on recent feminist scholarship, Lois Harder provides a fascinating chronology of propertied women's disenfranchisement during the first half of the nineteenth century and the prolonged struggle for universal franchise over the next 100 years. Harder's account refutes pat notions that women are "naturally" subordinate and that women have always been subordinated. Indeed, the coincidence of nation building in Canada with legislation and court decisions barring women from political roles and economic rights, raises important questions about the relation between the liberal nation-state and democratization.

Although the struggle to regain political rights was prolonged in Canada (women in Quebec secured the vote only in 1940, Asian women and men won voting rights only in 1948, and Native women and men living on tribal lands won suffrage only in 1960), the presence of multiple political parties, including a social democratic party, created important political spaces that women were able to use to press for progressive policies. In the aftermath of World War II, successive Canadian governments intentionally crafted a social-welfare state as part of an effort to shape a unique "Canadian identity." The "second wave" of feminism in Canada emerged in the context of the nation's growing commitments to social-welfare provision.

Various strands of liberal, socialist, and radical feminism across Canada were forged into a national coalition through the important work of the Royal Commission on the Status of Women. Appointed in 1967, the Royal Commission gathered systematic data concerning the dimensions of gender inequity in Canada and disseminated their findings in the context of public hearings, ostensibly set to gather evidence, in province after province, from coast to coast. Local and national press coverage of these hearings helped galvanize the women's movement long before the Commission's final report was published in 1970. To pressure the government to implement the 167 recommendations of the Royal Commission, women's groups across Canada formed the National Action Committee on the Status of Women (NAC), a coalition of women's groups from across the nation, which became the official voice of the women's movement in Canada in the late twentieth century.

Organized to influence legislation at both provincial and federal levels, NAC skillfully negotiated the complexities of Canadian federal politics, casting itself as an outsider for purposes of lobbying, working in conjunction with the newly created "state machinery for women" to craft government policy papers, and serving as recipient of federal funds, which could then be funneled into progressive feminist organizations at the local and provincial level. This astute combination of "outsider" and "insider" tactics enabled Canadian feminists to achieve a number of important policy successes, including the decriminalization of abortion, employment equity, pay equity, expanded childcare provision, antipornography legislation, and innovative strategies addressing violence against women. The most impressive feminist achievement of this era, however, involved constitutional reform. Demonstrating remarkable skill in building coalitions among provincial and federal legislators at a time of intensive fragmentation within the Canadian polity, feminist activists succeeded in adding *two* equality clauses to the Constitution Act of 1982, guaranteeing that constitutional equality commitments could not be overridden by either the federal or the provincial legislatures.

Despite this extraordinary political feat, Lois Harder reports that feminist initiatives in Canada began to encounter serious opposition in the mid-1980s, as a result of economic recession in combination with the embrace of neoliberalism by the Progressive Conservative government of Brian Mulroney. Demonstrating the fragility of feminist policy accomplishments, Harder traces two decades of retrenchment, as significant cuts have been made in Canada's social-welfare programs—cuts that disproportionately affect women, and as the Liberal government dismantled the "women's state machinery" in the government. Although a measure of economic recovery in the late 1990s allowed Canada to restore and enhance some social-welfare benefits, Lois Harder notes that feminist activism has declined during the past decade and many feminists, discouraged by domestic politics, have turned their attention to international organizations and globalization issues.

## The United States

In chapter 4, Mary Hawkesworth suggests that "democracy" looks very different when women's lives are placed at the center of the analysis. The proclamation of "equal and inalienable rights" in the Declaration of Independence, which launched and vindicated the American revolutionary war, masked practices of dispossession and dislocation of native peoples, enslavement of African and indigenous groups, and the introduction of new gender hierarchies within settler communities. The era of constitution making in the newly independent states, which followed the revolution, created requirements for political participation linked to male gender and white skin. Tracing the changing status of indigenous women, enslaved women, and settler women as the United States was founded, this chapter demonstrates how women were excluded from participation in the design of political institutions and from participation in the new polity. Rather than fulfilling a promise of equality, newly created constitutions excluded women from full citizenship and gave legal sanction to relations of domination and subordination tied to gender, race, and membership in indigenous communities.

In the late eighteenth century and throughout the nineteenth century, women protested against their exclusion and devised innovative strategies to change the rules of political life. They appealed to the courts for redress of their grievances. They organized public speaking campaigns and conferences to educate the public about women's rights. They collected hundreds of thousands of signatures on petitions to state and federal legislatures and lobbied legislators for changes in law and policy. They worked through the established political parties to secure commitments for policy transformation, and when the major parties betrayed them, women formed their own parties in attempts to gain political leverage. Through these intensive efforts, women developed new modes of political activism and expanded popular understandings of politics, creating practices that were more democratic, more participatory, and more issue driven than was the norm in politics at that time.

The results of such sustained effort were extensive, but slow in coming. During their "first century of struggle" for political equality, women won emancipation from slavery, property rights, access to education and the professions, the right to sue and be sued in court, rights to divorce and to custody of their children, minimum wage legislation, and occupational safety and health legislation. The right to vote and to hold elective office took longer to achieve, especially for women of color. Although women in the territories of Wyoming and Utah were enfranchised in 1869 and 1870, respectively; the 19th Amendment to the U.S. Constitution, which prohibited states from denying or abridging the right to vote on account of sex, was ratified only in 1920. Even then voting rights were not secured for all. Discriminatory laws that restricted the franchise of Native Americans were finally eliminated only in 1957; and restrictions on the voting rights of African Americans were eliminated only in 1965 with the passage of the Voting Rights Act.

In addition to fighting for formal rights of inclusion, feminists in the United States have struggled for equal treatment under the law and for changes in divisions of labor, traditional practices, and policies that disadvantage women. Beginning with the appointment of the President's Commission on the Status of Women in 1961, chapter 4 traces the contributions of women professionals, working-class women, African American women, Latinas, and women of the "New Left" to a range of feminist endeavors to achieve access to birth control and abortion; an end to sterilization abuse and pregnancy discrimination; access to education and employment on the basis of merit; access to childcare and early childhood education programs; access to credit; equitable divorce settlements and pension benefits, the politicization of issues such as sexual objectification, acquaintance rape, marital rape, domestic violence, and sexual harassment; creation of shelters for victims of rape and domestic violence and changes in police and court practices pertaining to these crimes; and to involve men in domestic and reproductive labor.

The impressive accomplishments of feminism during the 1960s and 1970s, however, did not eliminate all forms of sexual inequality. In the final section of this chapter, Mary Hawkesworth surveys the effects of neoliberal policies introduced in the last three decades on women and on feminism in the United States. In particular, she traces the growing inequalities among women created by cutbacks in social provision, as well as "casualization" of the labor force; and she explores the implications of neoliberal "privatization" for feminist social justice efforts, and the ways that neoliberal conceptions of the state place persistent gender-based inequities beyond redress.

## Part III: Gender and Globalization

Globalization's impact on women and men varies within and across regions, and differs significantly on the basis of race, ethnicity, nationality, class, sexuality, religion, and a host of other variables. Chapters 5, 6, and 7 trace economic, political, and technological transformations within and across the three countries of North America. In addition to providing an overview of the complex effects of globalization within each nation, each of these chapters analyzes the peculiarly gendered impacts of globalization, paying particular attention to changes that affect women and men differently.

### Mexico

In chapter 5, Laura Gonzalez demonstrates that globalization is not a new experience for the territory today known as Mexico, although the form of globalization in the last thirty years differs significantly from the form of globalization inaugurated by the Spanish Conquest in 1521. Both kinds of globalization profoundly transformed the area's economy and political institutions, establishing power structures that serve outside interests. The Spanish arrived in Mexico with tools, animals, plants, slaves, and ideas that had not been present in the New World. They also brought diseases that decimated the indigenous populations. They used military force to reorganize agricultural practices, to increase mining operations, and to impose or create new institutions to support the discovery, extraction, and transport of silver to Spain. In the twentieth century, international financial institutions have used the debt crisis to restructure Mexican institutions. Leveraging the government's need for new loans to reschedule old debts, international financial institutions, such as the International Monetary Fund and the World Bank, pressured Mexico to open its borders to free trade and foreign direct investment. As a result of this economic restructuring, a dual economy has been created in Mexico which provides impressive gains for multinational corporations and a Mexican elite that comprises only 10 percent of the population, but which does very little for indigenous Mexican industries, and which has lowered the incomes and deepened poverty of the remaining 90 percent of the Mexican population.

The chapter traces a variety of mechanisms within contemporary globalization that exacerbate inequalities within Mexico, demonstrating in concrete ways the effects of "institutional traps," the "debt trap," the "trade trap," and the "foreign direct investment trap." Transferring farm land to U.S. agribusiness, pushing Mexican peasants off the land, underselling Mexican agricultural producers and small businesses, forcing migration from rural to urban areas, and from Mexico to the United States, are all continuing consequences of global financial flows and structural adjustment policies in Mexico. Laura Gonzalez analyzes how these dramatic economic transformations are restructuring the lives of Mexicans, contrasting the experiences of those who migrate with those who remain in Mexico, and exploring the proliferation of transnational organizations, which build and strengthen ties between migrants and their home communities.

Investigating the gendered effects of globalization in Mexico, Gonzalez notes that economic opportunities within Mexico remain markedly sex segregated. In multinational-owned *maquiladoras*, as in factories in the export processing zones of many developing countries, the work force has been "feminized." Recruitment practices in textile, garment, and electronics plants have focused on young women, who now constitute 75 percent of this new, flexible, and highly insecure global labor force. Yet as globalizing transnational corporations relocate in search of cheaper labor in Central America and Southeast Asia, Mexican women are also being displaced from *maquila* factories and must struggle to produce subsistence from the informal sectors of the economy. This in turn contributes to increasing levels of migration among women. Shifts from subsistence agriculture to export production in Mexico are displacing many women from the land, generating migration from rural areas to cities within Mexico and across national borders. Increasing numbers of women are migrating, engendering a mode of existence which had once been nearly exclusively male. Male migration in search of gainful employment is simultaneously contributing to the "feminization of agriculture" and the feminization of local decision making in the communities men leave behind. In Mexico, youthful male migration to the north, combined with widespread government educational programs, are also creating a situation in which women are becoming more highly educated than men. Gender relationships in the home and the workplace are changing dramatically as a result of women's increased participation in the labor force, increasing levels of education, increasing responsibilities for local governance, and as a consequence of migration patterns within and across borders. The strains on family and community life created by rapid economic dislocations are multiple and manifested in many ways. One indicator of such strains is the increase in violence against women and girls on the job, on the street, and in homes, as the murder or disappearance of more than 500 young women in Juarez over a ten-year period makes clear.

Noting that the consequences of migration are not exclusively negative, Laura Gonzalez concludes her chapter with a discussion of the transformative effects of international migration on women who develop and come to appreciate new levels of autonomy and self-sufficiency; who are exposed to and learn to adapt to alternative modes of social, economic, and political life; who gain access to new forms of information and to transnational feminist networks, which foster progressive change. Indeed, Gonzalez notes the irony that the forces of globalization, which are reorganizing the Mexican economy and exploiting the vast preponderance of the Mexican people, are at the same time making Mexican women, and the Mexican government, aware of the gender hierarchies and power structures that have oppressed and silenced women. Moreover, transnational feminist networks developed through UN conferences are providing resources and identifying strategies that Mexican women's rights activists can use to promote change.

### Canada

Globalization also has unique gendered effects within social-welfare states such as Canada. In chapter 6, Laura Macdonald provides a comprehensive overview of Canada's changing political economy in the aftermath of the CUFTA in 1989 and the NAFTA in 1994. While deftly demonstrating the growing integration of the Canadian, U.S., and Mexican economies, she also argues that economic integration has not succeeded in providing the benefits for Canada that its proponents promised. On the contrary, her analysis of aggregate economic indicators suggests that Canada's record in growth and productivity levels has been "lackluster" at best. In addition, the benefits of economic growth have not been evenly distributed across the population. In Canada, as in Mexico, the levels of poverty and inequality have increased over the past 15 years.

The circulation of neoliberal ideology, first introduced by the Progressive Conservative government of Brian Mulroney in the 1980s, and consolidated by the Liberal government of Jean Chretien in the 1990s, contrasts sharply with long-standing Canadian ideas and practices concerning the appropriate role of the state in social-welfare provision. In keeping with its carefully crafted identity as a social-welfare state, Canada has been quite successful in using redistributive policies, such as social assistance or welfare, unemployment benefits, child tax credits, and pensions, to prevent inequality in living standards. While these tax and transfer programs continued to keep after-tax income fairly stable through the first half of the 1990s, cuts to social programs beginning in 1995 weakened the social safety net and inequalities began to rise. According to the 2001 census, for example, Canada was beginning to experience economic polarization, as the incomes of the top 10 percent of earners increased by 14.6 percent over the 1990s, while median family incomes stagnated, and the incomes of the lowest 10 percent of earners increased by less than 1 percent during the same period.

Women's labor force participation has increased in Canada, rising from 23 percent in 1953 to 56 percent in 2002; although it still remains lower than the labor force participation of men, which was 67 percent in 2002. Women remain more likely than men to be employed part-time: only 72 percent of women were working full-time in 2002 compared to 89 percent of men (Statistics Canada 2003). Although women in some sectors of the Canadian economy, such as the clothing industry where the work force is 75 percent female, have been particularly hard hit by the elimination of tariffs under CUFTA and NAFTA, globalization has not produced an increase in the earnings gap between men and women in Canada. Indeed, Laura Macdonald notes that Canadian women's income increased more quickly than men's during the 1990s, helping to reduce gender inequities in pay. She cautions, however, that the shrinking wage gap is due more to declining wages of men than to increasing wages of women. Inequalities have also been growing among women in Canada. As middle-class women pursue economic opportunities, women migrant workers from Mexico, the Philippines, and other nations of the global South are increasingly assuming responsibilities for domestic labor at very low wages. In Canada and the United States, such "outsourcing of reproductive labor" is a prime example of the impact of globalization, which carries important political, economic, and interpersonal repercussions.

While women's labor force participation per se does not appear to be tied to globalization, Macdonald notes that some women, most notably immigrant women, single-women heading families, and elderly women, are feeling the effects of globalization more than other women. Poverty is increasingly concentrated among particular categories of women. Single mothers and senior women living alone have far higher incidence of poverty than other Canadians: 95 percent of single mothers under the age of 25, 57 percent of single mothers under the age of 65 with children younger than 18 years of age, and 49 percent of elderly women living alone, are living in poverty. Laura Macdonald traces the feminization of poverty in Canada to the adoption of neoliberal policies, which break with long-standing commitments to social provision. In accordance with neoliberal principles, the 1995 federal budget dramatically reduced expenditures on social transfers, social programs, and education, and shifted more power to the provinces in determining social benefits, which enabled some provinces to introduce privatization of services and workfare requirements for recipients of social assistance. In Canada, as in the United States, neoliberalism, the ideological apparatus of globalization, endorses a shrinking of the state that disproportionately disadvantages women. Laura Macdonald points out, however, that despite the reductions in social programs and in redistributive policies that have occurred in Canada, these programs have been "weakened" rather than eliminated, and remain more robust than comparable programs in Mexico and the United States. Thus she concludes that although it has been susceptible to neoliberal influences, the Canadian state has insulated Canadians from the most negative economic dislocations of globalization.

### The United States

In chapter 7, Jane Bayes argues that the impact of globalization for any country depends to a large extent on the status of that country in the global economy. Unlike Canada and Mexico, the United States has been a global hegemon economically, politically, culturally, and militarily, since the end of World War II. The United States has also been one of the leading proponents of globalization. From 1944 to 1971, the United States helped to stabilize global currencies and thereby facilitated global trade by serving as lender of last resort to support a gold standard. During this period, the United States also devised particular industrial, tax, and foreign policies to encourage U.S. corporations to engage in international trade and foreign direct investment. This was the golden age of United States manufacturing as automobile, steel, chemical, electronics, and rubber companies among others were able to offer employees stable lifelong employment at quite decent wages. Unions were strong. The ruling political consensus was inspired by New Deal and Keynesian philosophies that held that government should provide citizens freedom from want and freedom from fear in addition to freedom of speech and freedom of religion. This meant that the government should regulate the economy with monetary and fiscal policies, that the government should provide for social services, disability, unemployment insurance, disability insurance, health care, and social security. Citizens had responsibility for the community.

Faced with a recession and overextended by the Vietnam War, by Great Society spending, and by the prospect of increasing oil prices as U.S. oil wells hit their peak of production in 1970, the Nixon administration in 1971 abandoned the gold standard. In the mid-1970s, faced with increased global competition from Japan and Europe, the United States began to remove government regulations that had previously controlled the size and opera-tions of U.S. corporations, a policy change that greatly increased corporate political power. Meanwhile the recession brought on by the oil crisis of 1973, when the Organisation of Petroleum Exporting Countries (OPEC) raised its oil prices multiple times, encouraged more and more U.S. corpor-ations to cut costs by moving their manufacturing operations offshore. The 1970s became the decade of deindustrialization in the United States as mil-lions of workers lost their jobs. Corporations downsized, hired cheaper women workers, hired more part-time workers. The workforce became feminized as many wives went to work themselves to provide an extra pay-check to support the family. Men often had to take two or three jobs to make the same income they had earned before in one.

In a stunning reversal of economic and political policy, the Reagan Administration came into office in the early 1980s and immediately aban-doned Keynesian economics, which recognized the need for state fiscal inter-vention to prevent prolonged downturns in the economy. Instead Reagan advocated neoliberal policy proposals that reduced the regulatory function of the government in the economy and promoted a reduced role for government in general. The market and market incentives were to replace governmental programs and governmental regulations. Governmental functions were to be privatized or eliminated insofar as possible. This neoliberal philosophy has subsequently become the ruling political consensus.

In many ways, globalization has strengthened the position of the United States and its economy vis-à-vis other states and has also strengthened the position of a small group of corporate elites while weakening the well-being of the middle and working classes. Chapter 7 identifies and discusses six major gendered consequences of globalization: (1) the feminization of the labor force; (2) changes in the structure of the family; (3) the ideologi-cal shift from Keynesian to neoliberal ideas especially with regard to social policies; (4) the simultaneous feminization of unions and decline in union power; (5) the increased flows of immigration; and (6) the growing inequal-ity between rich and poor especially as configured by race, ethnicity, and gender. The chapter suggests that rather than scrambling to cope with the effects of globalization as many smaller economies have had to do, the United States, because of its hegemonic position in the world, has been the architect and promoter of a globalizing agenda. Circulating universalist claims about the benefits of marketization for all people, the United States has ignored the growing evidence that the much acclaimed benefits of globalization are concentrated in the corporate sector and among the rich-est segments of its own population, while inequality grows exponentially within the United States and across the globe. The final chapter of the book returns to questions concerning the relation between globalization and democratization in North America, exploring factors that might contribute to very different futures for North America and its three constitutive states.

## PART 2

*Women and the Struggle for Democracy*

CHAPTER 2

# Women and the Struggle for Democracy in Mexico

PATRICIA BEGNÉ

This chapter provides a historical overview of the situation of women in Mexico. In contrast with Canada and the United States, the two nations with whom it shares the continent of North America, Mexico has only recently qualified as a "formal" democracy, characterized by competitive elections and peaceful transition of power from one elected political party to another. Only in the year 2000 did free and fair elections transfer power into the hands of a president elected from a party other than the *Partido Revolucionario Institucional* (PRI), the party that has dominated Mexican politics since the Mexican revolution in the early twentieth century. Consequently, Mexican women's struggles for political, economic, and social rights have taken place in a very different context from those of the other two North American countries. Mexican women's political activism is part of the broader, ongoing struggle for democratization of the country. Because Mexico's economy is less developed than that of its neighbors to the north, and because levels of poverty are far higher in Mexico, globalization has very different effects on Mexican women. This chapter explores the changing roles of women in Mexico since the sixteenth century, illuminating their many contributions to Mexican history, economy, culture, society, and politics, contributions that remain largely invisible in standard accounts of Mexican history. It also explores women's contemporary activism to promote public policies that reconcile the competing demands of work and family life, while fostering Mexico's sustainable development. For a brief overview of Mexico, see table 2.1.

## Panoramic Overview of Mexico

Mexico, located in southern half of North America, is currently bordered by Guatemala and Belize in the south and by the United States of America

**Table 2.1**  Mexico at a glance

| | |
|---|---|
| Geography | 1,972,542 square kilometers |
| Population | 104,000,000 |
| Political system | federal Republic: 31 states and the federal District (Mexico City) |
| Official name | United Mexican States |
| Income per capita | 5910 US$ (1) |
| Year women were granted right to vote | 1947–1953 |
| Percentage of women in federal Congress: | |
| Chamber of Deputies | 23 percent |
| Senate | 17 percent |
| Life expectancy: | |
| Male | 72.4 years |
| Female | 77.4 years |

*Source*:  Gross National Product per capita 2002, *World Bank Atlas 2003*.★

in the north. Mexico, whose official name is the United Mexican States, is a federal republic made up of 31 states and one federal district.

The Mexican population is the product of a mosaic of cultures, including indigenous, Spanish, and African. The ancient civilizations of the Olmecs, Toltecs, Aztecs or Nahuas, Mayas, Zapotecas, and Mixtecas, the original inhabitants of the territory, combined with the Spanish and the African and Caribbean brought as enslaved peoples, resulting in the ongoing *mestizaje*, or mixture, of indigenous, European, and Afro-Caribbean peoples and cultures. After the arrival and subsequent conquest of Mexico by the Spaniards, three centuries of colonial domination ensued, creating great economic, social, political, and cultural inequalities. The concentration of wealth by the Spanish conquistadors and the marginalization of the poorest groups, especially indigenous peoples and peasants, produced a society marked by inequality.

Every system of governance reflects both the conditions under which it was created and longer historical, cultural, and social legacies. Within Mexico, the long history of Spanish colonial rule, the struggle for independence from Spain, and the recently drafted Constitution of the United States influenced the design of the Mexican political system in the early nineteenth century. The "criollos," white descendants of the European settlers born in the "New World," and the mestizos launched an independence struggle against Spain in 1810, achieving full victory over Spanish colonial forces in 1821. During the war of independence, Mexican nationalists drafted two documents envisioning a free Mexican Republic, incorporating liberal political institutions and respect for individual rights. One was José María Morelos y Pavón's *Los sentimientos de la Nación* (1813), and the other was the Constitution of *Apatzingán* (1814). This vision was subsequently incorporated into the 1824 Constitution (*Acta Constitutiva de la Federación*

*Mexicana*), which created a government modeled on the federal system in the United States. Under the 1824 Constitution, the powers of governance were divided between a federal government and nineteen state legislatures. Within the federal government, the constitution called for a separation of powers between the president, a bicameral congress, and the judiciary. Although on paper, the Mexican Constitution was designed to prevent the accumulation of power in any one office, the challenges facing the emerging Mexican nation contributed to significant disparities between constitutional provisions and actual political practices.

For four decades following the adoption of the 1824 Constitution, Mexico experienced considerable political instability as a consequence of continuing power struggles between liberal and conservative elites, as well as contestations among powerful regional leaders (*caudillos*). In addition, between 1824 and 1870, the new republic suffered military incursions from Spain, France, and the United States, culminating in the loss of more than half its national territory to the United States in the aftermath of the Mexican–American War (1846–1848). In 1863, French troops invaded Mexico and proclaimed a new "empire" under the leadership of Austrian Archduke Ferdinand Maximilian Joseph von Hapsburg. For the following four years, Mexico had two governments, the Hapsburg dynasty ruling in southern portions of the nation, while the Mexican government continued to rule in the territories it controlled in the northern sectors of the country. These internal and external competitions for power gave rise to a form of politico-military leadership, which tended to concentrate power in the presidency, and which contributed to a pattern of multiple and violent changes of government.

In the midst of these violent political conflicts in the middle of the nineteenth century, the triumph of liberal political forces consolidated the Republic and created the basis for liberal reforms. The Constitution of 1857 restricted the power of the military and the Catholic Church and imposed limits on the property holdings of the Catholic Church, which at that time claimed control over nearly half the land within Mexico. In addition, the 1857 Constitution introduced a "Bill of Rights" and abolished slavery within the nation. In response to these liberal policies, conservatives, supported by the Catholic Church, unleashed the War of the Reform (1858–1861), a three-year civil war that gave the French a pretext for their invasion to support the Catholic Church and to extract compensation for damages to property incurred during the civil war. In 1867 the Austrian archduke, Maximilian von Hapsburg, who had been installed as the emperor of Mexico by Napoleon, was overthrown, and the liberal leader Benito Juárez, came to power. In 1876 Porfirio Díaz assumed the presidency, resulting in a 35-year dictatorship. Díaz adopted modernization policies, opening up the country to foreign capital. At the same time, these policies aggravated social inequalities, resulting in the explosion of the Mexican Revolution in 1910, led by Francisco Madero and peasant leaders like Emiliano Zapata and Pancho Villa.

The Mexican Constitution of 1917, embodying the social justice principles of the revolution, was the first socialist constitution ever created. While this constitution preserved the federal system, the formal separation of powers within three branches of government at the national level, and a bill of rights; it also recognized social rights and workers' rights; introduced a formal separation of church and state; and granted "universal" male suffrage. The 1917 Constitution accords power to the federal government, to 31 state governments, and to a federal district, where the capitol is located. Although the constitution divides power among the executive, legislative, and judicial branches of government at the federal level, the president has far more power than either the congress or the judiciary. The president has the ultimate power to decide what will become law. The president's signature is required to enact all legislation and the congress possesses no power to force a president to sign a bill into law. In addition, the president has the power to issue basic rules (*reglamentos*) without any consultation with the congress, and these statutory regulations carry the full force of law. Under the constitution, the president is limited to one, six-year term (*sexenio*).

The 1917 Constitution recognized certain social rights for workers and peasants and for the organizations that represented them in the political process. Article 123 granted workers the right to organize and to strike, established a maximum eight-hour work day, provided certain protections for women and children in the work place, established a "minimum wage sufficient to satisfy the normal necessities of life" for workers, and guaranteed a right to equal pay for equal work regardless of race, ethnicity, or gender. In addition, this constitution laid the foundation for "corporatist" politics, which gives particular interest groups, such as those representing workers, peasants, and their employers, a formal role in the political process. Article 123 establishes processes of consultation between the government and the representatives of management and labor. Indeed, it establishes mandatory processes of arbitration and conciliation in all cases of labor disputes. Beyond recognizing the rights of workers and peasants, the 1917 Constitution also establishes the principle of "economic nationalism." In keeping with the socialist principles of the Mexican Revolution, Article 27 grants the government broad powers to expropriate private property "in the public interest" and to redistribute land.

Although it has been modified and amended many times over the past nine decades, the Constitution of 1917 remains in force today. In addition to formal practices of amendment, the provisions established in the constitution have also been structured by political practices of party governance. At the end of the 1920s, the *Partido Nacional Revolucionario* (PNR, National Revolutionary Party) was created. Later renamed the *Partido Revolucionario Institucional* (PRI, Institutional Revolutionary Party), this party dominated Mexican politics until 2000. With only sporadic political opposition, the PRI developed a form of "clientelist" politics, through which it used its control of the official institutions of state to provide benefits to the particular constituencies it served in return for their continuing support in elections.

For example, in the 1930s, President Lázaro Cárdenas (1934–1940) redistributed land to landless peasants, creating state-sponsored communal farms (*ejidos*), which secured the popular support of the peasants for the PRI. Cárdenas also nationalized the oil industry in 1937, displacing foreign oil companies, and creating a new governmental agency (*Petróleos Mexicanos* or Pemex), which created jobs and sources of enrichment for upwardly mobile members of the middle class. The symbiotic relationship between the government and the PRI, combined with clientelist political relations between party officials, government officials, and particular segments of the Mexican population also created the possibility for systemic forms of political corruption which have haunted the PRI. The centralization of power in the presidency, combined with the president's deployment of the military in the twentieth century to provide domestic "stability" and "order" have also given an authoritarian cast to PRI rule. During the 1950s, for example, Mexico experienced several important strikes and land occupations related to economic grievances. In the 1960s and 1970s, students launched a series of protests against political corruption and economic policies that exacerbated inequalities, culminating in the 1968 killing of hundreds of student demonstrators by police and paramilitary forces in the Tlaltelolco section of Mexico City.

During the 1980s, as mounting economic crises led to massive inflation and the devaluation of the peso, cracks began to open in the edifice of the ruling party, a party that had permitted only a very gradual and limited process of political liberalization up to this point. Some democratic reformers within the PRI left the party to form a new center-left party, the *Partido de la Revolución Democrática* (PRD, Revolutionary Democratic Party). One of these reformers, Cuauhtemoc Cardenas, grandson of the revered populist president of the 1930s, Lázaro Cárdenas, became leader of the PRD and mounted a strong opposition to the PRI candidate, Carlos Salinas de Gortari, in the 1988 elections. The official count declared that Salinas won the presidency with a bare 50.3 percent majority after a suspicious 13-hour crash of the election computers. Widespread charges of electoral fraud created the most important political crisis in Mexico's recent history. As in many other Latin American states, pressures for democratization came partly from within the governing elites, but mounting pressures for change from below, including from newly mobilized women, contributed to the pace and extent of democratization.

During the 1990s, despite the signing of the North America Free Trade Agreement (NAFTA) with the United States and Canada, the political crisis intensified, and in 1994, the *Ejército Zapatista de Liberación Nacional* (EZLN, Zapatista National Liberation Front) started an armed rebellion in the southern state of Chiapas. This indigenous movement became famous worldwide, using the technology afforded by the internet to circulate information globally about the plight of indigenous peasants who were being displaced from their land and subjected to increasing environmental devastation. Shortly thereafter, both the PRI candidate for the presidency of the Republic and the president of the party were assassinated.

These events suggested that the PRI had lost its famous capacity to "maintain political order." After many years of rejecting formal processes of electoral politics under the PRI, many political activists began to dedicate themselves to a nonpartisan campaign to reform the country's electoral system. A group called *Alianza Cívica* composed of hundreds of small NGOs formed a campaign to clean up the electoral system (Franceschet and Macdonald 2004, 15). Mexico also experienced increased international pressure to democratize, after years in which the United States and other international actors had ignored the country's human rights abuses. In addition to the challenge from the left, the PRI faced a strong challenge from the political right, from the *Partido Acción Nacional* (PAN, National Action Party), which organized its campaigns for political offices around the theme of free and fair elections and an end to political corruption. While PRI candidate Ernesto Zedillo was able to win the presidency in a relatively clean election in 1994; the PAN presidential candidate Vicente Fox won the 2000 election, marking the first time in Mexican history that presidential power changed hands in free and fair elections.

## Women in Mexican History

### Pre-Hispanic Mexico

Pre-Hispanic Mesoamerican women engaged in a wide variety of activities, ranging from domestic activities like preparing food for their families and providing heirs for their husbands, to productive activities such as weaving cotton and producing clothing, to medicinal practices—gathering herbs and mushrooms and administering them to cure illness, and to artistic endeavors such as embroidery, writing poetry, and designing jewelry. They also learned multiple indigenous languages and served as interpreters, engaged in trade, and provided entertainment as dancers and singers. As horticulturists, they gathered food important to the staple diet of their families and communities (Flores 2000, 6). Women were valued for their diverse contributions to their communities, and in warrior societies, women who had several sons received particular honor.

Girls learned the arts central to survival, such as grinding corn, preparing food, spinning, and weaving in their homes. According to the *Mendocino Codice*, a book codifying traditional practices, mothers taught their daughters domestic duties. In addition to this education within the home, girls and boys could enter into one of two types of schools, *Calmécac* (schools for the children of the nobility) or *Tepochcalli* (public schools). According to class and talent, children were educated to become warriors, priests, historians, hydraulic engineers, biologists, experts in languages, or painters, artisans, or musicians. While most pre-Hispanic cultures adhered to a strict division of labor with regard to the activities carried out by men and the activities performed by women, in a number of these societies, women took up arms and fought beside the men when needed. In his 1521 chronicle, *Mexicayotl*, Fernando de Alvarado Tezozomac depicts indigenous women as valiant, manifesting strong character and firm personality, and as participants in the war against the Spanish conquistadors, assisting and encouraging the soldiers, guarding bridges, and raising alarms (Cosmes, 1979, 850). Chichimeca women, for example, helped the men in battle, shooting their arrows with greater precision than the men, and displaying more classic techniques in handling the bow and arrow than the men (Flores 2000, 3). In Totonac culture as well, women not only worked at home but were also involved in defending the territory, fighting beside the men.

## The Spanish Conquest 1519–1521

During the Conquest, women's conditions underwent enormous change. Apart from their various roles within indigenous communities, indigenous women became the lovers and servants of the Spanish. Without question the indigenous women experienced brutality and degradation during the Conquest, but they also seized opportunities to resist the Spanish, sometimes with recourse to arms. One anecdote captures women's contributions to armed resistance against the conquistadors. As the story goes, the number of male warriors was depleted during the defense of Tenochtitlan, so women joined their men, taking up arms and forming a line of defense along the roofs of the houses. From that height, they made themselves partially visible, so the conquistadors would know that women were actively fighting against them. Hoping that the ignominy of defeat would be heightened by the knowledge that the Spanish had been vanquished by women, the female warriors fought bravely, demonstrating the value of their military skills and helping to defend their city. Such a demonstration of military prowess also had an unintended consequence. It reduced the abuse suffered by indigenous women at the hands of the Spanish.

In indigenous culture, some women were *ahuainimes*, serving as lovers and offering pleasure to the men as a way to encourage and strengthen the warriors during battle. These women were considered an important part of society and were treated with respect and admiration. In contrast, the Europeans considered women who carried out this role immoral, and scorned them. These attitudes, among others, created a culture shock. The Europeans, as conquerors, imposed their principles and laws on an indigenous population that did not understand the Spanish worldview, a worldview that challenged many if not all indigenous assumptions.

Some women from this period played key roles for the conquerors serving as interpreters for the Spaniards and for the indigenous people. Besides acting as servants, lovers, and cooks, they also delivered important information about the logic, rules, principles, cultural traits, customs, behavior, and manner of thought of the pre-Hispanic societies. A famous example was *La Malinche*, whose real name, according to some authors, was Malinalli or Malitzin. An astute and intelligent indigenous woman of noble origins, who spoke various

languages and served as an interpreter for the Spaniards, Malinche was given as
a gift to the conqueror Hernán Cortés on his arrival in 1519. Scholars estimate
that she was approximately 13 years old when given to Cortés (Flores 2000, 6).

## The Viceroy Period 1521–1821

During the period of European rule after the Conquest, the marginalization of indigenous women reached extreme levels, and their situation
declined. Their inferiority to men was firmly established, and they were
obliged to play roles as lovers and servants. Gradually, the women of New
Spain began to take on new roles in the public sphere as cooks, waiters,
washerwomen, and prostitutes in addition to their domestic duties. Only
the few who enjoyed a good social and economic position had access to
education (Foppa Alaíde 1975, 240).

When Mexico gained its independence from Spain in 1821, the laws,
orders, and decrees promulgated earlier remained in place. Little by little,
beginning with the Constitution of 1824, new laws were created to replace
those put in place during the Viceroyalty. Few of these favored women.

## Women during the Mexican Revolution 1910–1917

The Mexican Revolution, disrupted women's traditional roles and opened
new political spaces for women's political activity. Many women of all
classes joined the struggle participating in a variety of activities that had
previously been reserved for men. While women's struggle to occupy a
central space in Mexican society was not new, the Mexican revolution was
critical in involving large numbers of women in political activities, a
political activism that did not die with the 1917 Constitution.

Because their activities were often clandestine and not recorded in history,
not much is known about the women veterans of the Mexican Revolution.
The stereotypical image of these women is as self-sacrificing, valiant soldiers,
heroines, and *guerrilleras* (warriors); however, these women's activities were not
limited to the support of men and armed fighting. They also served as spies,
confidential agents, liaisons, couriers, arms and munition transporters, and as
propagandists. As one commentator noted, all of these were secret activities:

In the period 1910–1914, female teachers, journalists and nurses were
proselytizers, writing, printing, and disseminating revolutionary
propaganda, carrying it to the camps and distributing it among the
rebels and the civilian population, transporting arms, correspondence,
messages, moving throughout diverse parts of the country. All of these
clandestine activities left no trail and were forgotten in the official male
history. The revolution openly incorporated women in military and
political activities within the constitutionalist movement and the feminist struggle, habits of participation that did not end in 1917 when the
new Constitution was adopted. (Consejo Nacional 2001)

In postrevolutionary Mexico, some women veterans continued to promote feminist projects, either as leaders or as members of diverse organizations. They put forward demands that still had not been satisfied: demands for education and work, as well as for the right to vote. Some remained teachers or worked in the government bureaucracy; a few continued to study and remained committed to revolutionary projects, participating in literacy campaigns and in rural education. Eulalia Guzmán, Julia Nava, and Elena Torres are a few of the veterans that should be mentioned (Begné 2004, 14). Hermila Galindo, publisher of the magazine, *La Mujer Moderna* (The Modern Woman), and often characterized as the "first Mexican feminist," used her political ties to President Venustiano Carranza to persuade him to pass a series of laws granting women more rights, including the rights to divorce and remarry in 1914. Hermila Galindo also played an important role in securing passage of the Family Relations Law of 1917, which accorded women the right to own property, to retain custody of their children, and to receive alimony following a divorce (Rodríguez 2003, 96–97).

The ongoing presence of women in the political, economic, and social life of the country, combined with their roles in the armed uprising against authority in 1910, encouraged women to question their subordinate condition. The Revolution marked a change for women from many different walks of life (Begné 2004, 14). As a politico-social process it altered attitudes, forged personalities key to the armed struggle, and changed the customs and habits among individuals of distinct social origin. This dynamic process also created a change in the relations between the sexes themselves (Begné 2004, 14).

### *The First Feminist Congress in Yucatán 1916*

After the revolution of 1910, the feminist movement began "to demand for women the same rights that exist for men" (Mora 1985, 49). In 1916, with the help and support of socialist Governor Salvador Alvarado, women in Mérida, Yucatán organized the first feminist congresses in Mexico (Miller 1991, 76; Rodríguez 2003, 95). Convened in January and November, the conferences attracted nearly 700 women who debated a number of important issues, including secular education, the need for sex education, suffrage, and the political participation of women (Ramos Escandón 1994, 200). Although suffrage and sex education were particularly contested issues, the women participating in the congresses reached a series of compromises on these policy issues and developed a "platform" that they presented to the Constitutional Convention in the spring of 1917. Although the women's platform endorsed municipal suffrage for women, the all-male members of the Constitutional Convention had markedly different views of women's appropriate roles in society. Stating that "women were not prepared to participate in the political sphere," the members of the Constitutional Convention enacted a series of laws that excluded women from political participation (Silva 1989, 272). Although participants in the Women's

Congress clearly demonstrated that "we want for the women of our country rights and functions similar to those of men in education, life and democracy, in accordance with the program of the Mexican Social Revolution" (Mora 1985, 59), their struggle for full political rights would continue for another 35 years.

## Law on Family Relations 1917

Since the end of the nineteenth century in Europe and the United States, many middle-class women have sought to modify their situation through social movements for reform. Mexico has been no exception. A small group of Mexican women from the middle class tried to transform the reigning patriarchal system, achieving isolated victories by appealing to powerful allies within the government. For example, in 1917, as noted above, women, including Hermila Galindo, succeeded in persuading President Venustiano Carranza to use his extraordinary legislative powers to pass the Law on Family Relations. In a nation that had been profoundly influenced by the power of the Catholic Church, the Family Relations law had a number of progressive features. Most notably, this law defined marriage as a civil and dissolvable contract, thereby legalizing divorce, and radically departing from Church doctrines concerning the indissolubility of the sacrament of marriage. In effect from 1917 to 1932, the law also included provisions that were far less progressive. Specifying the "duties" of married men and women, the law accorded married women authority over the children and all domestic affairs; while assigning married men the responsibility of providing food. In addition to codifying a gendered division of labor within the household, the law also required married women to obtain the permission of their husbands to work outside the home, have a job or profession, establish a business, or hire employees (*Diario de Debates del Congreso Constituyente 1916–1917*, 1990, 829).

In the state of Yucatán during the 1920s, Felipe Carrillo Puerto rose to power and established a series of measures designed to improve the situation of women. A member of the socialist party and a strong supporter of women's equality, Governor Carrillo Puerto granted women the right to vote in local and state elections and encouraged women, including his sister, to run for elected offices. In 1923, Elvia Carrillo Puerto, along with teachers Rachel Dzib and Beatriz Peniche, were elected to Yucatán's state legislature, the first women to win elective offices in Mexico. In the same year, Rosa Torres was elected to the city council of Mérida, where she served as mayor. Despite their popular election, elected women in this early period were completely dependent on the power of their male supporters. When Governor Carrillo Puerto was assassinated, for example, the three women serving as deputies were expelled from the state legislature.

Two other Mexican states enfranchised women in municipal and state elections during the early 1920s. Governor Rafael Nieto gave literate women in San Luis Potosi the right to vote in municipal elections in 1924 and in state elections in 1925; women in Chiapas were also enfranchised in both state and municipal elections in 1925 (Cano 1991, 281; Morton 1962, 10–12). Following her brother's assassination, Elvia Carrillo Puerto subsequently moved to San Luis Potosi, where she ran for federal deputy. Although she won the election by a wide margin, the federal Congress refused to grant her a seat in the Chamber of Deputies (Rodríguez 2003, 97).

A group of affluent Mexican women who had been active in international suffrage movements convened the *Congreso Feminista Panamericano* (Pan-American Feminist Congress) in Mexico City in 1923. Calling for full political equality between men and women and the elevation of Mexican women, more than 100 participants in the Congress passed a resolution demanding the right of suffrage, which they presented to the Mexican Congress in 1923. During this same period, a coalition of working-class and peasant women also began mobilizing on behalf of women's rights. Founding the *Congreso Nacional de Mujeres Obreras y Campesinas* (National Congress of Worker and Peasant Women), the coalition tried to work within the socialist and communist parties to press for political equality for women, including increased representation of women in party leadership and the development of party platforms that addressed women's needs. Frustrated by their inability to make significant changes within the parties, members of the *Congreso Nacional de Mujeres Obreras y Campesinas* decided to join ranks with the *Congreso Feminista Panamericano* to create a national women's suffrage organization *Frente Unico Pro Derechos de la Mujer* (FUPDM, United Front for Women's Rights), the first effective mass feminist organization in Mexico (Ramos Escandón 1994).

### Civil Code of 1928

Article 2 of the 1928 Civil Code proclaims that men's and women's legal capacities are equal; as a consequence, women are not subjected, by reason of their sex, to any restriction on the acquisition and exercise of political rights. Despite this broad statement of political equality and nondiscrimination, other articles in the civil code assign the care of the home to women and stipulate that women can hold jobs outside the home only if they do not neglect their domestic duties and if their husbands consent to their employment. In cases where husbands withhold consent, the civil code allows women to appeal to the courts to resolve the dispute. This legally sanctioned inequality remained in place until 1974.

While the Civil Code has been modified many times, the following provisions remain in effect:

- The capacities of men and women are comparable and complementary; thus women are granted their "own domain" as well as equality with their husbands;
- The Code establishes a married woman's right to arrange the spacing of her children, to direct the children's education and to oversee administration of the children's property or possessions;

- The Code accords a woman the right to have a job, exercise a profession, or dedicate herself to a business or industry, on the condition that her activity does not violate good manners and moral principles;
- A married woman can freely administer her property and dispose of her possessions without the authorization of her husband;
- A woman of the age of majority (18 years old) and with full capacities has the freedom to dispose of her person and her goods, being legally recognized to carry out all types of contracts;
- A woman does not lose the *patria potestad* (right of care) over her children after a divorce, even if she contracts subsequent nuptials;
- The Code eliminates the difference between legitimate children and children born out of wedlock;
- The Code gives children born out of wedlock the right to investigate who their father is; it also establishes the presumption that children born out of wedlock are the natural children of the male and female partners (*Diario de Debates. Congreso del Estado de Guanajuato, Guanajuato, México* 1967).

### The Struggle for Political Rights 1930–1953

In the 1930s women began to make an important mark on the national political scene, pressuring the PNR (later renamed PRI) to support women's demand for suffrage. The election of President Lázaro Cárdenas in 1934 brought dramatic political changes to the country, reviving many of the dreams of the Mexican Revolution that had been unfulfilled in the intervening years. Cárdenas constructed a top-down, populist political system based on corporatism, involving peasant, worker, and middle-class groups in official organizations with special ties to the ruling party. Through formal consultation with these organizations, the PNR devised a means to preserve political order, heighten its own legitimacy, and co-opt dissent. While these peasant, worker, and middle-class groups gained important benefits under this system, including extensive land reform, especially during Cárdenas's *sexenio*, the system was authoritarian and became increasingly so in the middle decades of the twentieth century.

Women's political activism attracted Cárdenas's attention as part of his broader agenda to build support for his party and promote social change. At its peak, the FUPDM brought together more than 800 women's organizations with 50,000 members throughout the country, including Communists, Liberals, Catholics, and supporters of distinct factions within the PNR. Focusing their efforts on the Cárdenas administration, the FUPDM demanded women's suffrage, while also pressing for legislation to address the problems faced by women in their daily lives, including demands for lower electricity rates, rents and taxes on market women, reform of labor laws and the civil code, equal rights for the indigenous and the poor, and the creation of a children's bureau. At this point, the movement was cross-class in character and included important working-class leaders in grassroots organizations (Ramos Escandón 1998, 92–95).

As a result of the lobbying by the FUPDM, Cárdenas sent a bill to the Senate in November 1937 that would reform the constitution to give women the vote. This amendment was initially approved by the Congress and ratified by all 28 states; but subsequently Congress decided to reconsider the matter and defeated the amendment. Given the degree of presidential power in Mexico, an outright defeat of a presidential initiative is highly unusual. For this reason, some analysts suggest that Cárdenas must have had a hand in this reversal. Despite his pledge of support for women's suffrage, toward the end of his mandate Cárdenas apparently feared that the amendment could divide the party; he also worried that women's political participation would support conservative forces, since women were perceived as close to and easily manipulated by the conservative Catholic church. Thus he changed his position on the issue (Ramos Escandón 1998, 97–98; Rodríguez 2003, 98–101). In the aftermath of this political setback, the FUPDM severed its ties with the PNR and began running its own candidates for elective office in defiance of the discriminatory election laws. It also continued to press for childcare centers, cooperatives for indigenous women, and legislation to protect domestic servants and for women's suffrage. In 1947, during the term of President Miguel Alemán, the FUPDM succeeded in getting the constitution amended to enfranchise women in local and municipal elections, but not in state and federal elections.

In the early 1950s, the FUPDM helped organize the *Alianza de Mujeres Mexicanas* (Mexican Women's Alliance) under the leadership of Amalia Caballero de Castillo Ledón, who had spent twenty years as an activist for women's rights in the international arena, serving as Chair of the *Comisión Interamericana de Mujeres* (Inter-American Women's Commission), and as one of the founding members of the UN Commission on the Status of Women. Castillo Ledón promised Adolfo Ruiz Cortines that the *Alianza* would support his presidential bid if he pledged to grant women's suffrage. Testing the capacity of the *Alianza* to mobilize women, Ruiz Cortines agreed to support voting rights for women if 500,000 women signed a petition calling for enfranchisement. Orchestrating a national petition drive, Castillo Ledón delivered petitions with more than 500,000 signatures to the Congress, which changed the law to grant women's suffrage in state and federal elections in 1953. Following this victory, the *Alianza* turned its efforts to electing women to Congress and succeeded in electing five women within the next two years (Ramos Escandón 1994, 205).

Despite success in gaining formal citizenship rights, women's political influence was largely defused. As the PRI consolidated its political control over the country, it succeeded in co-opting most social interests, including the women's movement. The party created a women's sector (*sección femenil*) and some women entered the bureaucracy, but neither group was able to articulate women's interests effectively. Until the late 1960s, women's political participation occurred largely within the dominant party, which was the terrain of ambitious, well-connected women who were able to make their way into the political elite. Political violence and undemocratic conditions in the country limited women's capacity to influence the political and economic directions of the country.

### *Consolidation of the Mexican State—The Mexican Miracle*

The 1940–1970 period in Mexico was one of unprecedented economic prosperity brought on by the state's commitment to a nationalist import substitution industrialization (ISI) development strategy from the 1940s to the late 1970s. The era from 1940 to 1960 is known as the "Mexican Miracle" because of the government's success in achieving striking levels of economic growth (averaging 6 percent growth in gross national product (GNP) annually in this period) and its success in maintaining political order through the corporatist structures of the PRI. While some of this prosperity trickled down to all social groups and contributed to urbanization and the growth of a middle class, income inequality increased steadily from 1950 to 1968 (Babb 2001, 80). In 1969, the poorest 30 percent of Mexican families still had an income less than or equal to one-third of the average Mexican family income (Babb 2001, 108).

In the 1970s, "second wave" feminism emerged in Mexico as it did in Europe and in the United States. Mexican feminists sought to improve the situation for women in Mexico, raise consciousness concerning continuing discrimination and gender-based inequities, and eliminate women's oppression within Mexico. While feminist efforts were launched primarily by well-educated, middle-class women, some feminists attempted to forge alliances with working-class and indigenous women as well. As in many other countries, entrenched racial and class divisions fostered suspicions and rifts that made successful alliances difficult. In 1975, the United Nations held its First World Congress on Women in Mexico City, an event that helped Mexican women bring women's issues to the attention of the Mexican government and energized Mexican women activists to form rape centers, women's studies courses, and activist groups in areas outside of Mexico City (Rodríguez 2003, 105–106). Yet Mexican women did not all agree about the best ways to use the UN World Conference to improve women's condition. Indeed feminists decided to boycott the UN conference in order to call attention to the Mexican government's neglect of pressing problems confronting Mexican women. Demonstrating their strategic prowess, the feminists organized a "counter-congress," politicizing issues such as voluntary motherhood or reproductive freedom, violence against women, and sexual freedom. The counter-congress garnered a good deal of press coverage, which helped the feminists organize a political wing, the *Coalición de Mujeres Feministas* (Coalition of Feminist Women).

To offset the bad publicity created by feminist critiques of government neglect and indifference, the PRI introduced a series of constitutional reforms in 1974. Chief among these was a new constitutional guarantee of sexual equality. Article 40 declares that "men and women are equal before the law." The government cast this new equality amendment as part of a series of actions taken to advance women's interests, including its decisions to sign the UN *Declaration on the Elimination of Discrimination against Women* in 1967, to implement the recommendations of the 1974 World Population Conference, to proclaim 1975 as the "International Year of Women," and indeed to host the UN World Congress on Women (Mora 1985, 97). Demonstrating its "progressive" credentials to the world, the PRI passed the gender equality amendment eight years before Canadian women succeeded in winning a comparable constitutional guarantee of equality and eight years before the "Equal Rights Amendment" was defeated in the United States.

### The 1982 Crisis and the Turn to Neoliberalism

In the 1960s and 1970s, the import-substitution formula for economic success began to unwind. The subsidies initially designed to support infant industries had become institutionalized into long-term state payments to successful Mexican capitalists creating inefficiencies and corruption. State subsidies increased industrial input costs and raised domestic prices for manufactured goods. The high and uncompetitive cost of Mexican exports combined with a dependence on imported inputs generated a continuing balance of payments deficit. In 1948 and again in 1954, Mexico had to borrow from the International Monetary Fund and the World Bank. From 1955 to 1970, the government turned more to national and international financial markets to pay for its spending (Babb 2001, 78–79). In the 1970s, the Echeverria (1970–1976) and López Portillo (1976–1982) administrations, faced with growing domestic social unrest, embarked on debt-financed spending programs in health, housing, and education. This led to the debt crisis of 1982 in Mexico, the devaluation of the peso, the demise of the import-substitution development policy, a huge structural adjustment program imposed on the Mexican people, and a social and economic crisis that led to a reordering of the Mexican economy and society.

This 1982 crisis was very important in bringing women into the labor force. Faced with soaring costs for food and basic necessities, an inflation rate of around 100 percent in the mid-1980s, an enormous debt burden, falling oil prices, and extensive capital flight, the Mexican economy was reeling. The 1985 earthquakes added further destruction, devastation, and misery. These events encouraged a series of survival strategies for the Mexican people, including the initiation of a process in which women, who had long been active in the subsistence and informal sectors of the economy, were encouraged to take up work in the formal sector. Approximately 28 percent of all women participated in the waged-labor force in 1976 (Rodríguez 2003, 55–56). By 2002, this figure had increased to 36 percent (Committee on the Elimination of all forms Discrimination Against Women 2002 [CEDAW]). To cope with the economic situation, men migrated to urban areas and north to the United States looking for work. Female-headed households increased and women (whether in male- or female-headed households) were left responsible for all domestic work in addition to their labor in the waged economy or the informal and subsistence economies.

For the first time in Mexico, the multiple crises led to the emergence of a civil society relatively autonomous from the state that had previously acted as benefactor. Urban popular movements had begun to organize in the 1970s, and gradually women became the majority of participants in these local activist organizations. As in many other new social movements in Latin America, the predominance of female participation reflected the fact that local movements were making demands around social reproduction, which was traditionally women's responsibility (Bennett 1998, 120–121). These movements expanded in the face of the dramatic crisis of 1982 and the state's turn to neoliberalism. Popular women's groups, often encouraged by middle-class feminists from Mexico City, organized themselves into networks throughout the country in the late 1980s, often working on particular issues such as the Network against Violence Toward Women, the Feminist Peasant Network or the Network of Popular Educators (Rodríguez 2003, 108).

However, self-identified feminist organizations were small, marginalized, and largely composed of middle-class, highly educated women. Feminists repeatedly attempted to build links with working-class women, but had little success in building a unified cross-class movement. Any cooperation between popular sector women's organizations and explicitly feminist organizations was short-term and sporadic, and the movement as a whole remains atomized (Franceschet and Macdonald 2004, 15–16). The peso crisis of 1994 created another wave of economic hardship throughout the country to which women responded further strengthening the political organization of women.

Mexican women's political activism underwent another important shift in the late 1980s as a part of the rise of a pro-democracy movement in the country. Previously, Mexican feminists tended to reject participation in the formal political sphere, suspicious of the dominant party's skill at electoral fraud and co-opting opposition. However, after the 1988 elections, women became important actors in the demands to clean up the political system, both in mixed organizations of men and women like *Alianza Cívica*, and in women-only groups like *Mujeres en Lucha por la Democracia*. About half of the participants in *Alianza Cívica* are women, although they are not necessarily in leadership positions. Despite the critical role that women played in demanding democracy in Mexico, the results of the achievement of democracy have been mixed for women, partly as a result of the conservative ideological character of the PAN government. While President Fox himself is not as socially conservative as much of his party, leading members of his party and his cabinet have made antifeminist statements. Moreover, as an economic conservative, Fox has continued and extended the neoliberal policies of his predecessors in ways that do not favor poor women.

Women have made important gains as is evident in their increasing numbers in public office. While in the 2000 elections the number of women in the Congress declined, by 2003, Mexico had a higher percentage of women in its

**Table 2.2** Comparison of women in parliaments, Mexico, Canada, and the United States

| | | Lower house | | | | Upper house | | | |
|---|---|---|---|---|---|---|---|---|---|
| Rank | Country | Date of election | Seats | Women | % Women | Date of election | Seats | Women | % Women |
| 27 | Mexico | July 2003 | 500 | 113 | 22.6 | July 2000 | 128 | 20 | 15.6 |
| 31 | Canada | June 2004 | 308 | 65 | 21.1 | N.A. | 105 | 33 | 31.4 |
| 57 | United States | November 2004 | 435 | 65 | 14.9 | November 2004 | 100 | 14 | 14.0 |

Source: Interparliamentary Union 2005, *Women in Parliaments* at http://www.ipu.org/wmn-e/classif.htm accessed January 22, 05.

lower legislative chamber (22.6 percent) than did Canada or the United States (with 21.1 and 14.9 percent, respectively.) The Interparliamentary Union ranked Mexico twenty-seventh with respect to percentage of women in both houses of the legislature, Canada thirty-first and the United States fifty-seventh (see table 2.2).

The representation of women improved after two of the three main parties, the PRD and the PRI adopted quota systems that required that 30 percent of their candidates for elected office be women (Bruhn 2003, 110). In the executive and judicial branches, women have also gained representation. In 1999, 30 percent of all department heads in the federal government were women. The first woman was appointed to the Supreme Court in 1961. In 1994, 19 percent of Supreme Court justices, 15 percent of federal magistrates, and 24 percent of judges were women (Committee on the Elimination of Discrimination Against Women 1998).

### International Influences and State Feminism in Mexico

The international women's movement has had considerable impact on Mexican women and on the Mexican government. As described earlier, Amalia Caballero de Castillo Ledón came back to Mexico in 1950 to help lead the fight for women's suffrage at the national level after having been heavily involved in international organizing work in the 1930s and 1940s for the League of Nations, the United Nations, and the *Comisión Interamericana de Mujeres* under the auspices of the Organization of American States. She was also one of the first officers of the UN Commission on the Status of Women. As noted above, Mexico received particular international attention with regard to women's rights when the first UN World Congress on Women was held in Mexico City in 1975. Subsequent world congresses on women organized by the United Nations in Copenhagen in 1980, Nairobi in 1985, and in Beijing in 1995, as well as the Beijing Plus Five meetings in New York in 2000, and the Beijing Plus Ten meetings in New York in 2005, have been used by Mexican women's rights advocates to press the government for policies beneficial to women. Organizing around platform issues emerging from the UN conferences, women in Mexico have pressed for increased representation in governance, reproductive rights, improved health care, poverty reduction, and greater attention to problems of violence against women.

Structural adjustment policies negotiated with international financial institutions during periods of economic crisis have also made successive Mexican governments particularly receptive to recommendations of outside lenders, such as the World Bank and the International Monetary Fund, which link poverty reduction strategies to increased employment of women in the formal sectors of the economy. While the current priority of these international financial institutions is women's empowerment through employment, in the 1960s and 1970s their primary focus was birth control as the way to curb population growth. Some feminist critics of the Mexican government suggest that population control has been the only consistent public policy aimed at women in the last 25 years in Mexico.

In 1981, Mexico signed the United Nation's Convention on the Elimination of All Forms of Discrimination Against Women CEDAW. "Popular feminists" in Mexico, often working in alliance with transnational feminist coalitions, have used CEDAW to illuminate "structural violence" caused by poverty, economic dislocation, and environmental devastation, as well as physical violence manifested in rape, domestic violence, and sexual harassment, suggesting concrete policy proposals to remedy these systemic problems. In December 1999, Mexico signed a further commitment to CEDAW which allows the UN Commission on the Status of Women to "monitor" the Mexican government's progress in eliminating violence against women, discrimination in education and employment, sexual harassment, sexual trafficking, and rape. Since CEDAW's ratification by the legislature on March 15, 2002, feminists working within governmental agencies in Mexico have been using the UN monitoring process as a way to "leverage" policy improvements for women.

Mexico currently has two official governmental organizations devoted to women's affairs. The *Instituto Nacional de las Mujeres* (INMUJERES, National Women's Institute) was created in 2001 by President Vicente Fox. The National Women's Institute took the place of *Programa Nacional de la Mujer* (PRONAM), an organization established in 1996 by President Zedillo as a response to the 1995 UN Fourth World Conference on Women in Beijing. The Beijing meeting called for all member governments to establish "women's machinery" within their bureaucracies to coordinate programs and actions to implement the "Platform for Action" ratified at the Conference. PRONAM was charged with coordinating activities related to women, implementing women's programs at the regional and local levels, and maintaining contact with other NGOs, international organizations, and academics. Between 1996 and 2000 PRONAM's activities addressed problems of health, principally birth control and prenatal care, and education. However, it suffered from very limited funding. When President Vicente Fox abolished PRONAM and created INMUJERES in 2001, he allocated a budget almost ten times the size of PRONAM's. The National Women's Institute is charged with making policy recommendations, but has no enforcement powers. Its first project has been to sponsor training sessions on gender issues throughout the governmental bureaucracy in all regions of the country (Rodríguez 2003, 133–135). INMUJERES is a "decentralized entity" not under the control of any government ministry. Its governing board, however, is dominated by women from the PAN party, and Fox came under considerable criticism from women's organizations when he chose as director of INMUJERES, *panista* Patricia Espinosa—who had publicly opposed abortion—over two pro-choice candidates supported by independent women's organizations.

In June 2002, Espinosa presented Mexico's fifth periodic report to the UN Committee on the Elimination of All Forms of Discrimination Against Women. This report and the discussion it engendered within the United Nations demonstrates how INMUJERES uses the international monitoring process to address women's issues. Providing an overview of her agencies' priorities, Espinosa informed the UN Committee that INMUJERES had established an Interinstitutional Panel of Gender Liaisons to "mainstream" gender perspectives into all governmental institutions at the federal, state and municipal levels, and had launched new initiatives through the Women and Health Program in the Ministry of Health to fight against domestic violence, sexual aggression, and violence against women. Among the major challenges facing the Fox administration, Espinosa included conforming Mexican judicial practices to UN protocols on the "Rights of the Child," the "Involvement of Children in Armed Conflict," and the "Sale of Children, Child Prostitution and Child Pornography," all of which Mexico had recently ratified. Other challenges included efforts to protect the rights of indigenous women, eradicate the trafficking and prostitution of women across the country, foster changes in sexist and discriminatory attitudes, values, and practices, and incorporate a gender approach into public spending and budgeting. Modernizing labor legislation, promoting equal compensation for women, advocating equal access to job opportunities for women, ensuring that poor women receive adequate health and education services, developing reliable indicators for measuring the well-being of women in various sectors of society, and encouraging more participation by women in decision making and political life were other challenges the National Institute was attempting to address (Committee on the Elimination of Discrimination Against Women 2002).

The UN Committee, composed of 23 experts from around the world, expressed concern that the rate of progress had been "very slow" and that improvements for women were not evenly distributed throughout all of Mexico. They also raised specific questions concerning the effects of the 1997 poverty reduction program, and current efforts to suppress trafficking, prostitution, and the exploitation of girl children. The Committee also raised questions concerning the uneven inclusion of women in decision making, noting that although women's representation had increased in the

Senate, it had decreased in the Chamber of Deputies, and remained very low in local government. The Committee asked for additional information concerning the status of the many women immigrating to Mexico from Central America. They also sought information about the institutional power of INMUJERES itself, raising issues concerning the agency's decentralized structure, its exclusively "advisory" mission, and the adequacy of its funding. A range of questions also addressed women's economic status. For example, one expert asked whether the poverty alleviation programs were designed to assist women, in particular, or families more generally. Others expressed concern that only 36 percent of women were in the waged-labor force; that women were earning only 75 percent of what men earned; and that fair labor standards were not being enforced in the *maquiladoras*. The Committee also asked about the availability and administration of microcredit programs for women. In addition the experts sought additional information about "rumors" of involuntary sterilization of indigenous women, girls' and women's levels of educational attainment, the absence of labor protection for domestic workers, the murders of 284 women in Chihuahua, as well as the murders of women along the border. Designed to highlight the most pressing issues that the government must address, the Committee's questions also provided INMUJERES opportunities to craft its own priorities in reporting on the monitoring process to the Mexican government.

In shaping its response to the UN Committee, INMUJERES representatives indicated the issues to which they would devote their energies. For example, rather than placing the blame on government for the "slow progress," INMUJERES suggested that despite the government's efforts to eliminate discrimination against women, a "discriminatory culture" continues to exist in Mexico, a culture that is notoriously difficult to change. Moreover, explicit cultural change typically falls outside of neoliberal conceptions of appropriate state policy. Nonetheless, INMUJERES representatives noted that one program launched in 1997, *Oportunidades*, had met with success in helping women to become more autonomous in household decisions and in handling household budgets. Espinosa also catalogued a number of other accomplishments for which the government could claim credit. With respect to women's representation in elective offices, she reported that the 84 women who headed municipalities had created a network to heighten their efficacy. An amendment to the electoral law at the federal level was designed to enhance women's electoral participation; and 6 of Mexico's 32 states had passed laws mandating women's political participation. Moreover, Mexican law guarantees that at least 30 percent of officeholders will be women as no more than 70 percent of electoral candidates can be of one sex. Espinosa also defended government programs to improve labor conditions in the *maquiladoras*, noting that workers were no longer subjected to mandatory pregnancy checks and were now provided with better access to training.

Signaling the areas that would be most likely to receive government attention, the Coordinator of the Program for Indigenous Women admitted that poverty was "the most important challenge for Mexico's development." Government programs for health and education often did not serve the most marginalized women and families in remote areas, although in some places government programs had doubled or tripled family incomes. In particular, microcredit programs were working for women, although the government did not have systematic data to support this claim. Resources remained a problem in providing health and education for indigenous and poor women. The retention of girls in schools continues to be a problem, although considerable progress had been made in this area. The government admitted that a few cases of involuntary sterilization had been reported, but claimed that this practice had stopped.

INMUJERES representatives also noted areas where changes in government policies were extremely unlikely. They noted that the government was aware of flagrant violations of human rights with regard to Central American migrants, but had no specific government policies to address them. The government had no information on the number of women who were victims of violence and relied on information from universities and NGOs. The INMUJERES spokesperson also admitted that the government was not prepared to deal with the trafficking of women and that the murders were a "painful indication of the kind of violence that existed throughout the country" (Committee 2002).

## Conclusion

This chapter has shown that Mexican women have had a wide variety of political and economic roles, roles that have varied over time depending largely on the economy and the political regime in power, although the country has from pre-Hispanic times differentiated between men and women's work. Changes in gender roles have tended to come with major disruptions in the society. In particular, events such as the Spanish Conquest, the Revolution of 1910, and the economic crises associated with globalization involving the devaluation of the peso especially in 1982 and 1994 have marked major changes not only in the government and in the economy, but also in the society as a whole, especially in gender relationships. While the Spanish Conquest involved the imposition of Spanish rule that did not recognize indigenous peoples as citizens and imposed Spanish family law that clearly relegated women to household and family duties under the husband's authority, the Revolution of 1910 and the economic crises caused by globalization created the opportunity for significant changes in race, class, and gender relations.

The economic crisis of 1982 generated still another shakeup in Mexican gender relations as women entered the formal labor force in very large numbers, migration increasingly separated family members from one another, and poverty mandated that women assume nontraditional economic roles in the formal sector. In 1910, 1982, and thereafter, the impetus for major gender role changes did not come from Mexican women's organized resistance to household chores or duties, but were instigated by civil or economic disruptions that necessitated change. Nevertheless, many Mexican women have seized the chance to participate economically and politically in light of these structural disruptions.

Class continues to define women's participation in politics, with formal participation in established political legislatures and bureaucracies being assumed predominately by university-educated elite women from political families. Mexican women are also divided by race, with indigenous women continuing to suffer extreme economic and political marginalization. Over the past 30 years, globalization has been accompanied by a burst of women's political participation in grassroots political and economic organizations, as well as in nongovernmental organizations. Industrialization and the 1982 economic crisis ushered in a "feminization" of the Mexican labor force as *maquiladoras* brought larger numbers of women into the waged-labor force. Many more women were drawn out of their subsistence agricultural economies to engage in small businesses, street vending, and other aspects of the informal economy including prostitution. Still other women migrated from one part of Mexico to another or to the United States, where they obtained employment as domestics, restaurant and hotel workers, janitors, and sweatshop workers.

Since women received the right to vote in 1953, Mexico has steadily increased the number of women in its governing legislatures, judiciary, and in its federal, state, and local bureaucracies. Mexico now has more women representatives in the federal legislative branch than does the United States. The social disruption brought on by the forces of globalization has increased the levels of inequality in Mexico, heightening inequalities among women, as well as between men and women. Levels of violence are increasing in Mexico City and along the border. While globalization has opened political spaces for some women, the increasing levels of poverty, violence, and inequality do not auger well for Mexican women or for Mexican democracy.

# CHAPTER 3

# Women and Politics in Canada

## LOIS HARDER

A distinctive feature of women's political power is its ghost-like quality. Often unacknowledged, but also strongly resisted, its existence, effects, and potential are evident in the vast array of structures and practices that have been devised to reinforce its obscurity. The phrase "women and politics" thus has a peculiar ring. It asserts that women have a role in the shaping of our collective well-being, thereby not only acknowledging the realm of domesticity and reproductive labor as sites of politics, but also claiming that women have a role in public power. Further, the relationship between women and power is not simply one of subjection. In fact, different groups of women at various times have reinforced, resisted, and reshaped the forces that work to structure the gender order (understood as the structures and norms that give meaning to masculinity and femininity (Orloff 1996) as well as the broader conditions of social life).

Using a four-part periodization, this chapter explores Canada's economic and political development, through a gendered lens, to trace the meaning and significance of women in the territory that came to be known as Canada. This review begins with: (1) the precontact era through the establishment of staples economies; (2) industrialization, suffrage, and temperance; (3) the second wave of the women's movement and the crisis of the welfare state; and (4) contemporary neoliberalism. From the perspective of women's role within governmental institutions, this trajectory might suggest a steady increase in women's political importance. However, such a conclusion repeats the error of obscuring the power that women commanded throughout Canada's history as well as ascribing a level of authority to contemporary political institutions and to the significance of women's gendered identities within these institutions that is not sustainable. In short, this chapter presents a paradox: women had power where we often presume they had none, and they may not have power where we presume that they should. For an overview of Canada, see table 3.1.

**Table 3.1**   Canada at a glance

| | |
|---|---|
| Geography | 9,922,000 square kilometers |
| Population: | 31,825,416 |
| White | 86.6% |
| Black | 2% |
| Latin American | 0.07% |
| Aboriginal | 4% |
| Asian | 4% |
| GDP | C$1.25 trillion |
| GDP per capita | C$28,500 |
| Political system | federal, parliamentary |
| Languages | bilingual: English and French |

- No permanent settlements in 90% of the country.
- 72% of the population lives within 150 km of the U.S. border.
- 62% of the population resides in the Toronto–Ottawa–Montreal corridor.
- 0.3% of the population lives in Yukon, Northwest territories, and Nunavut.

## Precontact Era and the Staples Trade

Prior to contact with Europeans, the territory that would become Canada was populated by a widely diverse range of Aboriginal peoples. At least 12 separate families of languages existed with further variations among each of these (Benoit 2000, 32). Cultures were shaped by the primary avenues to subsistence, ranging from fishing in coastal areas, hunting and gathering in the north and east, agricultural production in what is today's Ontario, and buffalo hunting on the prairies (Prentice et al. 1988, 17).

Feminist historians and anthropologists have uncovered evidence that hunting and gathering societies, such as the Montagnais–Nascapi and the agricultural communities of the Six Nations and the Huron were organized around relatively egalitarian gender orders. In particular, women enjoyed power in their sexual lives and marriage, they exercised influence in decision making and they participated in spiritual and ceremonial activities (Prentice et al. 1988, 31). The tribes of the prairies differed from this arrangement in that parents exercised greater control over marriage (p. 33). This role would become evident to Europeans, as the fur trade necessitated close ties with Aboriginal peoples and marriages became an integral part of this dynamic. In the context of west coast Indians, we see further variation in the place of women. Many of these groups were matrilineal, but marriages tended to be arranged by men. On the other hand, women were involved in trade and in the religious life of their communities (p. 34).

Among political economists, the standard tale of Canada's economic development is built around the staples theory. First articulated by Harold Innis in the 1930s, the theory asserts that Canada's economy was shaped by the development for export of a successive series of primary commodities, these being fish, fur, timber, and wheat. The character of production for each of the staples gave rise to specific forms of community and to supporting infrastructure. Demand for staples was driven by European markets (or the metropole), thus leaving the colony (or the hinterland) vulnerable to the changing fashions and desires of the colonizer. As the demand shifted, a new staple would be identified to replace its predecessor and would give rise to new infrastructural requirements and relations of power.

Initial forays into North America by Europeans were thus driven by a desire to plunder the continent's rich resources for the benefit of kings and countries. In Canada, the French were the first Europeans to establish settlements. Seasonal fishing villages appeared on the coast of Newfoundland, but permanent European settlements would await the fur trade. The European demand for furs, especially beaver pelts, grew in the early 1600s, and, as supplies were exhausted, a steady westward pursuit of the animals was established (Innis 1977, 14). This required both strong relationships with Indian nations as well as a more permanent presence by the French.

Women were integral to the establishment of settlements, since they signaled France's intention to cultivate an enduring presence in North America. This desire to increase the French population in the New World was driven by both mercantilism and the Catholic Counter-Reformation (Prentice et al. 1988, 19–20); expressed in the New World as the drive to stem the rising tide of Protestants who were simultaneously settling the British colonies further south. European women first ventured to New France in the 1600s, and while many women came as wives and daughters, single women also made the arduous Atlantic journey (Foulché-Delbosc 1977, 15, 17). Single female immigrants fell into two general categories. The first, who began to arrive in 1639, were religious figures, daughters of highly placed wealthy families (Noël 1991, 30). The second group was the *filles du roi*; migrants sponsored by the government who arrived between 1663 and 1673 (p. 30). In addition, some single women came as domestic help (Foulché-Delbosc 1977, 15).

Feminist historian Jan Noël (1991) argues that women in New France enjoyed a relatively favorable existence in comparison to their compatriots in France and the women of New England. Several factors account for this, including the flexibility of women's roles that characterized Western Europe under the *ancien régime* and were transported to New France; the demographic configuration of the new colony; and the dynamics of the colonial economy itself, in which the centrality of war and the fur trade created opportunities for women (p. 36).

Noël asserts that the distinction between the public and the private had not yet been drawn in seventeenth-century Europe and hence, women and men readily traversed the ground that would later be demarcated by domesticity and "public" life (p. 31). The existence of New France as a predominantly military society and a staging ground for the fur trade, meant that men were often absent, leaving the commercial endeavors of the colony as well as the defense of many communities in the hands of women (p. 40).

Moreover, men's lives tended to be extremely hazardous, leaving many women without husbands and responsible for the well-being of their families and the commercial viability of the new colony. Indeed, in 1663, women held the majority of the colony's land holdings (p. 45).

Women's capacity to acquire property and run commercial enterprises was enabled by French law. The *Coutume de Paris*, which underpinned the legal system in New France, was relatively egalitarian. It protected women's rights by assuring that husbands could not alienate the family property (Noël 1991, 33). Moreover wives often brought substantial family property to their marriages and retained their rights to it (p. 33). The *filles du roi* are notable here as they brought a considerable dowry with them as part of the incentive to migrate to the new colony.

Women in New France were also relatively well-educated. Once the Ursulines and the Hospitalières—the most prominent female religious societies—had abandoned their efforts to "civilize" and convert the native peoples, they turned their attention to the health of the colony and the education of its girls (Prentice et al. 1988, 41–42). While this education was quite brief, perhaps only for a year, students did learn to read and write in anticipation of their first communion and were educated, in the words of Marie de l'Incarnation, founder of the Ursuline convent in Quebec City, in "all sorts of work proper to their sex" (p. 58). As a result of their urban origins, migrants to New France tended to be better educated than the people who remained in France.

The white women of New France also enjoyed advantages relative to their American and European counterparts due to their small numbers. In Montreal in 1663, for example, there were eight marriageable men for every marriageable woman (Noël 1991, 39). The scarcity of women thus accounted for their lenient treatment in cases of adultery; a relative tolerance for women's insubordination to authority; and the complete lack of persecution for witchcraft, which was at its high point at this time in both Europe and New England (pp. 39–40). This numerical gender imbalance, however, did not persist due to the short and dangerous lives of men. By the end of the seventeenth century women were the majority, maintaining this numerical advantage until the British conquest of New France in 1763.

In addition to their significance within their own communities, Aboriginal women were also extremely important to Europeans, playing an integral role in the fur trade (1670–1870). Native communities recognized the advantages of strategic alliances with the companies of the fur trade and marriages between native women and traders were a key part of these relationships (Prentice et al. 1988, 34). From the perspective of the Europeans (both French and English), native women made excellent guides and negotiators as well as companions. Moreover, native women were essential for the provisioning of expeditions. As Sylvia van Kirk observes, "one wonders . . . how the famed 1789 expedition of Alexander Mackenzie would have fared without the work of the wives of his two French-Canadian voyageurs. The women scarcely ever left the canoes, being 'continually employ'd making shoes of moose skin as a pair does not last us above one Day' " (1991, 76).

Sanctions against "mixed marriages" were difficult to sustain, given the importance of native peoples to the success of the fur trade and the absence of white women from Rupert's Land, which was later to become western Canada, until the 1800s. While the church maintained its refusal to recognize such marriages, the practice of *mariage à la façon du pays* or "country marriage" was widespread. Marriage required the consent of the family of the Indian girl as well as her own agreement and involved the payment of a substantial bride price to the native family (van Kirk 1991, 75). The ceremonies were conducted according to local native customs but also involved a declaration of "man and wife" at the trading fort (p. 75). In addition to their economic significance, marriages between Europeans and native women also enabled some approximation of a domestic life that would otherwise have been impossible for the Europeans.

Despite the commonness of the practice, neither British missionaries nor the managers of the trading companies still residing in Britain really came to terms with "country marriage." A Canadian court did uphold the marriage between Chief Factor William Connolly and his Cree wife, asserting that the marriage had been conducted according to the practices of the wife's people, it had the consent of both parties, and had been a publicly acknowledged relationship for 28 years (van Kirk 1991, 75). However, as the wheat economy began to overtake the fur trade and white women began to make their way to the prairies, the sanctions against mixed marriages became stronger. In 1806, for example, the North West Company permitted marriages between white men and the daughters of white men, but prohibited marriage to "full-blooded Indian women" (p. 78). Native women who, despite the significance of customary marriages, had always been vulnerable to sexual abuse, neglect, and family breakup, were increasingly "turned out" or cast aside (Brown 2001, 62). Further, the presence of a white wife signaled the superior-class position of their husbands (Driscoll 2001, 99). White women themselves contributed to the demeaning of native women, asserting that 'country marriages' were relics of a more barbaric and depraved age (van Kirk 1991, 71). Thus, as Sylvia van Kirk observes, "the vital role that native women had played in opening up the Canadian west was demeaned or forgotten" (p. 79).

## From British Conquest to Canadian Confederation

The period between the Conquest of New France by the British (1763) and Confederation (1867) extended the diversity of immigrants to the now British colonies and frontier. The Loyalist migration from the United States including escaping slaves, European refugees from the Napoleonic wars and the Irish potato famines, and British immigrants escaping the political unrest in England in the 1830s and 1840s were the major constituents of these migratory waves (Prentice et al. 1988, 66). The "underground railroad" helped to shepherd fleeing slaves from the United States to the British territory, where slavery had been abolished in 1834.

Whereas the separation of the public and private spheres was intensifying for the middle and upper classes during the nineteenth century in Europe and in the United States, the dividing line continued to be hazy in British North America and less gender demarcated. Certainly industrialization was occurring, with Montreal being the largest urban and commercial center in the British colonies, but even this development did not relegate women to domesticity. Many women had to support their families through their work in factories, or as domestics and in response, religious orders established a number of day care centers to assist women who were involved in waged labor (Cross 1977, 67).

Women in rural areas were also fundamental to the survival of their families. Far from the feminine idleness celebrated in upper class, Victorian social norms, women in the British colonies labored alongside their husbands and often alone or with their children, in order to feed, clothe, and house their families. The disjuncture between the realities of life in the wilds of Canada and the "civility" of Britain was famously captured in the writings of Susannah Moodie. Her pioneer tale *Roughing it in the Bush*, was a bittersweet chronicle of her experiences learning the skills of backwoods farming (Prentice et al. 1988, 69). And while the Moodie family would eventually find their way to a more genteel life in a southern Ontario town, Susannah Moodie's description of the back-breaking labor involved in homesteading would resonate for thousands of women in the British colonies, across the North West Territory, and in British Columbia, as they worked to establish farms and communities.

Patriarchal social customs and laws, including changes to the customary law that had protected the property rights of the women of New France, defined the institutional framework of women's subordination in nineteenth-century Canada. But again, the necessity of women's work to the functioning of British North America as well as to their families gave women authority and influence that was not reflected in the formal declarations of social order. In terms of political participation, women's exclusion was more a matter of custom than law. New Brunswick had specifically prohibited women from voting in 1791 but no similar formal exclusions were articulated in the other colonies (Prentice et al. 1988, 98). As propertied men became increasingly active in newly established elected assemblies, some evidence suggests that propertied women also felt entitled to exercise their ambiguous democratic rights. In Lower Canada, which would later become Quebec, women voted in elections in 1809 and 1820 (p. 98). Because the franchise was tied to property ownership rather than construed as an individual democratic right, however, an election in Bedford county was declared void when 22 married women duplicated the votes of their husbands on the same properties (p. 98). In the aftermath of this election, the Assembly declared that voting by wives was illegal, whether or not their husbands voted (p. 99).

The ambiguity surrounding women's voting rights continued to play out in the British colonies until the middle of the nineteenth century. Articulating arguments that would be replayed in the suffrage campaigns several decades later, petitioners contested the denial of a widow's efforts to vote in a Quebec election in 1828 arguing that "it would be impolitic and tyrannical to circumscribe [woman's] efforts in society—to say that she shall not have the strongest interest in the fate of her country, and the security of her common rights . . ." (Backhouse cited in Prentice et al. 1988, 99). Ultimately such pleas would be rejected. Prince Edward Island excluded women from the franchise in 1836; women were forbidden from voting in both Upper Canada (Ontario) and Lower Canada (Quebec) in 1849; and Nova Scotia followed suit in 1851 (p. 99).

In the century between Britain's conquest of New France and the establishment of Canada, a number of strategies for the governance of British North America were attempted. Primary issues concerned the degree of local autonomy over decision making that would be permitted by the colonial authorities, and whether Quebec's French language and culture should be addressed through accommodation or assimilation. These issues were played out within the broader context of Britain's ambivalence regarding its North American colonies—expressed through its termination of preferential treatment for colonial goods—and fear of American expansionist ambitions. These fears were exacerbated during the American Civil War, which stimulated discussions about unification among the remaining British colonies in North America. After a series of negotiations, four British colonies, Nova Scotia, New Brunswick, Ontario, and Quebec, agreed to form the Dominion of Canada in 1867.

## Confederation and the Formation of
## Canada's Contemporary Political Institutions

According to the terms established in the "British North America Act of 1867," the first constitution of the new nation, Canada's federal government is divided into two houses, the elected House of Commons and the appointed Senate. The Senate was to serve as a body of regional representation while the House of Commons is based on representation by population. With its property and age requirements for membership, the Senate was expected to serve as a "house of sober second thought," an antidote to the potential capriciousness of the House of Commons. Over time, however, appointments to the Canadian Senate have been criticized as being tools of political patronage rather than ensuring regional representation or policy reflection.

Canada's political system also distinguishes between the head of state and the head of government. The head of state is a primarily ceremonial position, held by the British monarch, represented in Canada by the governor-general. The substantive executive decision-making power resides with the prime minister who is the head of government, as well as his/her cabinet. Canada uses the Westminster or responsible government system. Rather than all Canadian voters electing the prime minister directly, the prime minister is the leader of the party that wins the most seats. S/he is elected like any other representative, by winning the most votes within a particular constituency. The party leader then selects her/his cabinet from among the party members, and the prime minister and cabinet form the political executive. The executive is then held responsible to the legislature and theoretically, can be defeated at any time if it fails to maintain the confidence of the House of Commons. Practically, however, the use of party discipline generally ensures that all members of the party that forms the government will vote in support of the executive.

Canada's federal design was a strategic imperative necessitated by the task of uniting four disparate colonies into the provinces of a broader nation-state. To secure their agreement, each former colony was granted a specific, autonomous domain of decision making. The federal government was empowered to manage issues that concerned the country as a whole and to ensure its ongoing development. Although "Confederation" is the term used to denote the establishment of Canada through the British North America Act of 1867 (later renamed the Constitution Act 1867), the initial plan for the relationship among the former colonies was much more centralized than a strictly confederal system would suggest. The federal government laid claim to the preeminent means of raising money at the time (customs duties), as well as all forms of taxation; while the provinces were restricted to direct taxation (income tax), which was not well developed at the time. The federal government controlled national defense, currency, international trade, and commerce—all matters that had bedeviled the initial union of America's original 13 colonies. In addition, the national government had the power to override provincial legislation and by virtue of its responsibility for the "Peace, Order, and Good Government" of the country, laid claim to any new governmental matters, or matters that were not strictly within the purview of the provinces. For their part, the provinces controlled their natural resources and were responsible for the health, education, and social well-being of their residents.

This division of powers would prove to be a central and perpetual source of tension between the federal and provincial governments. Initially, however, the arrangement served the new country well, as the federal government undertook the early process of nation building through a collection of policies that would come to be known as the First National Policy (1870–1890s). As a country that was claimed to have "too much geography and not enough history," the process of nation building entailed the establishment of a national railway that would unite the country "from sea to shining sea," the imposition of high tariffs to encourage the development of Canadian manufactured goods, but which also led to the establishment of foreign, especially American, subsidiaries on Canadian soil, and the settlement of the west, primarily by European immigrants.

Although the westward drive of the fur trade had resulted in the establishment of trading forts and surrounding communities, the migratory character of trapping lent a temporary quality to the resulting settlements. With the shift to the wheat economy, long-term, permanent settlements became possible. Nonetheless, the drive for settlement was tempered by a racial prejudice which ensured that only white and preferably northern European or American immigrants would be permitted to make their homes in the west. The Liberal government actively recruited eastern European agriculturalists, though many British settlers viewed Ukrainian and Russian farmers as "ruled by violence, pagan excess, and idleness" (Stasiulus 1997, 146). With regard to Asian settlement, however, both the Liberal government and British settlers uniformly resisted permanency, despite recruiting Chinese men to construct the railway. Rather than rewarding these men for their sacrifices in carrying out this dangerous work (it is estimated that one man died for every mile of track), the Canadian and British Columbia governments thwarted their desires to establish lives in Canada. The government imposed costly head taxes on Asian migrants, thereby blocking the efforts of Asian men to bring their wives to Canada.[1] As in the earliest days of colonization, women were widely held to be the key to permanent settlement.

The process of railroad building and western settlement also entailed treaty making with the native population to ensure that the railroad companies would have secure access to land. And while treaty making suggests some acknowledgement of a nation-to-nation relationship, the treaties favored the interests of the Europeans over the Aboriginal peoples.[2] Further defining the relationship between the Canadian state and the Aboriginal peoples was the passage of the first consolidated Indian Act in 1876. This law, which still exists in modified form, outlined almost limitless powers for the federal government over the lives of "Indian" peoples—including deeming who would be understood as an "Indian," that is, granting "status" under the *Act*. The *Indian Act* negated existing structures of Aboriginal power and authority, imposing patrilineal and patriarchal modes of social organization where they may not have previously existed. In particular, male status Indians who married non-Indians could transfer their status to their wives and children, whereas female status Indians who married non-Indian men actually lost their status entirely. Aboriginal women in this situation would lose their homes and their entitlement to federal benefits. As we will see, the sexual inequality written into the Indian Act would become a major impetus behind future efforts to protect gender equality through the passage of the Canadian Charter of Rights and Freedoms a century later.[3]

The First National Policy also entailed the inclusion of more British colonies within the Dominion and the division of territories into provinces. Between 1867 and 1905, British Columbia, Prince Edward Island, Manitoba, Saskatchewan, and Alberta became provinces. Newfoundland would not join Confederation until 1949. For women, the dynamics of Canadian federalism have been both a strategic boon and a source of frustration.

The federal structure not only necessitates organizing at both levels of government, but also enables activists to play the various governments against each other. Tensions within the federation can also spill over into the women's movement, as has often been the case between the women's movements in Quebec and in the rest of Canada. One of the first issues to conflate federalism and feminism, and to illuminate the strategic opportunities and challenges of Canada's particular political configuration, was the struggle for the vote.

## Suffrage and Women's Political Activity in the Late Nineteenth and Early Twentieth Centuries

Women's aspirations for themselves and their families ran parallel to the dreams that attended the First National Policy and the process of Canadian nation building generally. The late nineteenth century saw a number of milestones for women in the professions, including the opening of medical schools to women in 1879 and law schools in the 1890s (Cook and Mitchinson 1976, 167). These achievements, however, were overwritten by the prevailing view of women's inferiority. The hostility of male medical students toward their female classmates resulted in the reimposition of bans on women at the medical faculties of Queen's and Toronto in 1883, and the establishment of separate training institutions for women (de la Cour and Sheinin 1991, 208). But gaining the educational credentials did not ensure access to hospitals or the capacity to establish a viable private practice. As a result, medical research and overseas medical missionary work were the venues to which women doctors gravitated (Prentice et al. 1988, 132).

In terms of the legal profession, Canadian women were the first to gain access to formal legal education in the British Empire, but they encountered many hurdles along the way. Claire Brett Martin, the first Canadian woman to become a fully fledged member of the legal profession, was initially barred from the Law Society of Upper Canada, on the grounds that women were not "persons" (Prentice et al. 1988, 132). She enlisted the help of Dr. Emily Stowe, a medical doctor who had been a key mover in securing women's access to medical education, and the Dominion Women's Enfranchisement Association in her struggle (p. 132). Their efforts eventually culminated in 1891 in the passage of a bill in the Ontario legislature to enable women to study law. This success, however, was tempered by the fact that the legislation appears to have been a means to stave off the more controversial demand for women's suffrage and by the fact that it did not enable women to *practice* law (p. 133). In order to become a barrister, Brett Martin had to enlist the help of another prominent activist, Lady Aberdeen, wife of the governor-general, and the organization she founded, the National Council of Women of Canada (NCWC). Brett Martin eventually became a full fledged member of the Ontario legal profession in 1897, but given the fact that provinces controlled legal licensing, her success was confined to

Ontario (p. 133). In Quebec, for example, women did not gain access to law schools until 1914, and could not practice until 1941 (p. 133).

In the "professions" as a general category of employment, women attained numeric equality in 1901 (Prentice et al. 1988, 129). Not surprisingly, this achievement was overwhelmingly attributed to the number of women teachers, but their prevalence in the profession did not translate into opportunities for advancement. The ranks of school principals and inspectors were overwhelmingly populated by men. Interestingly, in contrast to the situation of Quebec's aspiring women lawyers, Quebec's women teachers enjoyed better opportunities for advancement in teaching than their Anglophone compatriots. The sex segregation of the Catholic school system largely accounted for this (p. 130).

The professions were only one site of women's employment. Most women engaged in paid work were employed as domestics, but they also worked in factories and increasingly in the service economy. Women's work was also essential to farming operations, and indeed, unmarried male farmers were known to be less successful than their married counterparts because of their lack of access to women's labor.

Clearly women were actively involved in building the new country, but whether, and how, their contributions should receive formal public recognition was the subject of intense debate and struggle. The sharpest expression of these debates over "the Woman Question" would come in the context of suffrage efforts.

### Suffrage

The extension of the vote to Canadian women was a piecemeal process. As we have already seen, some women property owners had been able to vote in local and colonial elections prior to Confederation, although this right was systematically removed over the early decades of the 1800s. By the latter part of the century, the tide was again turning, with women property holders gaining the right to vote in municipal elections in British Columbia in 1873 (Prentice et al. 1988, 175). In 1884 in Ontario, unmarried women who met property qualifications were also extended the right to vote in municipal elections, but they were barred from holding public office (pp. 175–176). This modest victory gave rise to the first organization explicitly organized to demand women's suffrage, but it would take another two decades before their objective was realized, first on a provincial scale, and then at the federal level.

As in the United States, Canadian women's clubs were the original sites for political mobilization, and ultimately, suffrage struggles. Women's clubs were strongly tied to religion and were narrowly denominational in their early formations, despite the fact that many clubs were formed to address similar purposes: the ills of urbanization, industrialization, moral decay, and in some cases, immigration (Strong-Boag 1977, 87). In terms of the demand for enfranchisement specifically, the failure of governments to prohibit the sale and consumption of alcohol was the single most important inspiration for women to seek the vote. The Women's Christian Temperance Union, having been unable to persuade politicians that alcohol was the source of societal ills, concluded that only through their votes could they mount sufficient pressure to change the law.

The link between temperance and suffrage, however, did not sit well with all women's groups. Catholic women, in particular, rejected the temperance cause (Strong-Boag 1977, 91). This religious division, tied as it was to the French–English divide in Canada, also contributed to a division between the French and English-speaking women's movement. Anti-immigrant sentiment also affected the suffrage movement. Icelandic women who had settled in Manitoba in the 1890s, for example, were strong supporters of women's rights to vote and to equality rights generally, but they were geographically isolated from the larger women's groups in central Canada and, in any case, were discounted on the basis of their ethnic origin (Prentice et al. 1988, 185). Nonetheless, the Icelandic Suffrage Association did become the first affiliate of the Canadian Women's Suffrage Association in 1907 (p. 191).

For some suffrage activists, the religious and ethnic divisions among women were viewed as a central obstacle that would have to be overcome if their struggle for women's voting rights was to be won. Lady Aberdeen was the key figure in the effort to unite women across these divides; a task she undertook through the founding of the NCWC. Because of her position as the wife of the governor-general, as well as her extensive experience with a number of charitable causes, her religious tolerance, and her travels across Canada, Lady Aberdeen was able to take a leadership role in drawing together activists from the Canadian women's club movement and to overcome the criticisms of antifeminists (Strong-Boag 1977, 98). Her strategy was to create an organization that was nondenominational, nonpartisan, and respectful of local autonomy, and while this approach would ultimately succeed, the organization faced much opprobrium regarding its lack of an explicit religious affiliation. While Lady Aberdeen was a suffrage supporter, the NCWC did not initially endorse the franchise for women in an effort to limit the divisions that might prevent the creation of a strong national women's organization (Prentice et al. 1988, 181).

As in the United States, Canadian women demanded the vote on the grounds of feminine virtue and, less explicitly, as a matter of natural justice (Strong-Boag 1991, 311). Accepting the widely held view that men and women were distinct if complementary, suffragists argued that women's strong morality and feminine virtue would provide the antidote to the corrupt tendencies of politics. And while some women also argued for sexual equality and hence the right of women to vote, many others believed that women's responsibility for the caring work of society was the strongest persuasive force in the demand for the vote.

Suffrage struggles took on different forms depending on where they were waged in the country. The west was most responsive, with male politicians often invoking the labor of pioneer women in establishing their communities (Prentice et al. 1988, 197). The obvious contribution that women made to the success of western agricultural development would lend a particular flavor to the suffrage debate, with prairie women encountering less resistance to the acquisition of voting rights than their central Canadian and maritime compatriots.

Ultimately, World War I would provide the final impetus for the extension of the franchise to women. On the basis of their contributions to the war effort, which ranged from suffering the loss of sons and husbands, working in factories at home, to serving as nurses overseas, the federal government acquiesced to the demands of the suffrage campaigners. But the vote was not extended to women as a matter of simple justice. Instead, in 1917, the federal government decided to begin the process of women's enfranchisement by first extending voting rights to nurses and then to women whose male relatives were serving overseas or had died in the war (Prentice *et al.* 1988, 207–208). This selective women's franchise was designed to shore up support for conscription, a highly divisive political issue, particularly along the French–English axis. And while these selected women were granted the vote, German immigrants, who were deemed enemies despite their citizenship in Canada, had their voting rights withdrawn. In 1918, the federal government finally passed the Women's Franchise Act which permitted women to vote if they were British subjects (i.e., Canadian citizens) and possessed the same qualifications as men under the provincial franchise (p. 208). See table 3.2.

Quebec was the last province to grant the franchise to women, in 1940. This long resistance was a product of the power of the Catholic Church in the administration of the province.[4] Until the 1950s, the Catholic Church

**Table 3.2**  Chronology of women's suffrage in Canada

| | |
|---|---|
| Federal franchise for women | 1918 |
| Provincial franchise | |
|     Manitoba, Saskatchewan, and Alberta | 1916 |
|     British Columbia | 1917 |
|     Nova Scotia | 1918 |
|     Ontario, New Brunswick | 1919 |
|     Prince Edward Island | 1922 |
|     Newfoundland | 1925 |
|     Quebec | 1940 |
| | |
| *Historic political achievements* | |
| First woman elected (provincial) | 1917 |
| First woman elected (federal) | 1921 |
| First black woman elected | 1972 |
| First Aboriginal woman elected | 1974 |
| First woman appointed to the Senate | 1930 |
| First woman appointed to federal Cabinet | 1957 |

in Quebec performed a variety of state functions, including the provision of education, health care, and social services. Through these functions, the Church was able to promote its teachings, quell dissent, and deny women their rights, including the franchise, on the basis of theology. Some indication of the arguments that were marshaled against women is provided in a letter sent by Cardinal Villeneuve to the Liberal government, which ultimately resisted the Church's objections and implemented voting rights for women. The Cardinal's objections, like those of so many opponents of woman's suffrage, were stated thus:

1. woman suffrage would militate against family unity;
2. it would expose women to all the passions of elections;
3. the great majority of women in the province did not want it, and
4. social and economic reforms could be as well achieved by women's organizations operating outside the realm of politics (Cleverdon 1974, 257).

While it was true that only a small number of Quebec women campaigned for voting rights, they were aided by federal government support and from a political situation in which modernity (represented by the Liberal party) versus insular paternalism (represented by its primary political opponent, the Union Nationale) formed a key axis of contestation (Cleverdon 1974, 253).

Finally, men and women of Asian and South Asian descent would have to wait until 1948 to vote; while Aboriginal men and women living on reserves did not obtain the right to vote until 1960. Prior to 1960, status Indians could vote if they renounced their claims to status under the Indian Act. Aboriginal peoples largely rejected this course of action as they rightly saw enfranchisement as a means of assimilation (Eisenberg 1998, 45).

Having obtained the right to vote, the first wave of Canada's feminist activists set about securing their constitutional claim to personhood. In 1927, five women from western Canada, "the Famous Five," spearheaded the campaign for a legal ruling on whether women were to be included as "qualified persons" for Senate appointments under the terms of the British North America Act 1867. In 1928, the Canadian Supreme Court ruled that women were not "qualified persons." The Famous Five then appealed to the British Judicial Committee of the Privy Council, which, at that time, served as Canada's highest court, and, in 1929, were successful (Prentice et al. 1988, 282). A set of statues on Parliament Hill celebrates this achievement, the only statues on the hill that do not commemorate former prime ministers.

The British Court handed down its "Persons Case" decision on the same day as the great stock market crash on Wall Street; a coincidence of great misfortune for Canadian women (Cavanaugh, 2005). In the economic contraction of the Great Depression, women who aspired to paid employment were thwarted as public sentiment overwhelmingly prioritized jobs for male breadwinners. And while a few women did gain elected office, they were more likely to do so under the auspices of protest parties (Bashevkin

1985, 16). Canada's first woman Member of Parliament, Agnes McPhail, for example, won election under the banner of the United Farmers of Ontario. More commonly, political parties restricted women's activities to fund raising and organizing. Only women in Canada's social democratic party, the Canadian Commonwealth Federation, attempted to assert their perspective. Other party women did not adopt this approach until the 1970s (pp. 99–100).

World War II would provide another opportunity for women to appear in the public realm. Initially, women took up the same kinds of tasks that they had performed during the Great War: collecting household items that could be recycled for the war effort, assembling care packages, running hospitality centers for the troops, and generally encouraging a sense of national pride and duty (Prentice et al. 1988, 297). Women in rural areas took on a greater share of agricultural production and women in the cities were again recruited into factory work. This time, however, women's labor was coordinated by the federal government, through the Women's Voluntary Services Division, established in 1941 (p. 297). The government established a national registration of women aged 20–24, with the objective of relocating single women to the factories of central Canada. However, the emphasis on employing single women could not be sustained as many of them left their lower-paying positions as domestics, clerks, and garment workers, creating a void in those positions (p. 298). As a result, married women were also increasingly drawn into the labor force. To support their labor force participation, the government established childcare centers and revised tax laws so as not to penalize men for the wages earned by their wives. Nonetheless, these initiatives were undertaken with a strong emphasis on their temporary character. Once the war was over, the childcare centers disappeared and the financial penalties for a working wife became even harsher than they had been prior to the war (pp. 298, 305–306).

World War II was also the first time that women were active members of the armed services. Nonetheless, very few women (other than nurses) were posted overseas, and their assignments were generally limited to serving as clerks, cooks, drivers, telephone operators etc. (Prentice et al. 1988, 302). Indeed, one unfortunate group from the Women's Division of the Royal Canadian Air Force found themselves assigned to washing the floors of the governor-general's mansion (p. 302).

The immediate post–World War II period was a moment of stark contradictions for women. Both men and women supported the enforced exclusion of women from high-paying factory and clerical jobs as part of the logical return to peacetime social order. Yet, the improving educational attainment of women, technological developments that eased the burdens of domestic labor, the positive experience of wartime employment, and an industrialized economy in which consumption was central, all helped to fuel the growing presence and need for women's engagement in the labor market (Bashevkin 1985, 22). Indeed, women did increasingly participate in the labor market in the 1950s and 1960s, while simultaneously confronting a prevailing ideology of domesticity (Prentice et al. 1988, 316). These contradictions would ultimately contribute to the second wave of the women's movement.

## The Second Wave

As with other industrialized nations, the postwar period in Canada witnessed unprecedented economic growth and the establishment of an array of social programs under the auspices of the welfare state. Like the United States, and unlike its European cousins who were quicker off the mark, Canada's post-war welfare state did not fully form until the mid-1960s, precisely at the time that the second wave of the women's movement was gathering momentum. In Canada, many explain this delay in terms of the division of powers between the federal and provincial governments. Because the provinces have responsibility for social programs while the federal government has superior revenue raising and spending capacity, federal–provincial collaboration is essential. Achieving this agreement, however, has not always been easy. Successive federal governments viewed the implementation of social programs that would be roughly equivalent across the country as a key mechanism in crafting a common citizenship. In the absence of a unifying national mythology, they would create a common Canadian identity.

The task of building a national identity involved the explicit articulation of what it meant to be Canadian. One of the first steps in this process was the effort to excise references to Britain as a synonym for the Canadian identity. Canada's post office changed its name from the Royal Post, to Canada Post; its military forces also lost the adjective "Royal" and became "Canadian" (e.g., the Royal Canadian Air Force became the Canadian Air Force); and the country selected its own national anthem and a flag. But the process of articulating a common identity gave rise to a series of challenges. Groups other than the British and the French objected to the formulation of a Royal Commission on Bilingualism and Biculturalism[5]—an objection, which eventually gave rise to Canada's "multiculturalism policy" and the adoption of French and English as the country's official languages. Despite claims to embrace multiculturalism, however, the government again launched an "assimilation" effort directed toward native peoples in 1969 by trying to strike down the Indian Act, an effort that became the spark for the mobilization of Aboriginal peoples, who rejected the demand for assimilation.

Second wave feminists inserted themselves into this milieu of identity articulation. The renewal of feminist activism came primarily from middle-class, white women, many of whom had met through peace activism and through the women's clubs that had been established during the first wave. They were not the only active feminists in Canada; indeed, socialist feminists generated much of the feminist economic critique, while radical feminists often took a lead role in drawing attention to violence against women. Nonetheless, the voice of feminism to which the Canadian state was willing to respond was that of mainstream women. In 1967, their first and enduring success was the appointment of the Royal Commission on the Status of Women (RCSW). In Canada, standard lore holds that governments appoint royal commissions as a means of avoiding complicated issues or decisions. The problem with this tactic is that ultimately commissions do release reports and make recommendations, often reinvigorating those groups that the government had hoped to depoliticize. Such was the case with the RCSW, whose report would provide the blueprint for 20 years of subsequent feminist activism.

The Commission traveled the country, hearing presentations and receiving written submissions. Many of their hearings were televised. For the commissioners and for the public, the hearings revealed much that was surprising and previously unacknowledged about how women were living their lives and the challenges they were facing. It also spurred women to organize for social change.

The Commission filed its report in 1970 and elaborated 167 recommendations around 4 principles:

1. Women should be free to choose whether or not to work outside the home.
2. The care of children is a responsibility to be shared by the mother, the father, and society.
3. Society has a responsibility for women because of pregnancy and childbirth and special treatment related to maternity will always be necessary.
4. In certain areas women will require special treatment to overcome the adverse effects of discriminatory practices (Prentice et al. 1988, 349).

Canada's feminists understood that public pressure would be required in order to ensure that the government would act on the Commission's report, a recognition that fuelled the establishment of "Status of Women Committees" in all provinces except Quebec, where feminists worked under the banner of the "Fédération des Femmes du Québec." The RCSW also gave rise to Canada's largest coalition of women's groups, the National Action Committee on the Status of Women (NAC), established in 1972, and the central voice of Canadian feminists for the following 25 years.

On the part of the federal government, the RCSW and Canadian women's activism resulted in the establishment of a "woman's state," whose components included: the appointment of a Minister Responsible for Women's Issues; the Secretary of State Women's Program, which was the primary funder for the organized women's movement in Canada; Status of Women Canada, a government office that was to promote gender equity within the federal civil service and in public policy; and the appointment of the arms-length Canadian Advisory Council on the Status of Women (CACSW). A precursor to these offices, the Women's Bureau in the Department of Labor had existed since 1954 and remains to the present day. Each of the provinces and territories eventually established similar offices.

The key issues around which feminists mobilized during this period included the decriminalization of abortion, which was achieved in 1988; employment and pay equity measures; childcare; and measures to restrict pornography and eliminate violence against women. But perhaps one of the biggest struggles, at least in terms of political symbolism, was the effort to secure gender equality provisions in the Charter of Rights and Freedoms.

As noted earlier, the postwar period saw many efforts to "Canadianize" important national symbols and political practices. However, a number of efforts to devise an amending formula for Canada's constitution had failed, leaving the final authority for constitutional change in the hands of the British Parliament. As an olive branch to Quebec in the aftermath of that province's failed 1980 referendum on sovereignty, Prime Minister Trudeau initiated the process of "patriating" the Constitution, in order to create a "made in Canada" amending formula. The Charter of Rights was a part of the constitutional package that would emerge from this initiative.

Prior to the Charter, rights were protected under the common law. Canada did pass a Bill of Rights in 1960, but this was not a constitutional document and only applied to the federal government. The courts made little use of it and when they did, the outcomes were often counter to what rights advocates had anticipated. Among the most notorious cases involving women were the Lavell and Bédard cases, which challenged the sexual discrimination involved in the treatment of men and women status Indians when they married non-status Indians, and the Bliss case regarding pregnancy. Yvonne Bédard was an Aboriginal woman who was evicted from her house after she returned to her home reserve following the breakdown of her marriage to a white man. The Supreme Court upheld the discrimination in the Indian Act, arguing that "equality before the law" only applied to the administration and enforcement of the law and not the law itself (Bourne 1993, 329). Because all status Indian women were treated the same way, the Indian Act was not discriminatory. As critics at the time argued, this reasoning could have been used to justify Hitler's Nuremburg laws, since they envisioned treating all Jews in the same way.

Stella Bliss launched a challenge to Canada's Unemployment Insurance (UI) regulations, which also cover maternity leave. The essence of Bliss' claim was that UI regulations discriminated against women because they required ten weeks of work in order to qualify, whereas eligibility for regular benefits only required eight weeks of work. In this case, the Supreme Court ruled that the law did not discriminate against women, but against pregnant "persons." Moreover, the court argued that since pregnancy was a voluntary state and not all women became pregnant, the discrimination was not based on sex but on pregnancy (Bourne 1993, 329).

The inadequacy of these judicial rulings as well as early indications that equality provisions might not be contemplated as part of the constitutional patriation package persuaded a core group of liberal feminists that the creation of a Canadian Charter of Rights would require their serious attention and vigilance.

The politics surrounding the Constitution Act 1982, of which the Charter is a part, were dramatic and have had profound consequences for subsequent federal–provincial relations. Women's efforts to secure constitutionally guaranteed sexual equality rights were situated in the midst of the federal–provincial conflict. From the perspective of many of the Canadian provinces, the protection of individual rights articulated in the Charter was an infringement on their autonomy. In order to gain provincial agreement on the constitutional package, federal negotiators acquiesced to the inclusion of section 33, "the notwithstanding clause." This clause allowed any government to pass a law, in force for a period of five years, notwithstanding sections 2 and 7–15 of the Charter. These sections include legal rights (e.g., the right not to be held without cause), fundamental freedoms (e.g., freedom of association, freedom of speech), and equality rights (e.g. protection against discrimination on the basis of sex, race, and religion). In its original formulation, the notwithstanding clause also covered section 28 that reiterates the sexual equality provisions in stating that the Charter applies to men and women equally.

The women who had organized to secure sexual equality guarantees in the Charter were horrified, but having witnessed the federal–provincial tensions that had marked the constitutional negotiations, they made a strategic decision. They decided to mobilize in an attempt to free section 28 from the notwithstanding clause (Dobrowolsky 2000, 58). To do this, they had to secure the agreement of all of the provinces, as well as the federal government, a daunting prospect involving a phenomenal organizational effort. Women politicians and senior bureaucrats worked from the inside, while grassroots women's groups were more public in their calls for provincial and federal responses. Ultimately, they succeeded (p. 62).

In the aftermath of this high pressure campaign, women gained substantial credibility as a political force. Indeed, the leaders of the major political parties even held a debate on women's issues during the 1984 election campaign for the federal Parliament. Further, the three major political parties (the Liberals, the Progressive Conservatives, and the New Democratic Party [NDP]) all adopted equity measures to increase the number of women they nominated. The NDP, as a social democratic party, had undertaken the most extensive measures, and their initiatives had a demonstration effect on the other parties (Trimble and Arscott 2003, 48). As a result of these initiatives, the number of women elected to Parliament and to provincial legislatures began to increase, reaching a historic high of 21 percent in the 2000 federal election. In 1993, women also marked a historic first in the selection of Kim Campbell to replace Brian Mulroney as the leader of the Progressive Conservative Party, and hence to become Canada's first (and only) woman prime minister. Campbell's tenure in office was brief, serving as prime minister only from June 25 to November 4, 1993; but her historic role was not greeted with warmth from feminist activists. Commenting on the new prime minister, Judy Rebick, then president of NAC, asserted that "women like that are going to become our most bitter opponents" (Young 2003, 79).

In retrospect, the post-Charter moment of the mid–1980s was the high-water mark of second wave feminism in Canada. From that point on, Canada began to adopt neoliberal policies of deficit restraint, liberalized trade, and a reduced role for the state in providing for the social well-being of citizens. Feminists and the cause of women's equality generally, were casualties of these policies.

## Neoliberalism

Canada's adoption of a neoliberal state form began in the 1980s under the Progressive Conservative government of Brian Mulroney, but was not fully articulated until the 1990s under Jean Chretien's Liberals. The impetus for the adoption of neoliberal governance was twofold. First, fiscal crisis brought on by economic recession in the mid–1980s, and again in the early 1990s, and developments in the international political economy, propelled decision makers to address the state's weakening fiscal health. Second, the social justice guarantees of the welfare state became increasingly difficult to sustain. While social activists had gained some legitimacy in the 1960s and 1970s, they were often disappointed with the translation of their demands into public policy. Neoliberal critics, on the other hand, alleged that the expansion of the state, which these social movements had precipitated, unduly infringed on the freedom of the individual and the market (Cohen and Arato 1992, 15).

In the face of these pressures, neoliberal prescriptions triumphed. The government addressed the fiscal crisis through dramatic spending reductions in social programs and in the size of the public sector workforce, areas in which women were disproportionately affected. By 2003, the federal government's share of program funding was roughly 12 percent of gross domestic product (GDP), the lowest level since the early 1950s (Prince 2004, 205). Between 1992 and 1997, the most dramatic of the neoliberal era, the government cut the federal public sector workforce by 73,000 jobs (Fudge 2002, 122). Further reductions were also meted out at the provincial level, where reductions in the federal contribution to social spending intensified already existing fiscal crises.

In addition to spending reductions, Canadian neoliberals also sought to diminish the state's role in ameliorating the conditions of social inequality. Achieving this objective involved delegitimating and depoliticizing the claims of social activists, particularly feminists. The branding of claims-makers as "special interests," the privatization of "care work," and the triumph of "freedom" over "equality" as the primary democratic value have been mobilized in the service of this goal. Although Canada's most recent social policy initiatives have retreated somewhat from the ferocity of neoliberalism, they continue to reinforce individual responsibility and privatized solutions to social needs.

The consequences of neoliberal governance for women and politics are evident at the levels of institutional participation, policy, and activism. As the federal government began to implement spending restraint, the offices of the "Women's State" were significantly affected. The Secretary of State Women's Program that had been so instrumental in funding feminist advocacy saw its budget fall from C$12.7 million in 1987 to C$9 million in 1990 (Burt and Hardman 2001, 208). Subsequently, in 1995, the Women's Program and Status of Women Canada were amalgamated, and the CACSW was eliminated (Jenson and Phillips 1996, 122). In addition, the cabinet position of Minister Responsible for the Status of Women was downgraded to the lower rank of Secretary of State Responsible for Status of Women (Burt and Hardman 2001, 208). The architects of this reorganization asserted that they were responding to the recommendations of the UN Fourth World Conference on Women (Beijing) that called for the application of a gender lens to policy development (p. 208). The women who had made this proposal at the Beijing conference had done so out of a concern that women's issues were often ghettoized within large bureaucratic structures (p. 208). Hence they argued that the application of gender-based analysis as a routine element of the policy-making process would alleviate this marginal status. But the Canadian government's response did little to advance the concerns expressed in Beijing. The responsibility for gender-based analysis continued to be housed within two marginal offices, Status of Women and the Women's Bureau in Human Resources and Development, and the resources available for its promotion and application were miniscule. In the 2000–2001 budget, the Gender-Based Analysis Directorate (GBA) expanded from one employee to three (p. 214). In 2004 there were five employees (Status of Women 2003–2004). And while they have established a network of GBA representatives in various government departments, it is not clear that these representatives command the authority or the resources necessary to ensure the application of a gendered lens to policy. Particularly when fiscal restraint continues to take priority over other policy concerns, the success of gender-based analysis is likely to be highly circumscribed.

The collision of gender equity and fiscal restraint in Canada's federal state also exists in the relationship between the government as an employer and its women workers. As the country's single largest employer of women, how the government of Canada articulates equality principles in its employment practices has an important demonstration effect (Fudge 2002, 86). Employment equity and pay equity (or comparable worth, which assesses and rewards jobs on the bases of skill, education, responsibility involved, rather than the gender of the worker) have been both challenged and trumpeted at various times, but the implementation of neoliberal governance has intensified the controversy surrounding these practices.

A pay equity complaint clearly illustrates the tension between neoliberalism and equity principles. The union representing federal employees, the Public Service Alliance of Canada (PSAC), brought the complaint to Canada's Human Rights Tribunal in 1984. Thirteen years passed before the Tribunal was convinced that an appropriate method of job comparison had been devised and that the federal government had an obligation to compensate its women workers with adjustments that would go back to 1985 (Fudge 2002, 86). Even with this outcome, however, the federal government balked, launching a legal challenge to the ruling, while claiming to be committed to paying women and men equally for work of equal value. The government had considerable support for its resistance at this point, since the hegemony of neoliberalism was well established. Critics argued that the definition of pay equity was contentious, that it punished taxpayers for past injustices, and that, ultimately, the value of work could only be determined by the market (p. 116). After all, went the argument, if workers didn't like the salary that was offered, they were not required to accept the position. Nonetheless, one year later, the Federal Court found fault against the government. With a substantial surplus and a renewed commitment to social spending, the government and the union finally came to an agreement. Approximately C\$3.5 billion would be paid to 230,000 current and former public service employees (p. 119). As this struggle demonstrates, it is possible for gender equality principles to be realized in the context of neoliberalism. Nonetheless, changes to employment patterns, especially the flexibilization of the labor force, and challenges to equality norms pose new and complex obstacles for the attainment of gender equity.

Less success in overcoming the challenges of neoliberalism has been realized at the level of women's representation in elected assemblies. Arscott and Trimble assert that women have reached a glass ceiling of 21 percent representation in the federal House of Commons and, on average, 20 percent in provincial and territorial legislatures. While Canada surpasses the United States on this measure, Canada ranks thirty-fourth among industrialized nations for the number of women elected to its national legislature (Trimble and Arscott 2003, 43–44). The 21 percent level has remained constant through the 1997 and 2000 federal elections, but declined slightly in the 2004 election. Given the very low numbers of women elected prior to the 1980s, 20 percent might appear as a remarkable achievement. Nonetheless, the fact that women's representation appears to have stagnated, particularly as neoliberalism has taken hold, is cause for concern. Scholars have attributed this stagnation to feminists' reduced encouragement of women's electoral participation and political parties' diminished efforts to recruit women candidates. Further, changes to Canada's party system, first manifested in the 1993 federal election and related to the rise of neoliberalism, have had a significant impact on the saliency of women's issues on the political agenda (Young 2003).

With the decline of liberal feminism as the primary impetus behind feminist activism, the pressure on political parties to nominate women candidates diminished. NAC, which had strong ties to the three main political parties in the 1970s and 1980s, began to distance itself from institutional politics in the 1990s. The organization turned its attention to economic issues, developing a far-reaching analysis of the gendered impacts of the Canada–U.S. Free Trade Agreement (CUFTA), and later the North American Free Trade Agreement (NAFTA) (Young 2003, 79). Groups, such as the Committee for '94 continued to pursue the electoral route to gender equality, but they would prove unable to sustain their momentum and had diminished or disappeared by the late 1990s (p. 80). Moreover, feminists were frustrated with the institutional reform approach, since the results were relatively meager given the incredible amount of energy invested in them.

Feminists' frustrations were fuelled by the backsliding and, in some cases, active resistance of the political parties to their demands. Throughout the 1990s, support for the social democratic NDP dropped significantly. The NDP, as we have seen, was the federal party that was most supportive of women's equality aspirations. Hence, its fall in popularity boded poorly for women. On the other end of the political spectrum, the House of Commons saw the emergence of the populist Reform Party that effectively replaced the Progressive Conservatives in the 1993 election.[6] As the party of the far right (and of "western alienation"), the Reform party was ideologically opposed to any positive measures to ameliorate disadvantage. The party openly challenged Canada's commitment to multiculturalism, trumpeted conservative family values, and denied the need to nominate members of underrepresented groups to run as party candidates. In the Reform Party's view, identity was a purely private issue. Its public recognition, they argued, would only lead to divisiveness and would undermine the stability of the community (Young 2003, 86). The irony here, however, was that, in asserting the privacy of identity, the Reform Party was responsible for politicizing precisely those issues that it had deemed extraneous to politics. Reactionary sentiment toward women's equality demands, immigration, pay and employment equity, and multiculturalism more broadly were sufficiently strong that the Reform's message, in conjunction with the popularity of its advocacy of fiscal restraint would contribute to a significant rightward shift of Canada's political debate.

The Reform Party's hostility to equality issues did provide an important opportunity for the Liberals, one that they have exploited to impressive effect in subsequent elections. Nonetheless, the legislative record of successive liberal governments would suggest that the party has been a rather weak champion for women.

Social policy reforms reflect the government's inattention to the gendered effects of neoliberalism. In 1994, the Liberals embarked on an overhaul of Canada's Unemployment Insurance program, beginning by renaming it Employment Insurance (EI). As part of these reforms, the determination of benefit eligibility shifted from the number of weeks worked to the number of hours worked. Since women are more likely to be employed part time, the result of this change was to reduce substantially the number of claimants, particularly the number of women claimants.[7] One result of these changes has been the development of a C$45 billion surplus in the EI fund, an amount equivalent to five times the fund's total annual payments (Canadian Labour Congress 2003–2004). Moreover the number of workers eligible for EI has dropped dramatically, from 83 percent of unemployed Canadians in 1989 (Prince 1999, 181) to 38 percent in 2002 (Canadian

Labour Congress 2003). Further, because maternity and parental leave benefits are administered through the EI program, the initial effect of this policy change was to remove maternity benefits from a significant number of women. Sufficient outrage erupted that the Liberal government ultimately reduced the number of work hours required to receive benefits from 700 to 600 (Burt and Hardman 2001, 218).

Another significant policy reform for women was the implementation of the Canada Health and Social Transfer (CHST) in 1996. Because the CHST is a block grant and is transferred to the general revenues of the provinces, little oversight is available to citizens or to the federal government regarding the programs in which the money is actually invested (Harder 2003, 182). In general, provinces have chosen to direct the decreasing federal dollars toward cash-hungry health care programs. As a consequence, the federal government has effectively vacated the realm of needs-based programs (certainly for poor adults), leaving the financing of programs for Canada's most economically vulnerable citizens, of whom women form the majority, solely to the provinces (Battle and Torjman 1996, 57). In many provinces, then, the combination of reduced funding and a backlash to gender equality demands has resulted in the elimination or weakening of services, as well as the imposition of more punitive conditions on recipients. In other provinces, however, particularly in Quebec, more positive developments have ensued. Quebec's child-care program for which parents pay C$7 per day has become the standard to which child-care advocates throughout Canada aspire.[8]

As noted above, the expression of neoliberalism in Canada has been somewhat muted, since the federal government began posting budget surpluses in 1998. As a result, some new social policies of interest to women have recently been implemented, including extending parental and maternity leave benefits provided under EI to 50 weeks; an EI administered caregiver leave program, which enables people to exit the workforce temporarily in order to care for a dying family member; and the National Child Benefit, which provides a tax credit to low income families with children. Yet even if these programs do signal a softening of the neoliberal approach, they also reinforce a highly privatized understanding of responsibility for caregiving. Because the maternity and caregiver leave programs are administered through EI, benefit entitlement results from labor force participation. This link is also evident with regard to the National Child Benefit that enables provinces to claw back a portion of the benefit from welfare recipients.[9] Thus, Canada's newest social policy innovations reinforce women's responsibility for caring, while also underscoring the importance of labor force participation for everyone.

Not surprisingly, the adoption of neoliberalism has also posed considerable challenges for feminist activists. With the consolidation of the Women's Program within Status of Women and reduced funding for women's groups, the government implemented new eligibility requirements for women's groups to receive federal support. Federal funding now supports projects and service provision, but advocacy work and operational funding must be garnered through private sources (Jenson and Phillips 1996, 124). Since Canada's rules governing charitable organizations disqualify associations that engage in political advocacy, contributions to feminist groups are not tax deductible.

In addition to a hostile social climate and the removal of key financial supports from feminist organizations, the encounter between feminism and neoliberalism in Canada has also been shaped by transformations within feminist activism and social activism more broadly. Feminism's foundational claims to the primacy of gender oppression have been enriched by the recognition of the complexity of identities and the need to analyze the workings of oppression on numerous registers. Yet the sophistication of this analysis and the demands to which it gives rise are incomprehensible to the neoliberal state. Indeed, a central purpose in adopting neoliberal governance was to displace demands for recognition and redistribution away from the state and onto the market and the community. That many feminist groups have given up on national and provincial governments, perhaps with the exception of Quebec, and have turned their attention to international organizations and issues arising from globalization is hardly surprising.

## Conclusion

The history of Canadian women's struggles for power and political legitimacy is simultaneously a history of efforts to make visible the significance of women's contributions to the shaping of the country. As we have seen, various social forces managed to obscure women's work. The refusal of the Church to acknowledge customary marriage during the fur trade and the disdain of European women settlers for Aboriginal women masked the significance of native women in Canada's early staples economy and in enabling European settlement. The important role of French women in sustaining the commercial viability of New France in the context of war and the hardships of settlement was later erased from the historical record as women's property rights were undercut and fierce resistance was mounted against granting women political power. More recently, we have witnessed the myth making surrounding "women's domesticity" during the 1950s, myth making that masks women's growing labor force participation during that period, and obscures the economy's need for women's paid work to fuel mass consumption. The myth of women's domesticity continues to inform policy making in the present day, despite the abundance of contradictory evidence.

Eruptions of resistance have disrupted this trajectory of efforts to repress evidence of women's contributions and subterranean political power. Demands for inclusion in professional schools, property rights, the vote, to be acknowledged as "persons," to engage in active military duty, and later, demands for reproductive freedom, equality in employment, protection against sexual discrimination, childcare, and parental leave have appeared on the political agenda when the techniques of suppression failed. Currently, the significance of women's contributions to Canada's globalizing economy and the social and political structures that support it are again feeling the heavy weight of delegitimation. As this chapter has argued, however, women's invisibility in the public realm belies their very real and important work and thus the potential power that women continue to wield.

## Notes

1. Currently, the Canadian government imposes a head tax of C$975 Canadian on immigrants—a practice for which it has been roundly criticized by human rights groups.

2. At least 50 percent of the First Nations population was not included in the treaties, nor were the Métis or the Inuit, creating a situation of uncertain entitlement to land and ambiguous legal relationships that persist to the present day. The Aboriginal communities are broadly categorized in public policy as follows: "First Nations" refers to the widely diverse Aboriginal communities living below the tree line, the Inuit live north of the tree line; and the Métis are either the culturally distinct descendants of unions between Scottish and French fur traders and Indigenous women or other people of mixed Indigenous and non-Indigenous heritage (Abele 1997, 119–120).

3. The politics surrounding the Indian Act are complex since the law is both harsh and racist as well as providing recognition for Aboriginal peoples and compelling federal responsibility to address the consequences of colonization. Efforts to repeal the Act have generally met with resistance from Canada's Aboriginal peoples, who interpret such initiatives as efforts on the part of non-Aboriginals to escape their obligation and/or to impose an assimilationist policy.

4. The Church had not always played such an important role in Quebec society, but its significance grew in the aftermath of the conquest of New France. With the success of the British forces, the more affluent French settlers returned to France, leaving a power vacuum that would be filled by the Catholic Church and English commercial interests. The entwining of the Church with the provincial government created an overwhelming force.

5. The Government of Canada continues to establish "Royal" Commissions.

6. The Progressive Conservatives (PC) were left with two seats after the 1993 election. Subsequently, efforts were undertaken to unite the Reform and PC parties to avoid vote splitting among conservative voters. The first manifestation of this was the rebranding of the Reform party as the Alliance Party. Then, in 2004, a more successful union was undertaken, with both parties now subsumed under the banner of the Conservative Party of Canada.

7. Human Resources and Development Canada noted, in 1998, that the change in eligibility determination meant that the number of women who successfully qualified fell by 20 percent while the number of men who successfully qualified dropped by 16 percent (Burt and Hardman 2001, 217).

8. As part of the interest in protecting Quebec's unique language and culture, the province has implemented a number of innovative social programs. In reaction against the dominance of the Catholic Church in the first half of the twentieth century, Quebec politics and society has become highly secular. The province has the lowest fertility rate in Canada, the highest rate of cohabiting couples, and relatedly, the highest number of children born out of wedlock.

9. The amount that is clawed back by the provinces approximates what the provinces provide as the child portion of social assistance payments to families. Hence for social assistance recipients, the benefit is supposed to be revenue neutral. For an extended discussion of the National Child Benefit, see Durst 1999.

# CHAPTER 4

# Women's Struggle for Political Equality in the United States

## MARY HAWKESWORTH

The practice of politics in the United States looks very different when women's lives are placed at the center of analysis. Narratives that begin with proclamations of equality and inalienable rights and relate tales of the progressive unfolding of freedom do not capture women's political experiences. Discussions of the history and development of the official institutions of state depict a terrain from which women have been excluded by law and by custom. Studies of the constitution and the legal system often fail to note that unequal treatment on the basis of race and gender has been the rule rather than the exception. Many accounts of U.S. politics also fail to mention the critical contributions of women to the development of inclusive and participatory democratic practices. This chapter will provide an overview of women's political engagements in the United States and consider how women's political activism challenges many assumptions about American political life. Table 4.1 provides basic demographic information about the United States.

## Origin Stories

Eurocentric accounts of the origins of the Americas emphasize moments of "discovery" by Christopher Columbus (1492), Amerigo Vespucci (1498), and John Cabot (1498), and the beginnings of colonization with the establishment of the first permanent European settlements in Villa Rica de la Vera Cruz (1519), Roanoke Island (1584), Jamestown, Virginia (1607), and Plymouth, Massachusetts (1620). Reflecting the struggles of European colonizers, these narratives often erase the histories of the vibrant indigenous peoples who populated the land for 20,000 years prior to colonization and whose land, livelihoods, and lives were appropriated by the settlers. Omitting the histories of some 2,000 native peoples with distinct languages

**Table 4.1**   The United States at a glance

| | |
|---|---|
| Geography | 9,629,091 square kilometers |
| Population | 290,342,554 |
| African American | 12.7% |
| Asian American | 4.0% |
| Latino/a | 13.4% |
| Native American | 1.0% |
| White | 69.0% |
| GDP | $10,082 trillion |
| Per capita GDP | $36,300 |
| Political system | Federal Republic |

and cultures also enables settler stories to leave out detailed discussions of the ravages of disease, dislocation, warfare, and forced relocation that came close to annihilating the indigenous peoples of North America.

## Indigenous Women

The indigenous women of North America differed from one another by language, culture, and traditions, yet they played vital roles in producing and sustaining the livelihoods of their people, gathering food, building shelters, transporting goods, trading, managing family wealth and resources, and in some instances, serving as chiefs and shamans (spiritual leaders and medical practitioners). In some of the "First Nations," women played crucial political roles. Iroquois women, for example, had rights to representation at all councils, to nominate council elders and depose chiefs who failed to promote the community good, to make and abrogate treaties, and to supervise domestic and foreign policies (Albers and Medicine 1983; Etienne and Leacock 1980; Niethammer 1977; Shoemaker 1995). Within many indigenous communities, women had far more equal relations with men, especially in the spheres of religious and political decision making, than was characteristic of European settler communities in the "New World." As nineteenth-century Anglo women's rights advocates noted, "Indian women," whom "civilized men pitied as drudges" had enjoyed political equality for centuries, while settler women were still struggling to obtain political rights (Evans 1997). Indeed, for many indigenous women, one consequence of sustained contact with Anglo settlers was the importation of gender hierarchies into indigenous communities.

## Enslaved Women

Some narratives of colonial life point out that the earliest settlers were disproportionately male. The ratio of women settlers to men was one woman for every three men in New England and one woman for every seven men in Virginia (Kerber 1980). Yet these demographic claims omit statistics about enslaved people in the colonies. When race and gender are taken into account, colonial experience in the "New World" looks dramatically different. Path-breaking research on African American women has revealed that 80 percent of all women who crossed the Atlantic prior to 1800 were African (Morgan 2004). Enslaved women's labor, productive and reproductive, was central to every aspect of social, economic, and cultural life in the American colonies. In stark contrast to the iconographic image of the male slave that has dominated historical accounts of slavery, African American women's historian, Jennifer Morgan, provides systematic evidence that women constituted 40 percent of the African captives subjected to "Middle Passage" from the fifteenth to the eighteenth centuries. Sold into settler communities and households that had markedly different linguistic, religious, and traditional practices than their communities of origin, enslaved women struggled mightily to survive. The majority of enslaved women (76 percent) performed grueling field work, comprising the majority of the agricultural labor force in the British colonies. In addition to their physical labor, their reproductive labor was also exploited. Given the paucity of Anglo women in the colonies, the sexual exploitation of enslaved African women was deemed essential to satisfy the desire of slave owners, as well as enslaved men. Appropriation of the reproductive labor of enslaved women was indispensable to the production, maintenance, and distribution of slave owners' wealth. Indeed, Morgan notes that for a significant part of the colonial period, the economic value of enslaved women and their children, as calculated by slave owners themselves, exceeded the value of enslaved men. In discussions of law and order in colonial settlements, slave owners and colonial administrators explicitly considered the uses of enslaved women "as a preventive against social unrest," as a strategic mechanism of social control indispensable to the stability and perpetuation of colonial regimes.

### Settler Women

Settler women's reproductive and productive labor was also vital to the home-based colonial economy. Anglo women bore eight children on average. One child in four died during the first year; half died before reaching adulthood (Kerber 1980). Women's work was highly valued and essential for the survival of the community. In a preindustrial world where home and worksite were not separate, women engaged in domestic gardening, producing subsistence crops for family consumption, and in home manufacture, including spinning, weaving, the production of clothes and staples such as soap and candles. Women also participated fully in family-run businesses. An early census in Philadelphia, for example, indicated that during the eighteenth-century women were 32 percent of the shopkeepers, 17 percent of the tavern keepers, and a large proportion of the innkeepers. Women also engaged in a wide array of trades, working as silversmiths, tinsmiths, barbers, bakers, fish picklers, brewers, woodworkers, founders, tanners, rope makers, lumberjacks, gunsmiths, butchers, milliners, tailors, net makers, harness makers, potash manufacturers, printers, morticians, flour processors, seamstresses, chandlers, coach makers, cleaners, dryers, braziers, and embroiderers (Kerber 1980).

Girls were excluded from the first free public schools created in New England in 1683 and were less likely to receive education at home. As a result, the rate of illiteracy among women was 50 percent higher than that of Anglo men in 1765 (Evans 1997). Nonetheless, some privileged women were well educated and practiced professions as early as the seventeenth century. Indeed, the first woman on record to have practiced law in the colonies was Margaret Brent of Maryland, whose legal cases appeared in colonial records in the 1630s. In 1648, she petitioned the colonial Governor of Maryland for equal rights for women, arguing that women should have "a voice and a vote" on the same terms as men.

## Women and the American Revolution

During the period of the Revolutionary War (1776–1783), women expanded their economic and political contributions in ways vital to the success of the war. Men left their homes and businesses during wartime for a variety of reasons. Some were revolutionaries, fighting as soldiers and as political leaders to win independence from the British. Some were loyalists to the British Crown and returned to England or fled to Canada. Some men were Quakers and pacifists who refused to fight as a matter of conscience and who were imprisoned for their refusal to bear arms. While their fathers, brothers, husbands, and sons were away from home, women managed the family farms and businesses and kept the economy functioning (Kerber 1980).

Women also provided the labor essential to the success of the boycott of British goods, the central economic weapon used by the American revolutionaries against the Crown. To ensure the success of the boycott, women had to change their purchasing practices and expand their production of essential goods to meet market demand. They produced sufficient homespun clothes to accommodate civilian populations and to supply revolutionary troops. They produced food, blankets, and medicines to provide for the troops. They removed lead weights from their windows and melted them down to make bullets. Some 12,000 "women of the army" fed the armies on the march, provided laundry and sexual services, and nursed the wounded. British and American war records indicate one woman "camp supporter" for every 10 members of a British regiment and for every 15 revolutionary soldiers. Because they could move more freely across enemy lines, women were recruited to serve as spies for both sides in the revolutionary conflict. Women who supported the American troops also launched fundraising efforts to cover the costs of the revolutionary effort. Women in Philadelphia, for example, raised US$300,000 in one campaign to support Washington's forces (Kerber 1980; Evans 1997).

The egalitarian commitments of Quakers fueled early efforts by women in Pennsylvania and New Jersey to secure rights of political participation.

As early as 1766, Philadelphia women circulated a pamphlet entitled, "Sentiments of an American Woman" proclaiming that women were "born for liberty" and "refused to be enchained by tyrannic governments." In Boston in 1776, Abigail Adams expressed similar sentiments to her husband, John, a prominent member of the Second Continental Congress, which was crafting the Declaration of Independence.

> I long to hear that you have declared an independency—and by the way, in the Code of Laws which I suppose it will be necessary for you to make, I desire you would Remember the Ladies, and be more generous and favourable to them than your ancestors. Do not put such unlimited power in the hands of Husbands. Remember all men would be tyrants if they could. If particular care and attention is not paid to the Ladies, we are determined to foment a Rebelion [*sic*], and will not hold ourselves bound by any Laws in which we have no voice, or Representation. (Butterfield 1963)

John Adams's response was telling: "As to your extraordinary Code of Laws, I cannot but laugh. . . . Depend upon it. We know better than to repeal our Masculine Systems" (Butterfield 1963).

Although Abigail Adams had no success in persuading her husband to abandon "masculine systems" of power, women in New Jersey had greater success. When the state constitution was being drafted in the aftermath of the Revolutionary War, New Jersey women insisted that "they had borne the weight of war and met danger in every corner"; and as such, were entitled to political rights on the same terms as men. They succeeded in persuading the state assembly to award voting rights to single women who owned property. Contrary to popular myths, some women in the United States had voting rights in the earliest years of the Republic, rights that were rescinded for partisan political reasons in 1807 (Apter Klinghoffer and Elkis 1992).

In developing their constitutions in the aftermath of the American Revolution, 12 of the original states, joined by New Jersey in 1807, set a precedent in "nation building" that has been widely replicated around the globe. Despite women's critical contributions to the revolutionary struggle, at the moment of victory, women were excluded from participation in the design of political institutions and from equal participation within those institutions. By excluding women from full citizenship, constitution making became a means of producing gender identities tied to legally sanctioned relations of male domination and women's subordination (Rai 2002). The gender inequalities enshrined in constitutional law often exacerbated inequalities entrenched in custom and tradition (Smart 1992). Feudal and colonial hierarchies had been grounded in class, family ties, nationality, gender, and race. Although the American Revolution claimed to break with such feudal hierarchies, the constitutions created within the first "liberal republic" replicated and strengthened hierarchies tied to gender, race, class, and membership in First Nations by denying equal citizenship and rights of political participation to these groups.

## The Design of the Federal System

Although the Declaration of Independence claimed to speak for all Americans, the original 13 colonies fought for political freedom as independent states. The original framework for governance, The Articles of Confederation, recognized the sovereignty of 13 states. Designed to forge a military and political alliance among these states to protect them from future European, particularly British, aggression, the Articles of Confederation created weak mechanisms to coordinate the foreign policy of the several states. It did not, however, coordinate policies governing the economy, commerce, and taxation, nor did it provide means to repay revolutionary war debts either to other nations or to individual soldiers who fought for the revolutionary army and had been paid in promissory notes.

Agitation to strengthen the bonds among the United States culminated in the Constitutional Convention held in Philadelphia in 1787. Although all 13 states sent delegates to the Constitutional Convention, representatives from many states walked out when it became clear that the goal of the gathering was to jettison rather than amend the Articles of Confederation. The new constitution, which emerged from a series of compromises at this convention, created a new form of government that differed in important respects from any government previously created. The framers of the constitution called their creation a "federal" republic.

Prior to 1787, history documented many experiments with *unitary* systems of governance in which sovereignty was centralized. Whether sovereignty—the power to make and enforce law, adjudicate disputes, and direct foreign relations—was lodged in the hands of one person (monarchy), a few people (aristocracy), or many people (democracy), within a unitary system the sovereign possesses the ultimate power to direct all political affairs within the state. The sovereign might choose to delegate some of that power to other officials, but as sovereign, she or he could reclaim any delegated power at any time. *Confederations* were alliances of unitary states for limited purposes, typically for common defense, for joint military actions, or for economic advantage. Members of a confederation would delegate limited power to their representatives to negotiate on behalf of the state. But any sovereign could withdraw from the confederation at any time or nullify the terms of any agreement negotiated by a representative.

The U.S. federal system was designed as a hybrid, incorporating certain aspects of a unitary system and certain aspects of confederation. It created two levels of sovereignty within the same geographic area, the federal government and state governments, but attempted to demarcate specific jurisdictions for each. The federal government was given the power to make war, regulate commerce, including creating a common currency, and represent the nation in foreign policy, negotiating treaties and establishing alliances with other nations. The state governments were to have authority over all other matters pertaining to the health, education, and welfare of the people, matters of criminal and civil law, criteria for citizenship, property ownership, marriage, and family life. The new system of dual sovereignty was called a "federal" system as part of a public relations campaign to convince the states to ratify this new constitution. Since "federal" sounded like "confederation," the term was chosen to foster the belief that states would be the most powerful entities in this new system.

Exactly how this new system of dual sovereignty would work was a subject of great contestation. John Adams, who was later to become the second president of the United States, was convinced that dual sovereignty was an impossibility: two supreme powers governing the same territory was, to his monotheistic mind, as unthinkable as two Gods reigning over heaven and earth. Many citizens were concerned that the proposed constitution would erode the liberties they had so recently won. They organized to oppose ratification of the constitution, calling themselves, anti-federalists. Alexander Hamilton, James Madison, and John Jay launched a campaign to defend the constitution, publishing hundreds of newspaper articles under the pseudonym, *Publius*. These essays, later republished as *The Federalist Papers* (Hamilton et al. 1961), provide a detailed discussion of the provisions of the constitution and the separation of powers envisioned by this new hybrid polity.

The *Federalist Papers* make clear that the federal system is designed to solve multiple political problems. In addition to providing for a "common defense" against outside aggressors, the new system was intended to safeguard against "majority tyranny," a "danger" perceived to be incident to democratic governments. Indirect election of the president by an Electoral College, the creation of a "republican" form of representative government involving a bicameral legislature, appointment of senators by state legislatures (this provision was altered to allow popular election of senators by the 17th Amendment to the Constitution, passed in 1913), and nomination of Supreme Court justices by the president with confirmation by the Senate, were all intended to curb the "dangers" of democracy. Indeed, the House of Representatives was the only part of the government elected directly by voters. Its members were envisioned as amateurs, who would serve as law makers only a few months of each year for a two-year term and then return to their families and their full-time occupations. Senate concurrence was required to pass any act approved by the House of Representatives, providing a mechanism to limit any "excesses" that might emerge from the people's representatives. And should the Senate fail to restrain the passions of the House, the President was also empowered to veto laws passed by the bicameral legislature.

The government was further insulated from the "passions of the people" by the restriction of voting rights to property-owning whites, which, after New Jersey rescinded women's suffrage in 1807, were further restricted to property-owning white men (Keyssar 2000). Article IV of the Constitution reserved the power to establish the criteria for citizenship to the states: "The citizens of each state shall be entitled to all privileges and immunities of citizens of the several states." In 1787, all state constitutions imposed property and racial (whiteness) requirements for citizenship; and all but New Jersey imposed gender (maleness) requirements as well. The framers of the Constitution employed only race-neutral and gender-neutral language in this document, referring to citizens, persons, electors, representatives, senators, justices, and the president; yet they knew full well they were constituting a citizenry that excluded women, blacks (enslaved and free), and Native Americans. Article I, Section 9 of the Constitution allowed the importation of slaves (i.e., "the importation of such Persons as any of the states now existing shall think proper to admit") until 1808. As members of "Sovereign Nations," Native Americans were excluded from and ineligible for citizenship. The only reference to women in the *Federalist Papers* involves a discussion of the "dangers posed to the safety of the state by the intrigues of courtesans and mistresses."

The ratification campaign spearheaded by the Federalists succeeded. The Constitution was adopted in 1789. Contestations over the meaning of the "enumerated powers" of the federal government, the residual powers reserved to the states, the rights of citizens, and the very definition of citizenship dominated much of nineteenth-century politics in the United States. The first ten Amendments to the Constitution, known as the Bill of Rights (1791), attempted to resolve some of these issues. Multiple rulings by the Supreme Court attempted to resolve questions concerning the distribution of powers between the federal government and the states, often accrediting the power of the federal government. Appealing to "states' rights," several states passed legislation to "nullify" laws passed by the federal government, which the states considered an unconstitutional invasion of the powers reserved to the states.

The American Civil War, fought bitterly from 1861–1865, ultimately established the "supremacy clause" of the federal constitution, eliminated the possibility of state nullification of federal laws, and emancipated enslaved blacks. The "Reconstruction Amendments" passed in the aftermath of the civil war ended one form of institutionalized racial oppression. The 13th Amendment (1865) abolished the institution of slavery. The 14th Amendment (1868) created federal citizenship, a notion of rights and immunities for all "persons born or naturalized in the U.S.," which could not be infringed by the states. The 14th Amendment also included an "equal protection clause," which pledged to guarantee that all U.S. citizens would receive equal protection of the laws. The 15th Amendment (1870) was designed to enfranchise African Americans, proclaiming that the "right of citizens of the United States to vote shall not be denied or abridged by the United States or by any State on account of race, color, or previous conditions of servitude." The civil war amendments use language that sounds inclusive. In a number of historic decisions, however, the Supreme Court ruled that only men were "persons" in the "constitutional" sense. In keeping with these rulings, the initial implementation of the 15th Amendment extended voting rights only to African American men; and within a decade of its passage, state laws, which were upheld by the U.S. Supreme Court, created literacy tests, poll taxes, and a range of restrictive registration measures that effectively disenfranchised black men as well as black women, a situation that was not remedied until the twentieth-century civil rights movement succeeded in securing passage of the Voting Rights Act of 1965.

## Expanding the Definition of Politics While Struggling for Political Equality

### Eighteenth-Century Initiatives

Excluded from participation in politics within the official institutions of state and federal governments, women in the early years of the Republic devised innovative strategies to change public policy, using litigation in the courts and developing a concept of public interest lobbying to change the law.

One of the first to seek recourse to the courts for redress of grievances was Bett, an enslaved woman in western Massachusetts owned by Colonel John Ashley, a leader of American forces in the revolutionary war. Serving the table while Colonel Ashley entertained revolutionists, Bett heard a good deal of discussion of the Declaration of Independence and the "self-evident truth" that "all men are created equal," which was also being used as a founding principle in the new constitution of the state of Massachusetts. She pointed out to two of Ashley's guests, Thomas Sedgwick and Tapping Reeves who were distinguished lawyers, that a constitutional principle of equality seemed markedly inconsistent with the practice of slavery. And she asked them if there was any way that the legality of slavery could be challenged by an appeal to the new state constitution. Sedgwick and Reeves agreed to bring a suit on her behalf to the state courts. Their first effort was thwarted by sex bias in the law. The judge ruled that as a woman, Bett was not recognized as a "person" in the eyes of the law, and hence lacked standing to sue in court. Bett then enlisted the aid of Brom, a fellow slave belonging to Colonel Ashley, to join her in the suit. Sedgwick and Reeves took *Brom and Bett v. Ashley* (1781) to the Massachusetts Supreme Court, where the justices vindicated Bett's insight and declared slavery a violation of the state's constitution. The institution of slavery was abolished in Massachusetts, 82 years before Lincoln's Emancipation Proclamation, due to an astute political intervention by an enslaved black woman. To celebrate this historic victory, Bett claimed the name, Elizabeth Freeman, quit the Ashley household, and took a job as a paid servant in the home of Thomas Sedgwick, where she worked for the rest of her life (Giddings 1984).

In addition to litigation, women in the eighteenth century began organizing "benevolent societies," precursors of public interest groups, to press for reforms that would benefit women and children in the new nation. One key target of this activism was education. In 1784, Judith Sargent Murray began publishing articles calling for the education of girls and women, envisioning a curriculum geared toward women's independence. She argued that topics in the liberal arts should be supplemented by the mastery of useful skills, affording women alternatives to marriage as a means of support. Proponents of women's education opened private schools catering to the daughters of affluent families. They also pressured local political leaders to open the public schools to girls and succeeded in persuading some local authorities to allow sessions for girls in the early mornings (6:00–8:00 a.m.) and in the summer months, when the boys were not using the buildings. These efforts produced palpable results. By the turn of the nineteenth century, literacy rates for white women began to equal those of white men (Evans 1997). Many states, however, continued to prohibit the education of black women and men.

### Nineteenth-Century Mobilizations

Throughout the nineteenth century, "woman rights" activists—black and white—advanced an encompassing vision of women's equality. They fought not only for the suffrage, but for the transformation of traditions and belief systems that truncated their humanity. They fought for the abolition of slavery and indentured servitude, for education for girls, for literacy training for adult women, for the right to speak in public, for the right to own property, for the right to contract, for the right to sue and be sued in court, for the right to divorce and to have custody of their children, for religious doctrines that enshrined the equality of men and women, for economic opportunities, for professions open to all who qualified, for married women's right to work, for all women's right to receive their own wages, for a living wage, for shorter working days and safer working conditions, and for an end to child labor.

In their work for these manifold causes, women demonstrated an acute understanding of state and federal politics. They also cultivated a conception of politics that was more democratic, more participatory, and more issue driven than was the norm in nineteenth-century American politics. Beginning with the courageous work of Maria Stewart, a free black woman, who in 1830 launched a public speaking tour to mobilize support for abolition and women's rights (Richardson 1987), women devised a strategy for political education, informing the public about issues that politicians sought to avoid, framing policy questions in terms of social justice, and mobilizing public opinion to pressure law makers to change policy. They invented public interest lobbying, gathering thousands of signatures on petitions to present to legislators, providing elected officials with expert testimony concerning the merits of proposed legislation, and demanding that elected representatives be accountable to the people. They became skilled grassroots mobilizers, organizing picnics, marches, and demonstrations through leafleting and the circulation of manifestos. They developed press strategies to encourage the media to cover the public events they orchestrated.

They wrote letters to the editor and opinion pieces to contest views they opposed. They also developed alternative media, such as *The Revolution* and the *National Woman's Journal* (Edwards 1997; Evans 1997).

In their efforts to achieve full citizenship, women worked within the Democratic and Republican parties, supporting candidates who pledged to work for legislation to empower women. They found, however, that candidates who accepted their assistance during campaigns for electoral office, all too often betrayed the women's rights agenda once they were in office (Edwards 1997). Frustration at such recurrent betrayal motivated women to form their own political parties, launching the Home Protection Party, the Prohibition Party, the Equal Rights Party in the last decades of the nineteenth century and the National Woman Party in the early twentieth century. They also created nonpartisan precinct clubs that would canvass electoral districts, house by house, trying to persuade voters to vote on the issues, rather than on the basis of a party label. Seeking a national platform for the cause of women's liberty, two women launched campaigns for the presidency of the United States: Victoria Woodhull ran for president in 1872; and Belva Lockwood ran for the presidency in 1884 and again in 1888.

As in the eighteenth century, some women attempted to use the courts to gain recognition of equal citizenship. In the presidential election of 1868, Susan B. Anthony went to the polls and cast a ballot, claiming that since she was required to pay taxes, she ought to be entitled to vote under the fundamental principle, "No taxation without representation," which fueled the American revolution. She was arrested, tried, and convicted of voter fraud. During her trial, the judge refused to allow her to testify on her own behalf, insisting that women had no legal standing in the courts. Fined $100 by the court, Susan B. Anthony continued her civil disobedience, refusing to pay the fine and mobilizing 30 women to join with her in casting "unlawful ballots" in the election of 1872.

Invoking the 14th Amendment, several cases argued that as "persons" born in the United States, women fit the definition of citizens established in this constitutional amendment and therefore qualified for full rights, including the right to practice professions such as law and medicine, the right to vote, and the right to hold elective office. In *Bradwell v. Illinois* (1873), *Minor v. Happersett* (1874), and *In re Lockwood* (1884), the Supreme Court consistently held that women were not "persons" in the constitutional sense. In the eyes of the law, "persons" were male, a constitutional interpretation that was not officially overturned until 1971 in *Reed v. Reed*.

Women's rights activists also championed certain tactics designed to help women to cultivate their political skills. As part of the long campaign for women's rights, women organized multiple "constitutional conventions," mock legislative assemblies in which women assumed the positions of law makers and drafted new laws to govern the republic. Although these laws had no binding force, participation in making them introduced women to practices of governance and honed their skills in speech making, legislative bargaining, and coalition building. The model laws passed also provided a glimpse of the difference it might make to have women serving in large numbers in elective offices (Buhle and Buhle 1978).

Resurrecting tactics from the revolutionary period, some women's rights activists organized economic boycotts as a way to enlist businesses in the cause for women's liberty. Excluded from rights of political participation, women deployed their market power as consumers in an effort indirectly to affect political outcomes. Knowing that many business leaders exercised considerable political influence, proponents of women's rights used their economic power to pressure business owners to support policies that would improve women's lives (Edwards 1997).

The *History of Woman Suffrage* records the prodigious energy that women devoted to political activism to secure their rights as citizens of the United States (Buhle and Buhle 1978). In their account of the political struggle to win equal citizenship, Carrie Chatman Catt and Nettie Rogers Shuler ([1926] 1969) computed the number of campaigns women organized to gain voting rights:

> Women conducted 56 campaigns of referenda to male voters; 480 campaigns to get legislatures to submit suffrage amendments to voters; 47 campaigns to get state constitutional conventions to write woman suffrage into state constitutions; 277 campaigns to get state party conventions to include woman suffrage planks; 30 campaigns to get presidential party conventions to adopt woman suffrage planks in party platforms; and 19 campaigns to 19 successive congresses to secure passage of the federal suffrage amendment.

The 19th Amendment to the U.S. Constitution, which establishes that "the right of citizens of the United States to vote shall not be denied or abridged by the United States or any State on account of sex," was ratified in 1920.

### Early Twentieth-Century Issues and Tactics

Many accounts of American women and politics stop with the successful passage of the 19th Amendment, creating the mistaken impression that women attained meaningful equality in 1920 and that women's political activism evaporated immediately thereafter. But women's campaign for equal opportunity, equal treatment before the law, and equal representation in the elective and appointive offices of this land did not end in the early twentieth century. The struggle for voting rights continued unabated for African Americans, whose constitutional entitlement to vote was not respected at state or federal levels until the passage of the Voting Rights Act in 1965. Moreover, the vision of meaningful equality developed by women's rights activists encompassed far more than voting rights. In the early 1920s, women mobilized on multiple fronts. Forming the Women's Joint Congressional Committee that became one of the most powerful lobbies in Washington, DC, proponents of women's liberty fought for legislation to meet the needs of women and children. They succeeded in getting the Shepperd-Towner Act, the first women's health bill, passed in 1921. A year later, they secured passage of the Cable Act, which ended the practice of stripping American women of their citizenship when they married men who were citizens of other nations. They built voting coalitions within the House and the Senate and won the requisite two-thirds majority to pass a constitutional amendment to end child labor, which was then sent to the states for ratification. In 1923, they introduced the Equal Rights Amendment to Congress (Anderson 1996).

Targeting the Democratic and Republican parties for transformation, women's rights activists launched "50/50" campaigns to ensure women's equal representation on national party committees and state party committees. Achieving this objective at the national level, and within 18 states by 1929, women working in the two major parties discovered to their dismay that a guarantee of equal participation did not ensure equal power in party decision making. Indeed, as Jo Freeman (2000) has brilliantly documented, both Democratic and Republican parties shifted the site of real decision making from party committees to backrooms once women gained equal representation in party committees.

During their first "century of struggle" for political equality, women's rights advocates achieved a number of singular accomplishments: emancipation, property rights, creation of universal, mandatory public education, access to higher education and professions, divorce and custody rights for women, creation of settlement houses, minimum wage legislation, occupational safety and health legislation, suffrage, and maternal and infant health care—to name a few (Flexner 1975).

"Progress" toward equality has been neither unilinear nor continuous, however. There have been setbacks, points at which racism, sexism, and heterosexism have been mobilized to thwart the legal recognition of equal humanity and equal rights. The Jim Crow legislation mandating racial segregation, the separate but equal doctrine announced by the U.S. Supreme Court in *Plessy v. Ferguson* in 1896, the successful campaign in the 1920s to defeat the ratification of the constitutional amendment to abolish child labor in the United States, the legislation that eliminated federal employment for married women during the Depression, are all examples of such defeats.

In the aftermath of World War II, after women had assumed critical roles in the war economy essential to the nation's victory, and after women had managed households, businesses and communities while so many men were away at war, many women argued that the time for the full realization of gender and racial equality had arrived.

### *Resurgence of Feminist Activism in the "Second Wave"*

Contrary to popular myths, women did not leave the labor force when World War II ended, but they were forced out of high-paying jobs, which they had performed successfully during the war years. After the war, women's labor force participation remained well above prewar years, but their share of professional and technical jobs diminished significantly. Between 1941 and 1948, women's share of professional and technical positions dropped from 45.4 percent to 38.6 percent while their proportion of clerical jobs increased from 52.6 percent to 72.6 percent (Freeman 1975, 38). As a consequence, pay inequalities, which had plagued women workers since their entry into the formal labor force in the mid-nineteenth century, were exacerbated. By the mid-1960s, the median income for women workers was US$1,638 compared to US$5,306 for men. Race further heightened these inequities. White women who worked full-time outside the home earned 58.2 percent of the median income earned by white men; black women who worked full-time outside the home earned only 71 percent median income earned by white women and 66 percent of the median income earned by black men (p. 30). During the 1950s, growing numbers of American women attended and graduated from colleges and universities. The number of women earning college degrees increased from 49,000 in 1930 to 139,000 in 1960 to 279,000 in 1968 (p. 29). Despite these qualifications, few were able to find professional careers comparable to those of male college graduates.

For most of the twentieth century, the Women's Bureau of the Department of Labor was the only agency of the federal government officially charged with responsibility for addressing the needs of women. Created during World War I as the Women's Division of the Ordnance Department, the agency's mission was to look after the needs of women working in the munitions industry. After the war, the office was renamed Women in Industry Service and moved to the Department of Labor. In June 1920, it was renamed again as the Women's Bureau, and was made a permanent bureau of the Department of Labor. As part of its mandate to formulate "standards and policies which shall promote the welfare of wage-earning women, improve their working conditions, increase their efficiency, and advance their opportunities for profitable employment," the Women's Bureau tracked a variety of inequities in women's employment, including pay inequality, job segregation by sex, unfair working conditions, and the "underutilization" of working women. Although its reports carefully documented forms of discrimination encountered by working women, as a government agency, the Women's Bureau's power to remedy such injustice was constrained by statute and bureaucratic politics (Duerst-Lahti 1989). To circumvent these limitations, Esther Peterson who had worked as an advocate for women and labor prior to her appointment as director of the Women's Bureau by President Kennedy, persuaded the president to create a Presidential Commission on the Status of Women.

Established in 1961, under the leadership of Eleanor Roosevelt and the direction of Esther Peterson, the President's Commission on the Status of Women launched a systematic study of the condition of American women in the second half of the twentieth century. Their report, *American Women*, published in 1963, documented in great detail systemic problems pertaining to discrimination in employment, unequal pay, lack of social services such as childcare, and unequal treatment by the law in all 50 states and at the federal level.

The President's Commission on the Status of Women had a number of direct and indirect effects. At the federal level, Congress passed the Equal Pay Act of 1963, which mandates equal pay for equal work. Congress also included "sex discrimination," along with racial, ethnic, and religious discrimination in Title VII of the Civil Rights Act of 1964, prohibiting these forms of discrimination in education and employment. Because so much of the discriminatory legislation unearthed by the commission was embedded in state statutes, the commission and the president urged the governors of each of the states to appoint State Commissions on the Status of Women to investigate and recommend remedies for state-specific issues. By 1967, State Commissions on the Status of Women were active in all 50 states. Annual conferences brought representatives from these State Commissions together, helping to lay the groundwork for a national network of women's rights activists, while also helping to consolidate a "women's agenda," identify strategies for social change, and strengthen the activists' understandings of the possibilities and limitations of "insider" techniques for social transformation. Indeed, acute awareness of the limitations of the State Commissions as vehicles for feminist transformation led a group of activists to launch the National Organization for Women (NOW) during the final days of the 1966 meeting of the State Commissions on the Status of Women (Freeman 1975; Hole and Levine 1971).

Feminist activism in the 1960s had multiple sources. The Women's Bureau and the President's Commission and the State Commissions on the Status of Women played important roles in providing the evidence to demonstrate that despite passage of the Women's Suffrage Amendment, women remained "second class" citizens. They also identified appropriate steps that might be taken within existing political, economic, and legal frameworks to redress women's legitimate grievances. For many American women, however, the pervasiveness of governmentally sanctioned racism and sexism afforded them little hope that "insider" strategies for social change would be effective.

Despite years of struggle in support of equality before the law, African American women had suffered repeated betrayals by activists who supposedly shared their cause and by politicians supposedly bound to uphold the Equal Protection Clause of the 14th Amendment to the Constitution. During the 1890s, the National American Women's Suffrage Association launched an overtly racist suffrage strategy designed to win support of Southern legislators. The "Southern strategy" urged law makers to enfranchise white women so their votes could "cancel" the votes cast by black men. On more than one occasion, concern for the "sensitivities" of suffragists from the South led white organizers of major suffrage marches to replicate "Jim Crow" policies during suffrage parades, requiring African American suffragists to march as a separate group behind white feminists, rather than as members of their state delegations. Poll taxes, literacy tests, citizenship examinations, and physical intimidation prohibited black women and men from casting their votes in elections across the United States. When social security legislation was passed during the height of the depression in the 1930s, the two professions in which the majority of African American workers were concentrated—agricultural labor and domestic work—were exempted from the provisions of the legislation. School segregation on the basis of race ensured that African Americans received substandard education.

Through clubs of the National Association of Colored Women and organizations such as the National Association of Negro Women, National Association for the Advancement of Colored People (NAACP), the Congress on Racial Equality (CORE), and Fellowship for Reconciliation (FOR), black women and men devised multiple strategies to advance their rights; but they met with continuing intransigence from whites (Gray White 1999). In the aftermath of World War II, African Americans responded to institutionalized racism in the United States with new initiatives that included renewed voter registration drives, public demonstrations for civil rights, and civil disobedience against unjust laws. Highly trained civil rights organizers such as Ella Baker, Rosa Parks, and Fannie Lou Hamer helped launch and lead the civil rights movement. Thousands of young women and men developed a vision of social justice and learned tactics of "direct action" under their auspices and through key organizations such as the Southern Christian Leadership Conference (SCLC), the Student Nonviolent Coordinating Committee (SNCC), and the Mississippi Freedom Democratic Party. Their vision of social justice encompassed gender, class, and racial equality. Thus the civil rights movement also played a crucial role in launching feminist activism in the 1960s (Greenberg 1998; White 2001).

Contrary to popular stereotypes, black women were more supportive of feminism than white women as the women's movement mobilized. A 1972 Virgina Slims poll recorded that 62 percent of black women and 45 percent of white women favored "efforts to strengthen women's status in society;" and 67 percent of black women compared to 35 percent of white women expressed "sympathy with the efforts of women's liberation groups" (Freeman 1975, 38). African American women were actively involved in the invention of the twentieth-century variant of American feminism, just as they had been in the nineteenth-century version, working within mass-based organizations such as NOW, union structures such as the Coalition of Labor Union Women (CLUW), informal city networks, and consciousness-raising groups. They also created feminist organizations such as the Combahee River Collective and the National Black Feminist Organization to combat the complex intersections of racism, sexism, and homophobia.

Union activism and community activism also provided key sites for the emergence of feminism. Latinas such as Aileen Hernandez and Delores Huerta worked within the International Ladies Garment Workers Union (ILGWU) and the United Farm Workers Union (UFW) respectively, to address issues of low wages, poor working conditions, and racism. In the course of this work, they also began to mobilize women around issues of their "triple oppression," that is, oppression rooted in race, class, and gender, and to raise consciousness about the unfairness of women's "double duty" (domestic labor in addition to work outside the home) and "triple shift" (paid labor in the workforce, unpaid labor in the home, and volunteer labor in community organizations). In places like Southern California, Texas, Florida, and New York City, Latinas also began creating women-only organizations and publishing newsletters and magazines focusing on women's issues. In Los Angeles, for example, Francisca Flores, cofounder of the California League of Mexican American Women, which encouraged political activism among Chicanas, went on to edit and publish *Regeneracion*, an activist magazine focusing on women's issues, found the Chicana Service Action Center, play a leading role in the establishment of *Comision Femenil*, and organize many of the first Latina conferences (Garcia 1997; Martin 1991; Pardo 1998; Perez 1999).

Among white women, feminism flourished particularly on university campuses and among women involved with "New Left" and antiwar organizations such as Students for a Democratic Society (SDS). Through civil rights activism, antipoverty work, and protests against the Vietnam War, many young women learned that sexism was as common among young men as it was among their elders. As their efforts to address sex discrimination within counter-culture and progressive organizations met derision and rebuff, some women began to meet separately to discuss social change tactics and to explore the politics of interpersonal and intimate relations. "Consciousness raising," "assertiveness training," a growing conviction that "the personal was political," and a commitment to forms of social change that encompassed public and private spheres became hallmarks of resurgent feminism (Evans 1979).

During the late 1960s and early 1970s, thousands of women took to the streets to publicize their causes, to educate the public about pervasive sex discrimination, to gather signatures on petitions, to pressure elected officials for legislation, and to press for social change and social justice. The magnitude of feminist accomplishments over the past few decades makes it easy to forget how much they had to fight for: access to birth control and abortion; an end to sterilization abuse and pregnancy discrimination; access to education and employment on the basis of merit; access to childcare and early childhood education programs; access to credit; equitable divorce settlements and pension benefits, the politicization of issues such as sexual objectification, acquaintance rape, marital rape, domestic violence, and sexual harassment; creation of shelters for victims of rape and domestic violence and changes in police and court practices pertaining to these crimes; the involvement of men in domestic and reproductive labor.

Feminism is often described as a "social movement" to capture the dimensions of self-generated, independent, and innovative collective action embodied in the activism of so many women during this period. While the conceptualization of feminism as a social movement captures important aspects of these mobilizations, thinking about feminism only as a social movement has a number of drawbacks. In playing to the media's fascination with spectacle, a social movement focus can mask feminist activity within social, religious, political, academic, and military institutions (Katzenstein 1998), making it appear that feminism has "ended" when women are no longer on the streets. Conflating feminism with forms of protest and mass demonstrations also sustains a representation of feminism as perpetual outsider. Since such outsider status is fundamentally incompatible with working within the system, feminism is condemned to temporary and fleeting manifestations, for the institutionalization of feminist principles and mobilization within institutions appears to lie beyond reach. Social movement frames also tend to reduce feminist goals to those amenable to legislative solutions. Once legislation has been passed, feminism is rendered obsolete. Thus while the conceptualization of feminism as a social movement highlights one form of feminist activism, it has the ironic effect of declaring feminism "dead" long before feminists have achieved the social transformations they envision. The movement is pronounced dead as feminists continue the struggle to achieve their unrealized agenda.

Feminist activism in the 1970s did generate a number of impressive legislative and legal victories. After nearly 50 years of effort, feminists succeeded in pressuring the Congress to pass the Equal Rights Amendment in 1972 and send it to the states for ratification. Under the leadership of Bernice Sandler, a task force of the Women's Equity Action League (WEAL) launched a class-action complaint of sex discrimination against colleges and universities in the United States. Using the affirmative action requirements for recipients of federal grants and contracts monitored by the Office of Federal Contract Compliance, WEAL worked with women inside institutions of higher education to pressure them to stop discriminating against women or risk losing their lucrative federal contracts (Sandler 1973). Congresswoman Martha Griffiths (Democrat-Michigan) worked within the Congress to build a voting coalition to pass Title IX of the 1972 Education Amendments that prohibits sex discrimination in educational programs receiving federal support. Amended several times, Title IX has been responsible for dramatic increases in the numbers of girls and women involved with school athletic programs and for the extension of college athletic scholarships to women athletes across a range of varsity sports. The Supreme Court decision in *Roe v. Wade* (1973), in combination with their earlier decision in *Griswold v. Connecticut* (1965), secured women's legal access to contraceptives and abortion. Through intensive efforts, feminists succeeded in heightening public awareness of violence against women, created shelters and services for rape victims and battered women, and pressured local, state, and federal governments to change laws, police and court practices, and to provide funding to address these important issues. In 1978, the federal government passed the Pregnancy Discrimination Act that made it illegal to fire, refuse to hire, or discriminate against a woman in any other way because of pregnancy.

Although these are impressive accomplishments, focusing exclusively on public policy in assessing feminism's impact would be a mistake. Equally important results of feminist activism are: increasing numbers of women in the medical and legal professions and in elective offices; changes in organization of domestic life, ranging from shared childcare and shared domestic labor in heterosexual households to some women's decisions to bear and rear children on their own; feminist mobilizations within institutions such as the Catholic Church and the military to redistribute power and responsibility; and innovative feminist scholarship across the humanities and social science disciplines that is reorienting popular understandings of the world. Within academic institutions, for example, women's and gender studies have flourished. From struggling programs launched by a handful of feminist scholars at a small number of American schools in 1969, women's and gender studies have grown exponentially. According to the National Women's Studies Association (NWSA), more than 800 colleges and universities in the United States now offer undergraduate and graduate degree programs in the field. Feminist scholarship has also made huge strides with more than 70 journals devoted exclusively to the publication of feminist research and with innovative book series published by virtually every major press. "Gender experts" are a growing field of professionals employed by governments, NGOs, and international institutions; and transnational feminist activists have built and continue to build global networks to advance common objectives. Within these diverse domains, feminist scholarship and activism are transforming the ways the world is viewed, analyzed, and lived.

As was the case with the first century of feminist struggle, "progress" for women has been neither uncontested nor constant. In the early 1980s the campaign to ratify the Equal Rights Amendment failed, three states short of the number required to make the Amendment operative. Affirmative action has been under sustained attack since the late 1970s and has been prohibited as the result of referenda passed by states such as California and Washington. Through litigation in other regions including the Midwest and the South, affirmative action programs have been severely curtailed and as a result the number of students of color admitted to elite universities has declined. In 1996, Congress passed the "Personal Responsibility and Work Opportunity Reconciliation Act" (PRWORA), which racialized and demonized poor women, and abolished welfare entitlements in the United States. Patterns of residential racism and white flight have perpetuated a racially segregated school system: 50 years after the *Brown v. Board of Education* decision, more than 80 percent of African American children are still being educated in institutions in which students of color are in the majority. Although women's reproductive freedom is supposed to be constitutionally protected, 88 percent of counties in the United States currently offer no abortion services. In March 2004, the U.S. Congress passed and the president signed the "Unborn Victims of Violence Act," which makes it a separate federal crime to kill or injure a fetus while committing a federal crime against a pregnant woman. This law declares that a "person" possessing full constitutional rights "exists from the moment of conception."

### Neoliberalism and Contemporary Struggles for Inclusion

Contemporary women's rights activists have noted that continuing struggles for inclusion are taking place in a political context of "backlash," an ongoing effort to reverse the gains that women and people of color have made in the United States (Faludi 1991). Backlash is occurring within a larger ideological shift toward neoliberalism, which subtly transforms perceptions of feminist activism and of the role of the state itself. In the United States, as in other liberal nations, during the struggle to create liberal democratic practices in the nineteenth century and during mobilizations to create social democracy in the aftermath of World War II, social justice activists understood the state as a viable site of political contestation. Through political party platforms as well as the politics of direct action, proponents of social justice engaged the nation state as the primary means by which to struggle against the enormous power of the capitalist market. Feminists, like other progressive activists, perceived the state as a unique vehicle in the struggle for social justice because the state had the capacity to bestow equal rights, to legislate policies to redress historic exclusions and inequities, to use its tax revenues toward redistributive ends, to provide all citizens with a decent quality of life, and to change exploitive conditions of labor. In devising multiple strategies to politicize women's issues, feminists intentionally sought to transform what had been construed as matters of private, intimate, or personal relations into objects of public concern. In forging their political agenda, feminists intentionally sought to redefine "public" issues. Thus they suggested that an issue is public:

1. if it is treated as politically important;
2. if it is understood as causally related to societal structures in which all citizens are implicated; and
3. if its solution is viewed as requiring a collective effort to bring about relief for victims and reform to prevent further occurrence (Kelly 2003, 77).

In targeting the state, feminists sought to force the official institutions of government to treat women and women's concerns as matters of political importance. Through court cases and legislative battles, they fought to demonstrate exactly how the law constructs and sustains public/private spheres and the relations of gender inequality that pervade them. By illuminating state complicity in the subordination of women, feminists tried to foster public awareness of the depths of collective responsibility for centuries of women's exclusion, marginalization, and exploitation in the hope that public knowledge of injustice would trigger collective action to change the laws, the social structures, and the personal relations shaped by them. In the United States and in nations around the globe, feminists have devoted and continue to devote extensive efforts to the formation of a feminist public sphere or "counterpublic" as a crucial step in the politics of social change. It is a step that presupposes engagement with the state as a critical venue for democratic politics.

The tenets of neoliberalism, however, transform the conditions under which feminist activists attempt to engage gender-based injustices. As we have seen, because of the exclusionary laws and practices of governmental institutions, feminists in the United States have relied heavily on "outsider strategies" for engaging the state, organizing grassroots campaigns, social movement organizations (such as NOW and Feminist Majority Foundation), and professionally staffed lobbying firms (e.g., WEAL and National Abortion Rights Action League [NARAL]). Because these outsider strategies fall within neoliberal definitions of the "private" sphere, neoliberalism characterizes feminist political activism as private interest group activity. What social movement feminists understand as a political struggle for social justice, the rights of women citizens, or for "women's rights as human rights," neoliberals construe as private mobilizations to gain public resources. For example, neoliberals frame feminist efforts to secure state funding for rape prevention, domestic violence prevention, and shelters for women who experience rape and domestic violence as "special interest" lobbying. In changing the framing assumptions from a discourse of social justice to a discourse of private pursuit of economic resources, feminist goals are depoliticized and resignified as "private" endeavors. By "privatizing" feminist appeals to the state for redress of grievances, neoliberals can depict feminist activists (as well as antiracism activists, gay and lesbian activists) as proponents of "special interests," who unfairly demand "special rights." As appeals to social justice are reduced to claims for "special treatment" within the neoliberal frame, they lose their justification and can be dismissed as violations of individual (i.e., white male) "rights" and "universal" norms. Caught within the privatization imperatives of neoliberalism, feminist claims for social justice are dismissed as special pleadings of private interest groups. Stripped by neoliberalism of a social justice context, feminist mobilizations have no greater claim on the public than the campaign of any interest group for private advantage. The moral suasion afforded by demands to remedy injustice is effectively neutralized as pluralist politics assumes the guise of providing an equal playing field for all private interests.

Neoliberalism privatizes feminist endeavors by subsuming them under interest group politics at the same time that it redefines the role of the state. Over the past few decades, neoliberalism has profoundly altered perceptions of the kinds of contestations possible within the nation-state (Hoover and Plant 1989). Resurrecting the classical view that inequality among people is natural rather than politically constituted and maintained, neoliberals insist that state efforts to reduce inequality are futile and necessarily oppressive. Rather than indulge utopian fantasies, the role of the state, on this view, is to promote individual freedom, understood as the individual's pursuit of material self-interest. The state can best advance this end by facilitating economic development, which in turn will resolve social problems. State strategies to foster economic development include deregulation of the corporate sector, provision of special incentives for economic development in free enterprise zones, reductions of income, estate, and corporate taxes, and elimination of welfare "dependency." Within the parameters set by neoliberalism, the political agenda should be winnowed down to the provision of essential business services and security (domestic and global). No space exists on this streamlined neoliberal agenda for feminist politics. At best, feminist efforts to expand the public agenda appear oddly anachronistic, a remnant of the misguided but buoyant politics of the sixties. At worst, feminist discourses are construed as petulant groveling in "victimization," which dupe women into practices that worsen their condition (Hoff Summers 1994).

While neoliberals actively advocate the cultivation of the corporate-friendly "night watchman" state as a matter of intentional public policy, many voices participating in contemporary globalization debates suggest that the retrenchment of the welfare state is less a matter of willful political design and more a consequence of the relentless forces of globalization. Whether advanced by proponents or opponents of globalization, discussions of the "hollowing out" of the state, the "erosion of sovereignty," and the "demise of the welfare state" accept the neoliberal conclusion that social justice politics have no place on the contemporary political horizon. As Peter Evans (1998, 86) has suggested: "The pervasive anti-state discourse in the Anglo-American global order has solidified into a domestic political climate that makes engaging the state as an ally seem farfetched." The consequences of this ideological shift are pronounced: "Strategies aimed at increasing state capacity in order to meet rising demand for collective goods and social protection look foolish in an ideological climate that resolutely denies the state's potential contribution to the general welfare" (Evans 1998, 84).

The shift toward neoliberalism has dire consequences for women that extend beyond the "privatization" of social justice issues. Persistent inequalities are placed beyond redress. Efforts to "cutback the state" translate into the elimination of a range of professional jobs that have afforded women a route to middle-class existence. In addition, elimination of entitlements to welfare and cutbacks in other forms of social provision increase class inequalities and heighten the poverty of the most vulnerable U.S. citizens, a group in which women and their children are overrepresented. Each of these consequences will be discussed briefly.

Despite more than 200 years of political effort, women remain at great remove from the achievement of legal, political, or economic equality in the United States. Feminist legal scholars have demonstrated that the failure to ratify the Equal Rights Amendment leaves women legally vulnerable to unequal treatment in state and federal law. In reviewing cases involving claims of sex discrimination, the U.S. Supreme Court has refused to declare sex a "suspect" classification, which means that state governments and the federal government may pass laws that treat men and women differently as long as they have a "rational basis" for doing so, and the legislative means adopted are substantially related to the ends the state seeks to accomplish. Despite the 14th Amendment's guarantee of equal protection of the law, then, men and women can be treated differently by the law in the contemporary United States. Feminist lawyers have estimated that some 15,000 statutes treating men and women differently remain on the books.

Women and politics scholars have pointed out that elective offices are one of the most glaring arenas of gender inequality. Although women constitute 52 percent of the U.S. population, no woman has ever served as president or vice president of the United States. Women currently hold only 79 of the 535 seats (14.8 percent) in the 109th U.S. Congress (14 of the 100 seats in the Senate; 65 or 14.9 percent of the 435 seats in the House of Representatives). The United States trails behind 57 other democratic nations in the percentages of women in elective office at the national level. Although women of color hold only 19 seats or 3.5 percent of the 535 seats in Congress (12 African American women and 7 Latinas serve in the House of Representatives, none currently serve in the Senate), black women and Latinas constitute a higher percentage of the African American and Latino delegations in Congress, than white women do in comparison with white men. African American women constitute 26.6 percent of the black delegation in Congress and Latinas comprise 31.2 percent of the Latino delegation; while white women make up only 17 percent of the white members of Congress. Within the states, women hold 25 percent of the statewide elective offices, but only 8 (16 percent) governorships, and 22.5 percent of the seats in legislative assemblies. While the numbers of women in office increased steadily between 1969 and 1995, in the past decade progress has stagnated, leaving women a very long way from achieving equal representation. Indeed, a recent study by the *Congressional Quarterly* projected that if women were to continue to move into federal elective offices at the same rate that they have been since 1917 when Jeannette Rankin first won election, it would take another 432 years for women to achieve equal representation in public office. Yet most mainstream politicians, journalists, and citizen activists fail to see women's deprivation of public roles as a political issue.

Women's continuing underrepresentation in elective offices is puzzling, in part, because women participate more actively in other aspects of politics than do men. Women have been out-voting men in every election since 1964. Since the 1950s, women have been 75–80 percent of the campaign workers in the Democratic party and more than 50 percent of the campaign workers in the Republican party. In both parties, women are more active as rank and file party activists at the precinct level (Freeman 2000; Sanbonmatsu 2002).

Political scientists have offered a range of explanations for the paucity of women in elective offices. Many of these accounts suggest that women choose not to engage in the rough and tumble of electoral politics. Maurice Duverger's *The Political Role of Women* (1955), one of the earliest comparative studies of women's political engagements, for example, suggested that women were unknowledgeable about and disinterested in politics, a view that was often cited to explain women's absence from elective offices. Since the 1970s, women and politics scholars have gathered considerable evidence to demonstrate the inadequacy of this account and to support other more illuminating explanations of women's underrepresentation in positions of political power.

Several of the early studies did not contest the idea that women were less politically active than men but investigated the role of gender socialization in producing women's "passivity" and suggested that strategies of "counter-socialization" be developed to enable women to participate fully (Flammang 1997; Fowlkes 1984; Kelly et al. 1991, chapter 5). Some scholars developed a "situational account," suggesting that the demands of motherhood left women little time to devote to full-time political careers that routinely involved evening engagements and extensive travel, but was much more compatible with local community activism, where many women invested their political energies (Lee 1976, 1977). Other scholars focused on structural barriers such as education, occupation, and income that made it more difficult for women to assume positions of political leadership. Prior to the 1980s, women's levels of educational attainment were lower than men's. Women were far less likely to hold advanced degrees and to practice professions such as law and business, which served as routes to political office. Women's incomes and control of wealth were significantly lower than men's, affording them fewer resources to devote to costly electoral campaigns for office (Bullock and Hays 1977). More recent studies have pointed out that the factors holding women back, whether pertaining to socialization, mothering, or socioeconomic status, are themselves socially produced. They are the result of laws, norms, and customary practices that enforced separate spheres and limited educational, citizenship, and political opportunities on the basis of race and gender (Flammang 1997; Siltanen 1994).

During the past two decades, scholarship in the field of women and politics has illuminated a range of distinctively "political" obstacles to women's election to public offices. Political scientists have long known that incumbency is a major factor in electoral success. Current office holders who seek reelection have a 95 percent chance of returning to office and 85–90 percent of incumbents typically seek reelection. As a consequence, winning elections when running as a "challenger" is extremely difficult. Since women were barred by law from most elective offices at state and federal levels until the second decade of the twentieth century, those who chose to run for office typically faced an incumbent, thus they faced a huge political obstacle to electoral success.

In a series of important studies, Wilma Rule and Joseph Zimmerman (1994) demonstrated that electoral systems themselves may constitute barriers to women's election to public office. In the United States, the electoral system creates single-member districts (only one person represents the district) with winner-take-all elections, decided by plurality rule (whoever wins the most votes is elected; a majority of votes is not required). Through multiple large, cross-national studies, Rule showed that single member districts with winner take all elections are far less hospitable to women's election than are multimember districts with proportional representation (i.e., districts in which political parties present slates of candidates to the voters and are awarded a percentage of seats in the legislature proportionate to the percentage of popular votes they win in the election).

Like public offices, political parties continue to be male-dominant institutions. Male party leaders tend to recruit other men to run for "winnable seats," thus playing a "gatekeeper" role that effectively excludes women. For years, party leaders claimed their preference for male candidates simply was a response to voter preferences, citing opinion polls from the 1930s that indicated that voters would not cast a ballot for a qualified woman. Public opinion polls since the 1970s, however, reveal that sex bias among voters is no longer a problem in the United States. Sex bias among male party elites remains a sizable obstacle to women seeking elective offices. Despite clear evidence of the role of political institutions in creating and perpetuating inequality, neoliberalism provides no role for the state in redressing these gender-based inequities.

In addition to placing women's underrepresentation in elective offices beyond redress, neoliberalism's attempt to "shrink" the state also has direct effects on employment opportunities for women and people of color in the public sector. Employment in the federal bureaucracy, often in the "redistributive agencies" of the welfare state, has been the primary route to middle class existence for many American women. "Great society programs in the 1960s heightened the importance of social-welfare employment for all groups, particularly women. Between 1960 and 1980, human services accounted for 41% of the job gains for women compared with 21% for men. Among women, there were significant differences in the importance of human services employment for whites and blacks. For white women, the social-welfare economy accounted for 39% of the job gain between 1960 and 1980; for black women, an even more dramatic 58%" (Erie et al. 1983, 103). "Downsizing" the government, then, places the economic security, the precondition for autonomous citizenship, at risk for thousands of women who have positions in local, state and federal agencies. Neoliberal cutbacks threaten African American men as well. More than one-third of all African American lawyers, and 30 percent of all black scientists work for the federal government (Hacker 1992). Thus the neoliberal effort to shrink the state is neither race nor gender neutral.

In celebrating the capitalist market as a sphere of freedom in which individuals voluntarily contract with their employers to sell their labor power, neoliberalism not only falsifies the historical record, but also forecloses options for addressing sex- and gender-based biases in the occupational system. As discussed above, local, state, and federal laws have been used to restrict women's and minorities' participation in the waged-labor force, to prohibit their freedom to contract, and to structure the educational and work opportunities available to them. Neoliberal rhetoric about freedom to contract masks that history of gender, racial, and ethnic discrimination by the state, while ruling out contemporary state intervention to correct the long-term effects of those exclusionary practices.

In the contemporary labor force, women's underrepresentation in positions of power in the public sector mirrors women's position in the private sector, a phenomenon that economists have labeled the "glass ceiling." Over the past three decades, women have made important gains in the labor force and in the professions. In 1970, 43 percent of women over the age of 16 were employed outside the home. By 2002, 60 percent of women were working outside the home, constituting 48 percent of the paid labor force. Thirty-two percent of adult women had completed 4 or more years of college by 2001, compared with only 11 percent in 1970. In the first decade of the twenty-first century, 30 percent of the physicians and 29.3 percent of the lawyers and judges are women, up from less than 5 percent in 1970. Indeed, the U.S. Bureau of Labor Statistics (2004) reports that in 2002, women held 50 percent of the positions in "managerial and professional specialty" category. To arrive at this statistic, however, they rely upon a wide range of positions in middle and lower management, as well as self-employment. The top of the Executive/Managerial pyramid is still dominated by men. Women hold less than 5 percent of the senior management positions in Fortune 1000 corporations.

During the last three decades of the twentieth century, the nature of the U.S. economy changed dramatically. Deindustrialization shifted the U.S. economy from a manufacturing powerhouse to a service economy. At the outset of the twenty-first century, 72 percent of the jobs in the United States were in the service sector; only 2.5 percent of the jobs were in farming, fishing, and forestry. While the nature of both male and female employment has changed with deindustrialization, job segregation by sex persists and the kinds of service work that women do (e.g., nursing, secretarial work, and childcare) differs from the kind of service work that men do (e.g, marketing and public relations, funeral directors, and morticians). Studies of comparable worth have documented that jobs traditionally performed by women pay 32 percent less than jobs traditionally performed by men that require comparable levels of education, responsibility, and skill. Yet, neoliberalism's emphasis on free choices of individuals who voluntarily contract their labor services within a competitive market precludes state intervention to redress pay inequities tied to job segregation by sex.

Pay inequities continue to harm working women and their families. According to the Bureau of Labor Statistics (2002), white women's earnings were 78 percent of white men's earnings in 2001, while African American women's earnings were 67 percent and Latina's earnings were 54 percent of white men's earnings. Job segregation by sex accounts for a good deal but not all of the pay disparity between men and women workers. When researchers control for education, experience, and quality of job performance, women still earn 10 percent less than their perfectly matched male counterparts.

The cumulative impact of pay inequities over a working woman's lifetime can be staggering. According to the U.S. Census Bureau, a man and a woman who graduate from the same university, with identical grade point averages, and equally positive letters of recommendation, who begin their careers in the same field and who perform their duties with the same levels of dedication, skill, and alacrity, will not have the same lifetime earnings: a man can expect to earn 50 percent more over the course of his lifetime than a comparably situated woman will earn. Although a slight decline in the pay gap between men and women has occurred over the past ten years, the difference is due to declining male wages—not to increasing wages for women.

The term, "feminization of poverty," was coined by feminist economists to make visible the growing concentration of poverty among women and their children in the late twentieth century. Since 1969, the incidence of poverty among adult women has grown dramatically as the incidence of poverty among adult men has declined. In 2004, 36 million U.S. citizens (7 million families), 13 percent of the population, live below the poverty line: 80 percent of the adult poor are women.

Poverty is not equally distributed across the U.S. population: 9 percent of white Americans, 23 percent of African Americans, 21 percent Latino/as, 10 percent Asian Americans and 30 percent of Native Americans live in poverty (U.S. Census Bureau 2002). Poverty is particularly concentrated among single women heads-of-household, that is, among women who are raising their children alone: 22 percent white, 35 percent black, 37 percent Latina, and 15 percent Asian American women heads-of-household live on incomes below the poverty line, which the federal government set at US$8,890 for a single individual and US$18,400 for a family of four in 2004. The kind of poverty experienced by women household heads is acute; more than half are living with income less than 50 percent of the official poverty level.

Contrary to many popular beliefs, the vast preponderance of the poor work, but the wages they earn are insufficient to provide a decent standard of living. In 2004, the minimum wage in the United States was US$5.15 per hour, which would yield an annual wage of US$10,700 for full-time work. Sixty-one percent of minimum wage workers are adult women; of these, more than half have children to support. A minimum wage worker who devotes 40 hours per week for 50 weeks per year to employment earns US$1,400 less than the poverty level if she has one child to support and US$7,700 less than the poverty level if she has three children to support. To grasp the intensity of this level of poverty, consider a recent study by the Economic Policy Institute, which indicates that it takes an income of US$27,000 per year to afford a two bedroom apartment and meet basic needs in rural areas of the United States in 2004 and US$52,000 per year to have the same minimal standard of living in an urban area. Yet 24 percent of the U.S. labor force earns less than US$8.23 per hour or US$16,640 per year. In the richest nation of the world, the working poor, who are disproportionately women and their children, lead very difficult lives. Neoliberal premises preclude state intervention to redress these growing inequalities.

Although the context of women's struggle for full citizenship, equal rights, and a more equal share in decision making has changed with the advent of neoliberalism and backlash politics, many women's rights activists in the United States continue their efforts to address persistent political, economic, and social inequalities in the twenty-first century. Tens of thousands of organizations, created by women and for women, seek to develop women's political agendas, conduct gender audits and gender impact analyses of government policies, build progressive coalitions among women, deepen the meaning of democracy and democratization, deliver much needed services to women, and pressure public and private sectors to include more women and respond better to women's concerns. The substantive scope of such feminist work includes livelihood struggles; the politics of food, fuel, and housing; women's health and reproductive freedom; education for women and girls; employment opportunity, equal pay, safe working conditions, and protection against sexual harassment; rape and domestic violence; sexual trafficking; women's rights as human rights; militarization; peace making; environmentalism; sustainable development; democratization; welfare rights; AIDS; and parity in public office. In the United States as in the rest of the world, women's political activism continues on all these fronts.

# PART 3

*Gender and Globalization*

CHAPTER 5

# Women and Globalization in Mexico

LAURA GONZALEZ

The history of Mexico is one of globalization although the impact of investment, trade and commerce with outside entities has taken different forms in different eras and in different regions. Prior to the twentieth century, globalization in Mexico involved military conquest and colonialism, perpetrated initially by Spain in 1521, and later by France and United States, as each of these states struggled with one another and with the fledgling Mexican state for territory and control in the nineteenth century. Globalization continued in a different form in the twentieth century. While other major historical events, such as the war for independence in 1810 and the Revolution of 1910 have caused major changes in Mexican political and economic organization, the impact of outside forces has been most evident in the period of conquest beginning in 1521, when the Spanish created new institutions to extract silver and gold from Mexico, and again in the period since 1982, when the Mexican peso crisis brought political and financial intervention from international political and financial organizations. In these two periods, from 1521 to 1810 under Spanish rule, and from 1982 to the present, globalization reorganized the political and economic institutions, changed gender relations, and ordered the economy to serve outside interests.

## The Spanish Conquest

When the Spanish conquered the North American continent in 1521, their main goal was to extract resources, primarily silver and gold. At the end of the sixteenth and beginning of the seventeenth centuries, 80 percent of Mexican exports to Spain were silver and gold. Corn, cacao, and cochinilla (a red dye) were other lesser exports. To accomplish the goal of extracting and transporting silver and gold, the Spanish brought with them not only their own technology, but customs, laws, African slaves, and institutions.

The Spanish also had to learn, adapt, and create new institutions to organize the use of water, land, animals, and labor. The mines required food and clothes for the workers, hides for leather, and tallow for candles. A "symbiosis *minero-agro-ganadera*" (a symbiosis among enterprises dedicated to mining, cattle raising and agriculture) developed. Throughout this period, the institutions were a complex mixture of indigenous and European forms of producing, taxing, and distributing key resources, conditioned primarily by the economics of mining (Gonzalez 1992).

The Spanish brought with them livestock that did not exist in the New World: horses, bulls, pigs, goats, and cows. In pre-Hispanic times, indigenous people planted using a stick or "*coa*." The Spanish brought metal plows to cultivate the fields. To feed those working in the mines and themselves, the Spanish cultivated lands that had never been cultivated before with crops new to the New World, such as wheat, barley, rice, olives, and grapes. The Spanish did not bring women with them initially. They created new land tenure systems, new agricultural systems, and new relations of production oriented mainly toward the goal of mining. In their exploration of the north and west for silver, the Spanish killed those indigenous people who resisted and gathered others together in *repartimientos, encomiendas, haciendas, presidios, and misiones*, communities of different indigenous peoples, whom they taught to speak Spanish, cover their bodies, convert to Catholicism, and learn the arts and technology of the Europeans.

Overall, the process was very uneven across the various regions of Mexico. Some regions in the New World were able to keep their own indigenous economic and political institutions, and were recognized by the Spanish Crown as indigenous communities, to be taxed as separate entities. Thus the relations between men and women in the Spanish viceroy period were not the same everywhere. In some places, women had much more control over food production and trade than in others. The Spanish Crown divided the territory into districts, each governed by separate administrators. Some of these were quite progressive, while others were cruel and oppressive. Mining areas were often quite wealthy. Architecture and all forms of art flourished. Waged labor was more prevalent than sharecropping.

This interaction was not a one-way relationship. The silver extracted from Mexico made its way to Spain, where it was used to finance world trade with Holland, Europe, and even China and Africa, helping to generate the first world financial system. Mexico gave the rest of the world not only silver, but also corn, cacao, tomatoes, vanilla, chiles, and cochinilla.

At the end of the sixteenth and throughout the seventeenth, eighteenth, and nineteenth centuries, a few middle-class Spanish women began to accompany their husbands, fathers, or brothers to Mexico as members of the court. The Catholic Church sent nuns to teach girls to be good wives or nuns. They taught elite girls to sew, play the piano, write, and sing. Some became important feminists, like Sor Juana Inés de la Cruz (1648–1695) (Glantz 2000).

A class hierarchy developed. Spanish from Spain were on the top and the indigenous were on the bottom. A very complex social hierarchy developed based on physical appearance and language. Only the Spaniards and *criollos* were allowed to have authority positions as administrators. Because only a few women came from Spain, many Spanish men had children with indigenous women and with African slaves, creating the *mestizo*, which is the prototype of the Mexican population today.

As Patricia Begné explains in chapter 2, gender relations under the Spanish placed women legally under the control of their husbands and/or fathers and confined their activities to those of reproduction, childcare, and work inside the home. The Catholic Church reinforced this gender regime. Although not always practiced, it functioned as a norm wherever Spanish and Catholic institutions reached in Mexico. As Begné notes, this model of gender relations was most severely disrupted by the Revolution of 1910, when women of all classes took on a variety of economic, political, and military roles as a part of the struggle. Not until the Civil Code of 1928, however, did Mexican women achieve the "legal" recognition of being the equals of men, able to work outside of the home without their husband's permission.

## Globalization since 1970

In the 1970s, Mexico was a country plagued by international debt, committed to a model of development based on import substitution, and fearful of being dominated by the United States. Its government was under one-party rule and plagued by a series of corruption scandals. About 25 percent of the population lived in rural areas growing corn, maize, beans, and vegetables in subsistence forms of agriculture. Although Mexico possessed extensive oil reserves, they remained relatively undeveloped at this point. Because of the global oil crisis in the Middle East, Mexico's oil reserves encouraged international lenders to invest in Mexican banks and businesses during the 1970s, although later financial analyses revealed that these banks and businesses were over-extended. Having implemented import-substitution policies in the 1960s and 1970s, Mexico was trying to develop without becoming further intertwined with its powerful neighbor to the North. Toward that end, the country continued to borrow more money than it could repay, causing the Mexican peso devaluation in 1982.

In response to its own debt crisis and encouraged by international financial institutions and the United States, the Mexican de la Madrid government abandoned its import-substitution development policies in favor of a greater reliance on exports. In 1986, Mexico joined the General Agreement on Tariffs and Trade (GATT). Subsequently, President Carlos Salinas de Gortari embarked on a program of liberalization, privatization, and land ownership reform, and began negotiating what was to become the North American Free Trade Agreement (NAFTA) of 1994, the first trade agreement between developed and developing countries (Audley 2003, 6). The systemic changes that have occurred since the economic crisis of 1982 constitute the second major reorganization of the Mexican economy and society brought about by globalization. Instead of seeking to extract silver from Mexico as the Spanish had, the United States, international capital, and international financial institutions, such as the International Monetary Fund (IMF) and the World Bank, sought a "return on their investments." To achieve that return, they demanded the repayment of loans, the opening of Mexican markets, privatization, and opportunities for more foreign direct investment.

## Mexico's Dual Economy

The creation of a dual economy in Mexico has been one result of the most recent round of globalization. Mexican economist Carlos Heredia Zubieta (2000) notes that the Mexican economy looks relatively healthy in macro-economic terms, but two disparate economies become manifest when different sectors of the Mexican economy are examined. An expanding and prosperous economy is associated with multinational corporations, while Mexican companies are stagnant or even declining. Exports tend to be concentrated among subsidiaries of multinational corporations, which are engaged in inter-firm trade primarily with the United States (Heredia 2000). Eighty-nine percent of all Mexico's exports are sent to the United States. Foreign direct investment is also largely from the United States. According to the Mexican government, 80 percent of all economic activities "were open for foreign direct investment" (Ministry of Finance 2000). Foreign direct investment increased three times between 1993 and 2000, with the fastest growing and most important investments in the manufacturing sector. By 2000, the United States had 11,630 subsidiary companies established in Mexico, accounting for 60.4 percent of all foreign direct investment (Ministry of Finance 2000).

While multinational corporations are flourishing, Mexican-owned enterprises are floundering, and poverty is intensifying among the majority of Mexican people. Several factors help explain Mexico's dual economy, including "institutional traps," the "debt trap," the "trade trap," and the "foreign direct investment trap." Each of these will be discussed further.

## Institutional Traps

When economic institutions and policies within a nation promote the interests of elites at the expense of the needs of the majority, Robert Isaak (2005) suggests that an "institutional trap" generates inequality. Over the past three decades, the global economy has intensified "the institutional trap" in Mexico. Centuries of authoritarian rule under the Spanish, and decades of one-party rule by the *Partido Revolucionario Institucional* (PRI), established tight and long-standing relationships between large banks, government officials, and business interests, relationships that promote their mutual benefit far more than benefits for the poor. Privatization campaigns mandated by international financial institutions seeking "return on their investments" have exacerbated such inequities. The privatization of Mexican banks after they were bailed out by international loans in the crisis of 1982 provides a powerful example of this problem. As Heredia (2000) has demonstrated, when Mexican banks were sold to private investors, many of them located in the United States, the assets and future profits of the banks were transferred into private hands while the liabilities were transferred to Mexican taxpayers. The privileged, who bought the banks, were allowed by the government to transfer significant debt to the public. The same imposition of liabilities upon the public occurred with the privatization of the toll roads (Heredia 2000). Government bailouts that benefit the wealthy are not peculiar to Mexico or to developing countries, the same pattern occurred with the bailout of "Long Term Capital Management" by the U.S. government in 1998 (*Washington Times* October 1, 1998); but the severity of the inequalities that result from such "institutional traps" are particularly egregious in a nation like Mexico, where more than 40 percent of the population is living in poverty.

PEMEX, the state-owned Mexican oil company, provides another example of the institutional trap. The discovery of large oil reserves in Mexico has been accompanied by the creation of a bureaucracy clouded in secrecy, which is not accountable to the public. At the same time that the government has adopted neoliberal rhetoric condemning food and welfare subsidies to the people, it has supported subsidies to private banks and PEMEX bureaucrats, while shrouding such transfers to the rich in secrecy. Thus, institutional traps are particularly adept at making the wealthy wealthier (Heredia 2000).

### The Debt Trap

The "global debt crisis" is intimately intertwined with "the oil crisis" that was triggered when the Organization of Petroleum Exporting Countries (OPEC) decided to raise the price of oil three times in 1973, four times over the next year, and five more times by 1979. Advanced industrial nations dependent on oil imports, as well as industrializing nations trying to advance development agendas, found themselves faced with huge oil bills. Saudi Arabia and other OPEC countries, in contrast, found themselves awash in dollars. The Saudis invested their cash in global banks (many of them U.S. banks), which in turn made loans to developing countries at exorbitant interest rates. In order to finance their development agendas, developing countries were forced to accept the high interest rates. After several years, however, these cash-strapped nations threatened to default on their loans because they were unable to repay them. At this moment of debt crisis, international financial institutions, such as the IMF and the World Bank, intervened to stabilize the global economy. Toward this end, they negotiated changes in government policies that would enhance the debtor country's ability to repay future loans. Using the promise of additional loans and interest abatement as leverage, the international financial institutions exacted agreements from desperate states to conform with certain "conditionalities," or "structural adjustment policies," generating the "global debt trap." Although acceptance of structural adjustment policies enabled poor nations to receive additional loans and to "reschedule" their debt, the new loans often involved even higher interest rates that contributed to higher levels of indebtedness. Ensnared within the "debt trap," debtor countries are compelled to reorganize their economies, giving priority to projects that generate hard currency for debt repayment, rather than organizing their economies to serve the needs of their people. A typical strategy for production of hard currency, for example, is the shift of agricultural production toward export crops, while cutting food production to be consumed by their own people. Land once used for subsistence crops is planted with coffee, soybeans, or flowers, products in demand in affluent nations. In Mexico, traditional agricultural products, such as corn and beans for domestic consumption, have been replaced by the production of flowers, fruit, and vegetables for export. Thus the generation of hard currency for debt repayment coincides with declining living standards and increasing malnutrition among the poor. In addition to the shift from subsistence to export agriculture, structural adjustment policies place a premium on repayment of the interest on old debts so that debtor nations can maintain global credit ratings. To meet their interest payments, poor nations have had to cutback essential public services, such as the provision of clean water, power, education, and health care.

Mexico is a somewhat unusual case of the debt trap because unlike most developing countries, Mexico has large, if only partially developed oil reserves and does export oil. However, debt problems are not solely dependent on oil politics. Institutional problems have contributed significantly to Mexico's debt problem. In the 1970s, Mexico's international credit rating was high, precisely because it had proven oil reserves. The country's banking structure was not strong, however; and loans poured into Mexico, generating debt that could not be repaid in spite of the oil reserves. The debt crisis came to a head first in 1982, and again in 1994. In each instance, Mexico's banks had to be bailed out, creating a debt burden and the requirement that interest be paid each year with public money. Despite its oil reserves, Mexico has fallen into the debt trap, devoting public funds to debt repayment rather than to social programs (Heredia 2000). Thus the debt trap is another mechanism that heightens inequalities, a mechanism through which globalization generates increased hunger, disease, and economic dislocation, especially for the poor, 70 percent of whom are women. The poor become poorer.

### The Trade Trap

Classical economic theory holds that trade benefits all in the long run, but that there will be winners and losers in the short term. Globalization has perpetuated a particular geography of winners and losers, concentrating benefits in the affluent nations of the North, and losses in the struggling nations of the South. Trade in the global economy generates and perpetuates these inequalities, because the goods and services produced by developing countries are not as "valuable" or "stable" in price as the goods and services produced by developed countries. For example, many developing states were encouraged to plant coffee for export to meet the growing demand for coffee in the developed world. As more coffee was produced, however, the price of coffee in the international market plummeted as "supply outstripped demand." In the context of North American agriculture, economies of scale and capital-intensive farming methods enable U.S. agribusiness to produce basic products at a cheaper price than small Mexican farmers can. That these inequities will dissolve in the future is not at all apparent.

Many developing countries have one-crop agricultural economies (coffee, sugar, cotton) or are dependent on the sale of raw resources, such as minerals, ores, and metals. This situation makes them very dependent on global commodity prices, prices that fluctuate dramatically from year to year. To make matters worse, developed countries often impose tariffs or quotas on agricultural goods, such as oranges, sugar, tomatoes, and lumber, to protect their own domestic industries and workers. Mexico is not a one-crop economy, but in the 1960s its economy had a weak manufacturing sector and exports were primarily agricultural or extractive minerals. Thus they have been subject to the trade trap.

The major way that global trade generates inequality in Mexico is through imports from other countries, particularly the United States, which undercut Mexican products in price. This problem has long dominated U.S.–Mexican trade relations. Even before the NAFTA agreement in 1994, Mexico had a trade deficit in agriculture, services, and manufacturing with the United States. When U.S. producers capture Mexican markets, small and medium-sized Mexican farmers and businesses are destroyed because they cannot compete with U.S. large-scale and capital-intensive agriculture, especially when it is supported by U.S. farm subsidies. Mexican agricultural staples such as corn, beans, and oil seeds have been undercut by cheaper U.S. products. In addition, cheaper poultry, beef, pork, and cheese produced in the United States have flooded the Mexican market. Ranchers in Tabasco and Veracruz have gone out of business. Small local cheese makers could not compete with gigantic foreign retailers like Walmart, which imported a variety of cheeses from other countries to Guanajuato, Mexico, a place which used to have only a locally made cheese available. Neoliberal economists see this situation as beneficial in that it offers consumers more choice and perhaps provides a more efficient way of production. For the producers of the local Mexican products, however, this import trade is a generator of poverty. The situation is even more dramatic with regard to corn and beans, staples of the Mexican diet. The United States can produce cheaper corn and beans than those grown in Mexico, thus they supplant small Mexican producers of these products even in local markets. Mexican subsistence farmers can no longer make the income they once made selling their small agricultural surpluses because of cheap agricultural imports from abroad.

The "*maquiladora* program" is an example of an attempt by Mexico to skirt the trade dilemma by developing a capacity to manufacture products for trade—chiefly textiles, garments, electronic equipment, electronic components, and automobiles. Begun in 1965 as a "twin-plant" Border Industrial Program, which allowed U.S. corporations to take advantage of cheap Mexican labor without paying tariffs on goods produced in Mexico and sold in the United States, the *maquila* program spread from the border throughout the interior states of Mexico, and expanded rapidly growing 14 percent annually from 1978 to 1988 (Isaak 2005, 146). The *maquilas* are financed by foreign direct investment, staffed by Mexican labor, and their finished products are exported for consumption outside of Mexico. Because they rely on imported supplies and parts, they are not well integrated into the rest of the Mexican economy, and do not generate a "multiplier" effect of additional economic activity within the Mexican economy. By 2000, the *maquiladoras* accounted for 53 percent of total exports, and were a significant component of the prosperous part of the Mexican dual economy (Heredia 2000). They created jobs in Mexico, especially for women workers, jobs that often exploited these workers with low pay, unhealthy and sometimes dangerous working conditions, and slum-like living arrangements. In 1994 at the beginning of NAFTA, *maquiladoras* employed almost 700,000 workers. By 2001, the peak of *maquiladora* employment in Mexico, *maquiladoras* employed around 1.3 million workers. As a mechanism to redress the trade imbalance between Mexico and the United States, the *maquila* program has had some success. Although Mexico continued to have a growing trade deficit in agriculture and services with the United States, since 1994 this has been offset by a rapidly growing trade surplus in manufacturing, large enough to give Mexico an overall trade surplus with the United States (Polaski 2003, 15).

Although Mexico introduced the *maquiladoras* program in an effort to skirt the trade dilemma, in the early twenty-first century, Mexico encountered another dimension of the trade trap. As export processing zones were created across the global South, Mexico found itself in competition globally with other low-wage countries for the *maquila* plants. At the turn of the century, many of Mexico's *maquila* plants began to close and move to China, where labor costs were even cheaper. By 2003, Mexican *maquila* employment had fallen to slightly less than 1.1 million workers, about 550,000 more workers than were employed in *maquilas* in 1994. By comparison, non-*maquila* manufacturing in Mexico that employed slightly less than 1.4 million in 1994, dipped to about 1.275 million in 1996 following the 1994 peso crisis, rose to a peak of 1.47 million in 2000, and dropped rather precipitously to 1.32 million in 2003 in conjunction with the recession in the U.S. economy. Throughout the period, non-*maquila* manufacturing provided more employment than *maquilas*, although by 2003, employment in non-*maquila* manufacturing (1.32 million) was only slightly larger than employment in *maquila* assembly plants (1.1 million) (Polaski 2003, 15–16).

### Foreign Direct Investment as a Trap

In the contemporary period of globalization, foreign direct investment also has contributed to growing inequalities. As in the case of trade, foreign direct investment often crowds out local Mexican farmers and small to medium-sized businesses, because their small-scale enterprises cannot compete with the large-scale, capital-intensive foreign operations. Capital-intensive agricultural firms that buy local land, install large irrigation systems, use special fertilizer and special seeds to increase yields, for example, are driving small subsistence farmers off their land, further undercutting the prices of locally grown agricultural products. As a consequence, Mexican farmers have lost their food self-sufficiency. Many have left farming, often migrating to urban areas, or joining the migrant flows to the north. In 1993, 8.15 million Mexicans were employed in agriculture; by 2002, this number had shrunk to about 6.75 million (Polaski 2004, 20).

Foreign direct investment has shaped the dual economy in Mexico. Between 1994 and 2004, foreign direct investment in Mexico increased from US$3.87 billion to US$13.43 billion a year. Located primarily in the most developed areas of the country around the northern border, and in the big urban areas of Monterey and Mexico City, foreign direct investment is concentrated in manufacturing (49.5 percent), financial services (24.4 percent), and commerce (10.8 percent). Much of the foreign capital has been used to buy existing companies, such as banks and large commercial chains (Picard 2003, 36), and to establish *maquiladoras*—assembly plants that are not integrated into the Mexican economy. Of the 6 largest export firms in Mexico, 5 are 100 percent foreign owned (Picard 2003, 27). The geographic concentration of foreign direct investment creates still more inequality between the poorer southern and rural parts of Mexico and the more prosperous northern regions, while also driving a wedge between the flourishing multinational-driven economy and the struggling domestic economy in Mexico.

## The Overall Impact of Recent Globalization
## on Mexico

### Inequality

As indicated earlier, the impact of globalization on both men and women is structured by class, region, race, nationality, and level of urbanization. In each instance, the inequalities are increasing rather than decreasing. Ten percent of the population is better off than they were ten years ago, while 90 percent are the same or worse off (Polaski 2003, 26). The incidence of poverty is higher than it was in the late 1970s. In rural areas, 69 percent of the population is poor.

## Employment, Productivity, and Wages

Employment in Mexican non-*maquila* manufacturing continued to surpass employment in the multinational-driven *maquiladoras* from 1994 to 2003, but the size of that difference diminished significantly over the course of the decade. While non-*maquila* manufacturing exceeded *maquila* employment by 1.35 million jobs in 1994; the difference had shrunk to 260,000 jobs by 2000, 170,000 jobs by 2002, and 120,000 jobs in 2003 (Polaski 2003, 15). Many of the jobs in *maquiladoras* involve poor or dangerous working conditions, no benefits, and poor living conditions. Since 2000, *maquila* employment has fallen as multinational corporations have moved their plants to China and Central America, taking about 30 percent of all *maquila* jobs with them. Employment in domestic manufacturing has also fallen since 2000, due in part to the recession in the United States.

In agriculture, the employment situation is much worse. Globalization, especially since NAFTA, has reorganized Mexican agriculture, displacing many subsistence farmers, who had produced maize, beans, oil seeds, poultry, pork, and cheese, while creating some new jobs for export of crops such as horticulture, strawberries, watermelons, mangos, and vegetables. In general, globalization has not generated the employment for Mexicans that was expected. Instead, the disruptions caused by economic liberalization have increased the pressure to migrate.

Productivity has increased but real wages have gone down in Mexico since 1994, due at least in part to the peso crisis in 1994. The decline in wages has not been sufficient, however, to enable Mexico to compete with the prevailing wage rates in other countries, such as China, Honduras, or Costa Rica.

## Migration and Cross-Border Networks

Migration flows within Mexico from rural to urban areas, from the south to the north, as well as cross-border migration from Mexico to the United States, have been longstanding but have increased dramatically with the dislocations caused by recent globalization. Migration from rural areas has been particularly pronounced.

In addition to the Mexican population that remained on the lands occupied by the United States after the Treaty of Guadalupe Hidalgo in 1848 concluded the U.S war against Mexico, Mexicans continued to move back and forth across the border, seeking work on the railroads, in the cattle industry, in the fields, in the mines, and in factories. Those that settled permanently in the United States began to build some of the complex networks that directed migration from Mexico in the future to particular locations in the United States (Durand et al. 2002; Papademetriou 2004). Mexicans who migrated and established permanent residence in the United States early in the twentieth century built extensive networks, connecting local areas in the United States with specific towns or regions in Mexico based on family and friendship ties. Every permanent immigrant increased the migration flow by financing the migration of family and friends, providing information about employment, providing shelter, and facilitating the movement of others in a variety of ways.

In 1942, the governments of United States and Mexico established the Bracero Program to bring Mexican males to the United States to work under contract for periods of 18 months. In the 1950s this program brought more than half a million men per year from Central Mexico, primarily to build railroads, work in the mines of Arizona, and on the ranches and in the fields of South Texas, California, and elsewhere in the Southwest. Although these workers were supposed to return to Mexico after their allotted time in the United States, many did not. Many others would return to Mexico, wait a few years and then return to the United States for another 6, 9, or 18 months. Still others migrated even though they were not involved in the program. The prevailing pattern was for men to come for short periods, leaving their families in Mexico. In times of depression, such as the 1930s, local and state governments in the United States deported as many as 3 million Mexicans. In the 1960s, Mexicans in the United States constituted 6 percent of the population of the United States; 80 percent of these were living in the states of Texas, California, Arizona, and Colorado. Smaller numbers had migrated to work in the automobile industries in Illinois and Michigan and on the railroad tracks in Pennsylvania. These, too, established durable networks that have shaped the pattern of migration in the last 30 years. The Bracero Program ended in 1964, but this did not stop the flow of migrants. By the late 1970s, Mexican workers had moved into a much broader range of jobs, working in food processing, manufacturing, construction, and personal services, with larger numbers moving beyond the southwest to places like Chicago and New York.

In the 1980s, the passage of Proposition 187 in California that denied social services to Mexicans, encouraged agricultural migrants to go to North Carolina, Georgia, and Florida. The Immigration Reform and Control Act (IRCA), passed by the U.S. Congress in 1986, granted legal status to all unauthorized immigrants who could prove U.S. residence since 1982, or who had worked in U.S. agriculture for a specified period of time. Between 1989 and 1994, this enabled almost 2.5 million Mexicans to become legal residents, and laid the foundation for increased immigration in the future, as these new permanent residents brought their wives, children, parents, and other relatives, neighbors, and friends to join them.

The economic crises of 1982 and 1994, and the subsequent devaluation of the peso, sparked a collapse in Mexican employment and an increase in migration to the United States. Areas of Mexico that had not previously had a record of sending migrants to the United States, such as Oaxaca,

Guerrero, Puebla, Hildalgo, Veracruz, Morelos, and the State of Mexico, began to establish migrant networks not only in the traditional destinations, but all over the United States. By 2002, migration from rural areas in Mexico was 452 percent higher than it had been in 1980 (Papademetriou 2003, 51). Also, by 2002, the composition of the immigrant population had changed. More immigrants were coming from urban areas, and more were educated and of middle-class background.

Within Mexico, migration has also occurred. From 1970 to 2000, the percentage of Mexico's population living in rural areas dropped from 41.3 to 25.4 percent. While many of these migrants went directly to the United States; others migrated to urban areas within Mexico, especially to the cities and towns along the U.S.–Mexico border (Papademetriou 2003, 51).

## Remittances

Another important part of the migration story concerns "remittances," funds sent by Mexican immigrants in the United States to their families and communities living in Mexico. Remittances are a vital part of transnational migrant networks. They have also been an important contribution to the Mexican economy since the 1970s, increasing in importance in the twenty-first century. In 2000, remittances were the second or third largest source of foreign income after oil and tourism. By 2004, remittances surpassed oil as the number one source of transborder revenue. In 2004, 78 percent of US$13.3 billion in remittances to Mexico were sent to individual households to provide for basic needs, such as food, clothing, and medicine. Seven percent was spent on education, 8 percent placed in savings, 4 percent spent on luxuries, 1 percent was spent on homes, and 1 percent was used for investments. More than a million Mexican households received these remittances. The states of Guanajuato, Jalisco, Michoacán, San Luis Potosí, and Zacatecas received 44 percent of the total flow. The remainder went to all the other regions (Instituto de los Mexicanos en el Exterior 2004).

## Transnational Organizations

In addition to the informal transnational migrant networks, migrants have been encouraged by state and local governments in Mexico, and by the political parties to build formal transnational organizations. As migration has increased, these organizations have been strengthened and become more numerous. During the Mexican Revolution in the early twentieth century, Mexican transnational organizations were quite prevalent, consisting of groups both for and against Porfirio Díaz. They subsided somewhat during the Depression and the deportation of Mexicans from the United States to Mexico. During the 1950s–1970s, the Mexican government's interest in supporting or encouraging Mexican organizations in the United

States was fairly dormant. In the 1950s, migrants began to establish mutual aid societies or *mutualistas*. One of their primary purposes was to send the dead bodies of relatives or community members back to Mexico for burial. *Mutualistas* also served religious and cultural purposes, as Mexican migrants in the United States gathered to celebrate saint's days, to cook and eat the traditional foods of the communities they had left behind, to celebrate cultural standards of beauty, or to play soccer.

Despite the long history of such transnational organizations, most of the current associations are no more than 15–20 years old (Fitzgerald 2000, 32). The impetus to organize the more recent associations has come largely "from above," as the Mexican government's Program for Mexican Communities Abroad, created in 1990, has encouraged the creation of these transnational organizations. In 2001, the Mexican Embassy reported 691 of these organizations across the United States. The largest number of these organizations, 154, have been created by migrants from Zacatecas, followed by migrants from Jalisco with 120, and from Guanajato with 57. In the United States, the organizations are concentrated in 3 states, with California having 396, Illinois 165, and Texas 76. Thirty organizations have no specific state of origin within Mexico (Programa 2001).

The Mexican government encourages the formation and existence of these organizations because they are important stimulators of remittances to Mexico and remittances are the number one source of outside income for Mexico. These organizations engage in a variety of projects. Typically, they begin with a specific project in Mexico, such as church restoration, building plazas, water systems, electrical service, sports facilities, warehouses, or *maquiladoras*. Building new classrooms and equipping schools have also been popular kinds of projects (Fitzgerald 2000, 33). Other projects include construction of hospitals, clinics, purchase of ambulances for local communities, paving roads, and providing telephone service.

Mexican political parties only began to take an interest in organizing and mobilizing Mexican migrants living in the United States in the 1980s. In 1988, Cuauhtémoc Cárdenas (who a year later founded the *Partido de la Revolución Democrática*, PRD), campaigned in California against the *Partido Revolucionario Institucional*, PRI, in an attempt to rally Mexican emigrants disgruntled with the PRI's economic and social policies (Dresser 1993, 94–96; Fitzgerald 2000, 22). In response, several members of the PRI began an outreach campaign of their own to encourage Mexicans living in the United States to form an ethnic lobby, along the lines of the Jewish-American lobby or the Cuban-American lobby, and to stimulate the flow of remittances from Mexican migrants to their families in Mexico. In 1990, the Mexican government established the Program for Mexican Communities Abroad (PACME) under the Ministry of Foreign Relations. Two years later, Solidarity International was created as a part of President Salinas's National Solidarity Program (PRONASOL). Both programs encouraged migrants in the United States, and residents in various Mexican-sending communities, to carry out public works projects (Fitzgerald 2000, 23).

In 1996, in an attempt to maintain the allegiance and interest of Mexican emigrants, the Mexican Congress amended the Constitution to allow Mexicans to hold dual nationality. This change in the law allows children of Mexican citizens born abroad, as well as naturalized U.S. citizens of Mexican origin, to maintain property rights in Mexico, although they were not permitted to vote at that time. Mexican citizens living abroad are now allowed to vote through the mail (Diario Oficial Tomo DCXXI 2005).

In 1996, the Mexican Congress amended the Constitution to remove the restriction that Mexicans must vote for president in their district of residence. This amendment creates a possibility that Mexicans living abroad could vote in presidential elections, if the Federal Electoral Institute chose to create electoral mechanisms outside the country (Fitzgerald 2000, 26). Perhaps anticipating such a development, PRD candidate Cárdenas campaigned in Los Angeles in the 2000 election. Vicente Fox of the PAN party also campaigned in Texas and California, asking Mexicans to call their relatives in Mexico to tell them to vote, and to vote for Fox (Fitzgerald 2000, 27). In 2000, four Mexicans, who live at least part of the year in the United States, ran for the office of deputy in Mexico. Although the three PRD candidates lost, the fourth candidate, a member of PRI running in Mexico City, won the office. Most of his electoral support came from voters in Mexico City, for reasons other than his transborder ties.

Another impetus for the organization of transnational organizations from above has come from state governments. The state of Zacatecas took the lead in the 1970s and 1980s, celebrating the return of migrants from the United States, who came home to help with the harvest or to help plow and plant crops, before returning to the United States. In 1985, Governor Genaro Borrego established a Program for Zacatecanos Abroad, which committed the state government to match every dollar sent by migrants back to their home communities. Later, Governor Romo extended the program to allow federal and state governments to match the funds raised by the Zacatecanos living abroad on a two for one basis (Fitzgerald 2000, 30). In 2000, Zacatecas increased the incentive by inaugurating a three for one program. When serving as the governor of Guanajuato in 1997, Vicente Fox instituted a "three for one plan" for Guanajuato. For every dollar raised from migrants in the United States, the federal, state, and local governments provided a matching sum. When he was elected president, Fox created a three for one program for all of Mexico. The problem with this is that Mexicans living abroad are sending much more than the state expected and the state is unable to match the funds as originally planned.

### The Institute for Mexicans Abroad

On August 6, 2002, President Vicente Fox announced a radical change in Mexico's policy toward Mexican communities abroad, revealing a new institutional arrangement to promote ties between Mexicans on both sides of the border, and to help Mexicans living abroad, 98 percent of whom live in the United States. At the center of this new framework is the Institute of

Mexicans Abroad (IME), an entity initiated by the Ministry of Foreign Relations responding to pressure from the 25 million Mexicans living abroad. The *Consejo Consultivo de Instituto de Mexicanos en el Exterior* (CCIME) or the Consultative Council, an initiative of IME, was launched to include Mexicans living abroad in the policy-making process. Bringing together Mexican hometown associations, national Hispanic organizations, Mexican state governments, Mexican federal government agencies, and Mexican American intellectuals, CCIME is a representative body, comprising 100 counselors elected by Mexican communities in the United States, 4 counselors elected by Mexicans in Canada, 10 representatives of U.S. national organizations; 10–20 special advisors invited by the Mexican government, and several representatives of the Mexican states with highest levels of emigration. Thirty six of the one hundred and four counselors are women. The Consultative Council is charged with representing Mexican emigrants to the Mexican government. It meets twice a year, usually in Mexico. The Council's work is organized into six different commissions, which focus on education, health, political affairs, legal issues, border issues, and economics. Since its creation, the Council has taken up a range of issues, including: (1) allowing Mexicans living abroad to vote in the Presidential Mexican elections of 2006; (2) pressuring U.S. institutions to accept a *Matrícula Consular* certificate issued by any Mexican consulate for all Mexicans, whether documented or undocumented, as an identity certificate that can be used to obtain bank services; (3) helping to organize distance classes taught by Mexican educational institutions at all levels in Spanish for Mexicans living abroad; and (4) providing information about human rights, legal rights, health services, and disease prevention. CCIME has established a nonprofit organization in the United States, the Institute for Mexican Affairs (IMA), to ensure that CCIME's work will continue regardless of the changes in Mexican politics. In June, 2005, a major goal of CCIME was accomplished when the Mexican government passed a law permitting Mexicans living abroad to vote in Mexican federal elections through absentee vote or by mail (*Diario Official Tomo DC XXI* 2005; McKinley 2005).

## International Development Policies and State Apparatus for Women

Although Mexico had an import-substitution development policy until 1982, and was wary of being controlled by external political forces, it was not immune to influences from the international community. Population control, for example, was the primary focus of development policy during the 1960s. Between 1950 and 1970, Mexico's population grew by 3.2 percent per year, one of the highest growth rates in the world, despite the increased economic growth and urbanization that elsewhere have been associated with lower fertility rates. Responding to international pressure to curb population growth, the Mexican government established a nationwide family planning program in 1973. Spurred on by the 1974 UN Conference on Population in Bucharest, the Mexican government established over 3,000 rural health clinics and 73 regional hospitals in regions with less than 2,500 inhabitants between 1976 and 1982. The clinics and hospitals provided counseling concerning the benefits of small families, and recommended use of birth control, particularly in the form of inter-uterine devices (IUDs) or sterilization (Chen et al. 1990).

In 1980, Mexico signed the UN Convention on the Elimination of All Forms of Discrimination Against Women (CEDAW), and in 1999, Mexico signed the Optional Protocol of CEDAW that permits an international committee of experts to investigate and report on any forms of discrimination or abuse being suffered by women in Mexico. In response to the 1995 UN World Conference on Women in Beijing, the Mexican government under President Zedillo established the *Programa Nacional de la Mujer* (National Women's Program, PRONAM) in 1996, placing it in the Ministry of Interior (Gobernación) rather than in the National Population Council (CONAPO). PRONAM was charged with coordinating and implementing all women's programs at the state and local levels and with maintaining contact with NGOs, international organizations, and the larger society to advance the goals of the agency (Rodríguez 2003, 130–131). When Vicente Fox became president in 2000, he replaced PRONAM with the *Instituto Nacional de las Mujeres* (National Women's Institute, INMUJERES), decentralized its organization, and increased its budget from 26 million pesos to 230 million pesos. The agency was removed from the Ministry of the Interior and placed under the direction of a board, composed primarily of members of his own party, "*panista*" women (Rodríguez 2003, 130–134).

## The Impact of Globalization on
## Mexican Women

As discussed above, the forces of globalization in the last 30 years have meant

1. high rates of unemployment for both male and female subsistence farmers;
2. a "feminization" of the waged-labor force, that is, a large increase in the numbers of women working in factories and *maquiladoras*;
3. increased dependence of women, children, and elderly parents on remittances;
4. a dramatic increase in migratory flows from rural to urban, from south to north, and from Mexico to the United States;
5. the rise of the informal sector;
6. changes in the family structure;
7. the strengthening of old and the creation of new transnational networks and communities;
8. the growth of violence in the society;

9. the growth of undocumented populations working in the United States;
10. the "hollowing out" of local and urban communities as the most able of all classes and levels of education go north leaving behind the old, the sick, and the infirm;
11. a growing gap between the poor and the wealthy.

While these are primarily negative consequences, globalization has had positive impacts on women as well. Affluence has increased for 10 percent of the population, and at least half of these are women. In some instances, changes in the family structure have created new opportunities for women, supported higher rates of school attendance for girls, and given some women more economic independence. Women have been increasingly involved in business and in local, state, and national politics, suggesting that globalization has contributed to the creation of a small class of relatively self-sufficient women, who can and do take leadership positions in business, politics, and community affairs.

### The Impact of Poverty on Women in Mexico

For most women in Mexico, however, globalization has meant adjusting to lower levels of income, and in many cases, coping with poverty. It also has meant adjusting to sudden and abrupt disruptions in traditional ways of life in rural areas. Traditional village life in rural Mexico is quite sex segregated. Women perform the tasks of carrying water (if there is no water system), cooking, childcare, clothes washing, sewing, and the delivery of meals to the fields. Some women care for small plots of land (*ecuaros* and *huamiles*), near their homes, where they grow corn, beans, squashes and many other vegetables for household consumption, herbs for medicinal purposes, and trees for firewood. They carry *nixtamal* or soaked corn to the mill (*molino*) every morning to have it ground into *masa*. By tradition, men who bring corn to be ground at the mill are served ahead of all the women. Women sit in the back of the bus, while men sit in the front. The drinking of alcohol is a male, not a female, activity. Men are expected to be providers of cash income by plowing and working in the fields, or by selling extra crops in local markets. Any surplus income is generally invested in livestock or home improvements. When the men can no longer make money by selling their crops in the market, the traditional solution has been for the male family members to go to the city or go north to the United States to earn money. The men often return once a year, if they can, to help with the harvest and the planting. The remittances they send are critical for the survival of these families and villages. As migration has increased, especially in rural areas, many women have become heads-of-households for most, if not all, of the year. Many men maintain close contact with their families by telephone and continue to make decisions from afar, but others do not. In some families the men continue to send money, but start second families in the north. In still other households, the men leave and never return.

Women who remain in rural villages adopt a variety of coping strategies. Some farm the fields and do much of the agricultural work that men had done; some continue with their traditional domestic chores and wait for remittance checks to arrive; some get jobs in nearby *maquilas* or other factories and stores; some take in piece work from nearby garment factories. As more and more men migrate, bringing their wives and children with them, the women who remain in the village are left to care for the elderly, the sick, the injured, and the young. Some villages have taken on a ghostly quality, as many, if not most, of the houses are empty. When young men, who have been in gangs or prisons in the north, are deported back to Mexico, these village women are left to deal with the unruly and sometimes violent behavior of these young men, in communities where no adult males are available to exert control. With the dearth of males, some of these village women, especially those whose husbands send enough money in remittances to support them, become leaders, run the town telephone, the town store, or become elected *delegadas*.

When faced with reduced income, many women especially in the more urban areas of Mexico tend to join the informal economy, cooking food to sell on the street, doing piece work or assembly work in their homes for nearby factories, opening small convenience stores (*tiendas*) in their homes, doing laundry, cleaning, and providing childcare for others.

### Feminization of the Waged-Labor Force

A survival strategy for both urban and rural women has been to work in factory jobs—both *maquilas* and non-*maquilas*. Before *maquilas* spread beyond the border into the hinterland, young women would come to the border area to work, live in slum-like *colonias*, send money home to their families, or bring their families to the *colonias* to live. Textile and electronics firms hire primarily young women between the ages of 16 and 24. Working conditions for these women are often very bad involving low wages, dangerous working environments, monthly pregnancy checks, sexual harassment, rape, and no job security. Women in electronics firms suffer severe eye fatigue and must retire at an early age. Working conditions in textile and garment *maquilas* are hot, dusty, polluted with textile dye, and crowded. Now that *maquilas* operate throughout Mexico, and include auto and truck assembly, both women and men have *maquila* jobs. For some women, *maquila* work is a crushing experience. For others, the work is difficult but has the benefit of providing some independence. Being able to bring home money for the family or send remittances gives status to some women living in traditional patriarchal families (Fernandez-Kelly 1983, 1991). A few women have been able to emerge from the *maquila* work experience to become *promotoras*, organizers of women and men in the *colonias* or squatter communities, which house the *maquila* workers.

## Violence against Women

The UN Committee on the Elimination of Discrimination Against Women notes in its January 2005 Report on Mexico that "violence against women has increased steadily during the past decade with a consequent rise in the number of murders motivated by sex, domestic problems and disputes or drug trafficking and use" (p. 15). One of the more publicized instances of violence against women stimulated by the feminization of the waged-labor force is the case of Ciudad Juárez, where over 320 young women have been murdered since 1993. In addition, an unknown number of women (ranging from 44 reported by the state authorities to 400 reported by NGOs to 4,500 reported by the Human Rights Commission) have disappeared. The murder victims are mostly very young, slim, poor, and vulnerable. About one-third of those who have been murdered had been raped, some were sexually abused, and some were tortured or mutilated (p. 11). Most are *maquila* workers, students, or employees of commercial companies. The committee describes the situation in Ciudad Juárez as follows:

> The accelerated population growth has not been accompanied by the creation of public services needed to respond to the basic needs of this population, such as health and education, housing, and sanitation and lighting infrastructures. This has helped create serious situations of destitution and poverty, accompanied by tensions within individual families and within society as a whole. During a visit to the city's western district, the delegation was able to witness the extreme poverty of the local families; most of those households are headed by women and live in extreme destitution (p. 8) . . . The situation created by the establishment of the maquilas and the creation of jobs mainly for women, without the creation of enough alternatives for men, has changed the traditional dynamic of relations between the sexes, which is characterized by gender inequality. This gives rise to a situation of conflict towards the women-especially the youngest-employed in the *maquilas*. (pp. 8–9)

This situation is not peculiar to Ciudad Juárez. Chihuahua city has also been experiencing similar murders and disappearances, including cases of sexual violence, as have other regions of Mexico, namely Nogales, Tijuana, León, and Guadalajara (pp. 12–13).

## Migration and Women

Some controversy exists about the gendered composition of Mexican migration to the United States since World War II. An accepted view is that Mexican migration was almost entirely male during the Bracero Program from 1942 to 1964. Increasingly in the 1980s, married men sent for their wives and children to join them in the north, once they had established themselves there. This was particularly the case after the passage of the Immigration Reform and Control Act in 1986 (IRCA), which gave amnesty to those living and working in the United States since 1982, thereby allowing them to bring their families to the United States (Papademetriou 2003, 44). Based on the number of undocumented workers apprehended at the border, CONAPO (2005) estimates that women were 8 percent of the migrant flow before the Bracero Program; 5 percent during the Bracero Program; 18 percent between 1965 and 1986; and 16 percent from the 1986 until 1992. From 1993 to 1997, 14 percent of those detained were women, compared to 17.4 percent from 1998 to 2001, and 16.9 percent from 2001 to 2003. An independent study of Guanajuato migrants between 1994 and 1998 found that 90 percent of the migrants were men and 10 percent were women (CONAPO 2005).

The role played by women in international migrant networks is vital, although often unrecognized. As these networks have grown and matured, Mexican women have anchored them, linking migrants to family and community on both sides of the border. The women who stay at home maintain the religious, economic, and political structures of their communities while their husbands are away. They take care of the land, animals, stores, and other small businesses that sustain their families. They assume the multiple responsibilities of the head of the family, such as disciplining children, providing medical care, and taking care of the young, the sick, and the elderly. For some families, males living abroad continue to make family decisions as telephone contact is frequent. For others, the absence of men in local communities due to migration opens political spaces for women, not only to run their own households, but also to take decision-making positions in the community. Extended family relations at home and across the border remain a major resource for childcare, eldercare, and help in emergencies.

The women who migrate with their husbands to the north continue to perform household chores and often seek employment themselves. If they are unmarried, they may perform household chores for a relative in exchange for room and board until they can find work. They establish ties that give the family access to shared resources, as well as to governmental and nongovernmental agencies, offering health care, formal education, religious education, recreational areas, and political affiliations.

The women, who go north and return, are generally "transformed." They have learned to live in another economic system with different rules, different gender relations, and different ways of dealing with the state. Many of the returned women migrants transform their home communities by becoming municipal delegates, successful business people, entrepreneurs, heads of family, and active leaders in civil, religious, and political movements. Both women who migrate and those who stay in Mexico generate income for the home by working in the informal economy or in service or manufacturing jobs.

For many Mexican women in the United States, the exposure to "modernity" and "modernization" is overwhelming. Mexican domestic workers are exposed to families with divisions of labor in which men do the laundry, help with cooking, and with childcare, a radical departure from traditional practices in Mexico. Mexican women learn that women in the United States have a different conception of why they work. Mexican women often do not consider earning money outside of the home to be "work"; rather it is an activity directed toward providing a better life for their families. They consider it "helping" their husbands, their fathers, or their families.

Coming to another country and learning another system familiarizes women migrants with the idea that it is possible to have rights and to have leisure. They go back to Mexico and tell their mothers, sisters, and friends that there are blenders, washing machines, microwaves; that it is not necessary to spend hours every day making tortillas or doing heavy labor. Returning migrant women tell their relatives that they do not have to have so many children, that women can drive cars and even buses, and that women can be independent. Furthermore, they emphasize that it is okay to be independent. Returning migrant women also convey stories of different sexual mores, and different relations to desire and pleasure. They learn and report that women do not have to tolerate their husbands having mistresses or physical abuse in the home. They learn that young boys do not need to be taken to brothels as a rite of passage, and that the doctor can be a woman. Migrant women, who stay in the United States, cut their hair, wear pants, and change their culture. Through the migrant networks that connect women with their families in Mexico, migrant women introduce new ideas that question old patterns of behavior.

In recent years, remittances have become a pedagogical instrument of globalization for women. The government of Mexico is eager to encourage their citizens to make use of the banks. In 2002, banks, beginning in California, accepted the Matrícula Consular—an identity document issued by the Mexican government—to open a bank account to facilitate the transfer of money. This has helped to change the behavior of women in Mexico, because they now need to make use of the banks to receive remittances. The banks bring with them another culture. For women to have a teller card, to learn how to open a checking account, to get a debit or credit card, to use a teller machine, to read a bank statement, to manage money that is not cash, is a new experience. As women have been increasingly exposed to these new practices, they now use a new word, "*bancarizarnos*," meaning we have to learn how to use banks.

### Globalization and International Communication

Globalization has also provided women with new access to information. Never before have Mexican women had a Women's Institute, women in power, so many girls in schools, so many women owning and running their own businesses. Never before has the state paid so much attention to women's issues, such as reproduction, domestic violence, birth control, abortion, sexual harassment, leadership, education, and micro loans. Because of international influence, most notably the policies of the World Bank and other international lenders, which stipulate that women's advancement is key to economic development, the rights and needs of women have become much more visible in Mexico.

More and more women are working for wages out of their homes, in offices, factories, and *maquiladoras*. More women are now asking for help, reporting that they have been raped, that they want to open a business, or continue in school. These changes are all related to flows of information facilitated by globalization. Although globalization has had multiple negative consequences for women, it has also made Mexican women more aware of different systems of power. Before, these problems were secret, invisible, taboo. Now, these issues are in the open and women are able to talk about them.

Within Mexico, globalization brings to women TV programs, soap operas, and radio programs packed with new information. A star like Silvia Pinal, for example, uses her TV programs to create awareness about alcoholism, battered women, women's shelters, sex toys, rape, birth control, sexual harassment, and bigamy. The presence of women from all over the world coming to Mexico to march, to support the women in Chiapas, and the struggle in the Juarez–El Paso border for mothers of young women who had disappeared or were murdered, are additional examples of modes of transnational influence through which new information is shared and new possibilities explored.

Still another global influence within Mexico is the arrival and proliferation of evangelical pentacostal churches. These churches are particularly appealing to women because they preach that individuals can have a direct relationship with God without any mediation by a church (Alexander 2004). Eroding what has been the more or less monopolistic religious authority of the Catholic Church, these pentacostal churches also create new spaces for women's leadership. Many women have become leaders in these churches, something that has not been possible in the Catholic Church (Alexander 2004).

## Conclusion

This chapter has demonstrated that globalization in Mexico in different eras has involved the abrupt restructuring of Mexican institutions, changing basic power relations in ways that have profound consequences for women and their relationships with men. During the Spanish Conquest, globalization involved the use of brutal force to combine Spanish and indigenous institutions and practices, creating a society organized primarily around the extraction and transportation of silver from the New World to Europe. Spanish traditions and Catholic institutions served to train men and women about the separate and subordinate roles women should play in society.

Globalization in the last part of the twentieth century has involved the use of capital investment, debt, trade, and international agreements among states to restructure Mexican society once again. Rather than extracting silver and gold, the neoliberal ideology of the "Washington Consensus" has justified structural adjustment policies that "marketize" Mexican society and take advantage of the cheap labor that Mexico supplies without recognizing the human rights of six million undocumented Mexicans living and working in the United States. This process has dramatically favored existing elites, while increasing and intensifying poverty among the remaining 90 percent of the population, and has affected Mexican women disparately. Wealthy, educated, and middle-class women have benefited from having higher incomes, more opportunities for education and leadership. Poor women have suffered economically, as they have lost their land and their businesses, have taken work in *maquilas* under terrible working conditions, have assumed new roles in the formal and informal economies, while simultaneously running households and raising children by themselves while their husbands are away. Many poor women live in squalid slum-like conditions; others face the dangers and uncertainties of migrating to urban areas, the border, or the north. The dislocations for these women are stark and abrupt. Still other women have been the victims of sexual-trafficking rings, of senseless killings such as those in Juárez, and of drug trafficking.

Ironically, the restructuring of Mexican society, generated by global marketization in the last 30 years, has also brought to consciousness a hidden power structure involving the relations between men and women. More and more women have come to understand that they can question traditional divisions between the public and private arenas and between men and women. More have come to question the authority of the Catholic Church. Increased rates of migration, increased exposure to the waged-labor force, migration back and forth across the border, more access to technology in the form of TV and radio programs, internet connections, and even the telephone, have uncovered new possibilities for many rural, poorly educated women and even for many wealthier middle-class urban women. As a result, many women in Mexico are reorganizing their lives, their work, and their relationships with men.

While Mexican women have a long tradition of being politically active, the international women's movement, especially as organized by the United Nations, has had an enormous influence on the Mexican government and its desire to become a stronger member of the international global economy. Under the auspices of Mexican governments seeking international acceptance by complying with international gender-mainstreaming protocols, the NGOs of international women's movements and the women working within governmental agencies to advocate women's rights, have made remarkable progress in exposing (although unfortunately not necessarily changing) the hidden structures of power that have kept so many Mexican women bound in silence and submission.

# CHAPTER 6

# Globalization and Gender in Canada

## LAURA MACDONALD

As citizens of a small, relatively open economy, Canadian women have long been conscious of the ways in which their economic and political opportunities are buffeted by the forces of the global economy. Since the mid-1980s, however, Canada has undergone a dramatic intensification of its ties with the United States. Already heavily linked with the United States both economically and culturally, Canada's level of integration has increased quite dramatically in recent years as a result of the signing of the Canada–U.S. Free Trade Agreement (CUFTA), which came into effect in 1989, and the subsequent North American Free Trade Agreement (NAFTA) in 1994. Globalization thus takes a specific form in Canada—the importance of Canadian economic ties with other parts of the world has reduced in recent years, while relations with the United States have assumed ever-greater economic and political importance. For Canada, globalization primarily means growing interaction with and integration into the U.S. economy, not greater globalism. Canadians' ambivalent relationship with the U.S. hegemon dominates much of the nation's history and has helped shape Canadian national identity. Therefore, when considering globalization, this chapter will focus primarily on the impact of Canada's integration into the North American economy on Canadian women. However, other aspects of globalization should also be kept in mind, including the growth of the "new economy," technological change, changing rates of unionization, migration, and a range of state fiscal, monetary, and social welfare policies. The decision to pursue trade and investment liberalization in the late 1980s was part of an important shift in macroeconomic strategy toward market orientation, privatization, deregulation, and the pursuit of price stability and deficit elimination (Banting et al. 2001, 1).

The debate surrounding the decision to pursue a trade deal with the United States was one of the most intense in the nation's history. Yet despite the fact that the Canadian women's movement was raising questions from the beginning of the debate about the impact increased liberalization would have on women, women's voices were never taken into account in government decision making (Macdonald 2003). Canadian women's movements like the National Action Committee on the Status of Women (NAC) consistently argued that globalization "destabilizes existing social institutions and replaces them with impersonal market relationships and . . . reduces the power of nations to regulate business, tax corporations, and provide for the needs of people" (Cohen et al. 2002, 6). NAC argued that women would bear a disproportionate share of the burden of economic restructuring. But Canadian women's organizations also recognized that "the effects of globalization are not homogenous and that some groups of people are disproportionately affected as compared to others" (Macdonald 2003, 6).

The war in Iraq has to some extent understandably distracted attention in Canada from the effects of economic restructuring, and the decline of NAC in recent years has meant that no national-level women's organization has been promoting sustained attention to the gendered effects of globalization in Canada. However, economic integration is proceeding rapidly, and many business leaders and associated think tanks have been promoting deeper and more formalized forms of integration (Gabriel and Macdonald, 2004). What is the record concerning the effects of trade liberalization specifically, and globalization in general, on gender relations in Canada?

This chapter argues that the effects of globalization are more complex than what both advocates and critics of free trade initially expected. While globalization has not increased the gap in earnings between Canadian men and women in recent years, neither has North American economic integration succeeded in delivering the benefits its proponents promised. Overall, Canadian economic performance over the last 15 years has been disappointing, and the gap between living standards and productivity in the Canada and the United States continues to widen. However, two factors have mitigated the negative effects of globalization on women relative to men in the Canadian case. First, social programs and redistributive policies have been weakened, but not eliminated, despite globalization, and have remained more robust than those in the United States and Mexico. Since women benefit disproportionately from these programs (given their initial subordinate position), state action has reduced the negative impact of market forces on women and other vulnerable groups. Second, it seems that as Canadian feminist economist Marjorie Cohen has argued, intensified international competition has brought about the repression of wages of both men and women, resulting in little cost advantage to corporations from a strategy of feminization of the workforce (Cohen 1994, 105–106). Women's and men's participation in the workforce remains less divergent than in many other countries experiencing globalization.

The Canadian case provides an interesting perspective on the complexities of gender and economic restructuring in an advanced industrialized country demonstrating that states are not necessarily evaporating in the face of globalization, but continue to exercise positive efforts to mitigate the gender-differentiated effects of market forces. Nevertheless, the overall impact of globalization and regionalization in Canada has been decidedly mixed. Worrying trends are appearing in such areas as inequality in before-tax income, some areas of social policy, productivity, competitiveness, and the decline of the Canadian women's movement. The first part of this chapter outlines the impact of globalization on Canada, particularly regarding the increase in Canada–U.S. ties, and then discusses the social effects of globalization. The second part explores the implications of these changes for gender relations in Canada.

## Globalization and Social Progress in Canada—1980s to 2004

Globalization is not a new phenomenon for Canada. Canada has always been distinctive among industrialized states because of its high levels of dependence on trade, particularly trade in primary goods. Foreign investment has also played a decisive role in the Canadian economy, particularly after U.S.-based firms learned how to hop over the Canadian tariff wall to establish subsidiaries on Canadian soil in the early twentieth century. Canada was, in a sense, the training ground for U.S.-based corporations, whose strategies in Canada would later be extended to the rest of the world during the contemporary era of globalization. Since the decline of its ties with Britain, Canada has also established close military ties with the United States. Since the 1960s, these two countries have sought to integrate defense production, and both countries are members of both the North Atlantic Treaty Organization (NATO) and North American Aerospace Defense Command (NORAD). Nevertheless, throughout Canadian history, successive administrations also recognized the dangers to Canadian identity and sovereignty of overly close identification with the United States, and sought ways to distance Canada from its southern neighbor on many occasions. Not until the election of a conservative government led by Prime Minister Brian Mulroney in 1984 did Canada choose to pursue a free trade agreement with the United States (and subsequently Mexico in the NAFTA).

Despite historically high levels of trade openness in Canada, the degree of expansion of Canadian trade levels since the Free Trade Agreement (CUFTA) and NAFTA has surprised even supporters of the trade agreements. Exports of goods and services accounted for an astonishing 46 percent of national gross domestic product (GDP) in 2000, up from 28 percent in 1990 and 21 percent in 1970. In contrast, the U.S. economy remains relatively closed, with only 13 percent of the total GDP represented by exports, up from around 7 percent in the mid-1980s (Of the three countries, Mexico's trade orientation has risen the most dramatically, with imports rising from 12 percent of national GDP in 1987 to 52 percent by 2000, and exports from less than 10 percent of GDP in the 1970s to 45 percent in 2000) (Standing Committee 2002, 53). Nearly C$1.9 billion in goods and services cross the Canada–U.S. border every day, making this the largest bilateral trade relationship in the world (Department of Foreign Affairs 2003, 3). Canada and the United States remain each other's largest trade partners, but exhibit a striking asymmetry in levels of interdependence: while 87 percent of Canada's exports are sold to the United States, only 22 percent of U.S. exports are destined for Canada. However, rising imports from other countries like China and Mexico mean that imports from the United States represented 64 percent of total imports in 2001, down from a record high of 68 percent in 1998 (Standing Committee 2002, 58). Trade between Canada and Mexico has also risen rapidly since NAFTA—bilateral trade rose by 517 percent since 1990, and Mexico is now Canada's sixth largest export destination. However, Canada–Mexico trade represented only 1.6 percent of total intra-NAFTA trade, and only 0.7 percent of Canada's exports went to Mexico in 2001, up from 0.4 percent in 1990 (pp. 62–63).

Trade figures capture only part of the story of North American integration. Foreign direct investment levels have also risen dramatically within the region, reflecting higher levels of corporate transnational integration. Canadian investment in the United States rose from billion C$60 to C$154 billion between 1990 and 2000, representing an increase of 157 percent. U.S. investment in Canada rose less rapidly, by only 121 percent in the same period (Standing Committee 2002, 61). Overall, North American firms have become increasingly integrated across borders, particularly in the manufacturing sector, and within this sector especially among automobile and auto parts producers. A continental energy market is emerging, with increased trade in electricity, petroleum, and natural gas (p. 71).

The Canadian government and many analysts view NAFTA (and CUFTA before it), as clear success stories for Canada. The Canadian Department of International Trade declared that after ten years of NAFTA, "the verdict is clear—it has been a great success for Canada and its North American partners, and we are committed to ensuring that it continues to help us to realize the full potential of a more integrated and efficient North American economy" (Department of International Trade 2003a). In a recent summary of an evaluation of the record of NAFTA after ten years, the Department of International Trade claims that Canadians have experienced a wide range of benefits as a result of NAFTA, ranging from increased productivity and competitiveness for Canadian businesses, lower prices for consumers and increased movements of people within the continent, to improved environmental performance and labor rights (Department of International Trade, 2003b).

This glowing evaluation is clearly overstated. Government reports, like those of many NAFTA critics, generally fail even to attempt the difficult task of separating out the benefits (or costs) to the Canadian economy that can be attributed to NAFTA from those that derive from other factors. Even supporters of NAFTA recognize some clear weaknesses in Canada's economic position. Andrei Sulzenko, Assistant Deputy Minister in Industry Canada, points to several areas of concern, despite his overall positive evaluation of NAFTA's impact. Sulzenko claims that the main factor in the increase of Canadian exports to the United States during the 1990s was the growth of the U.S. economy, not the CUFTA and NAFTA. Sulzenko also points out that Canadian labor productivity increased at only about half the pace of U.S. performance.[1] The performance of Canadian productivity levels is particularly disappointing, since one of the main arguments in favor of Canada's forming a free trade agreement with the United States was that this would increase the competitiveness of Canadian industries. Sulzenko also notes that Canada faces growing competition with countries like Mexico and China for U.S. markets, and Canada's share of inward North American foreign direct investment has declined substantially in recent years (Sulzenko 2003, 39).

Critics of CUFTA and NAFTA claim that the benefits of NAFTA to the Canadian economy are vastly exaggerated by its supporters, even measured in aggregate economic terms. John Foster and John Dillon contend that real per capita growth rate of Canadian GDP averaged 1.6 percent a year during the free trade era from 1989 to 2002, a level below the average rate of 1.9 percent per year during the eight years prior to the implementation of the CUFTA. This low level of growth is largely attributed to the country's disastrous economic performance during the recession that Canada experienced in the first five years of CUFTA when real GDP growth averaged −0.4 percent a year. The recession was largely a result of the Bank of Canada's restrictive monetary policy in these years, which they claim was a consequence of an unannounced side deal made by the Canadian government with the United Stated as part of the CUFTA (Foster and Dillon 2003, 84–85). Strikingly, Satoshi Ikeda argues that Canada has dropped from the core to the semi-periphery of the global economy during this period, based on the drop of per capita GNP compared to U.S. levels (Ikeda 2004, 268).

Moving beyond aggregate economic indicators, when we begin to take distributional effects into account, further questions arise. The effects of Canada's lacklustre economic record in growth and productivity levels are not distributed evenly across the population but have resulted in growing levels of inequality and rising levels of poverty. Social progress essentially stalled in the period from 1989 to 1996 that saw a deep recession, followed by recovery and quite strong performance in the period 1996–2001. Canadians' average incomes also declined in the 1990s, from a peak in personal disposable income per capita in 1989, through a steady decline in the early 1980s. By 2000, incomes had not yet recovered to their 1989 levels. The gap between the standard of living in Canada and the United States also increased in this period, mostly due to the fall in productivity levels in Canada (Banting et al. 2001).

Income inequality also increased in Canada during the 1990s. Inequality of market income for economic level for families of two or more rose by 10.4 percent from 1989 to 1998 (based on the Gini coefficient). State redistributive measures like social assistance, Employment Insurance benefits, pensions, and child tax credits may act to prevent inequality in living standards, and the Canadian welfare state has traditionally been relatively successful in achieving this goal, particularly compared to the record in the United States.[2] However, Banting, Sharpe and St-Hilaire argue that the traditional role of the Canadian state in off-setting market-income inequalities diminished over the decade of the 1990s. In the first half of the 1990s, the tax and transfer system was quite successful in keeping after-tax income inequality relatively stable. However, after 1995, cuts to social programs weakened the social safety net and levels of inequality in after-tax income began to rise (Banting et al. 2001, 6).

The recession of the late 1980s and early 1990s also meant that unemployment figures were quite high for most of the free trade era. Unemployment levels rose from a low of 7.5 percent in 1989 to over 11 percent in the early 1990s, later decreasing to a current level of 7.6 percent. While job-creation levels have improved in recent years, most job creation takes the form of the growth of self-employment and involuntary part-time employment, increased work hours and "a significant intensification of work for most full-time, permanent workers" (Jackson 1999, 141). The "low-income gap" between the families below Statistics Canada's low-income cut-off (LICO)[3] and average families narrowed significantly during the 1990s, widened during the recession of 1991–1992, and, more surprisingly, continued to widen until 1997, despite strong growth rates. Heisz, Jackson and Picot claim that approximately 60 percent of the increase in the low-income gap was the result of decline in employment earnings and 40 percent the result of changes in social transfers (Heisz et al. 2001, 268). The 2001 census figures show the ongoing polarization of Canadian society, with the total incomes of the 10 percent of families in the top bracket increasing by over 14.6 percent over the 1990s, while median family incomes stagnated, despite significant economic recovery in the last half of the decade. The 10 percent of families with the lowest earnings saw their average income increase by less than 1 percent in the same period (Canadian Council 2003, 1). Poverty levels are particularly high among immigrant families, who make up a growing proportion of the Canadian population, and visible minorities (Heisz et al. 2001, 267).

While Canada's encounter with the current phase of globalization is mostly marked by an increasingly intense relationship with the United States, one aspect of the country's national development that reflects the greater influence of global flows is in the area of migration. Canada has long had one of the world's most open policies toward migration, and, like the United States, has been a nation of immigrants since Europeans began settling in the country in the 1600s. Since the early 1970s, the source of immigrants to Canada has shifted away from Europe and toward regions in the developing world such as the Caribbean, Latin America, Asia, Africa, and the Middle East (Stasiulus 1997, 142). While before 1961 about 90 percent of immigrants arrived from European countries, by the period between 1991 and 1996, only 19 percent came from Europe (Abu-Laban and Gabriel 2002, 14). The demographics of the Canadian population have thus shifted dramatically in the last 40 years. Both Canada and the United States accept many immigrants, but the Canadian immigration policy has several distinctive elements. According to Jeffrey Reitz, immigration policy plays a more important role in Canada's national development strategy than is the case in the United States and forms part of a continuing project of nation building. The flow of immigrants to Canada is higher as a share of the total population, and immigrants make up a large and growing percentage of the population in Canada's largest cities. More Canadians view immigration in a positive light than do Americans (Reitz 2002, 1). Gallup polls since 1975 show that at least 50 percent of the Canadian population have wanted either to maintain or increase current levels of immigration in every year except one (p. 12). Canada's multiculturalism policy and relatively high levels of immigration have helped the country "brand" itself as the model of a progressive, tolerant, and diverse nation. Nevertheless, recent evidence shows a steady downward trend in employment rates and earnings of new immigrants from most countries of origin, reflecting in part higher educational levels among native-born Canadians and also the effects of a shift toward a knowledge-based economy (p. 18).

## Gender and Globalization in Canada: The Complexities of Restructuring

How has Canada's encounter with globalization affected women's efforts to achieve greater gender equity? Feminists generally agree that globalization is not a gender-neutral process. Most believe that women are more likely to be among the "losers" rather than the "winners" from the globalization process because they have less access to resources and education, and are less likely to benefit from the opportunities presented by globalization. In most countries, one of the most important aspects of globalization has been the feminization of the workforce, as multinational corporations seek more flexible, more docile, and cheaper workers in order to become more competitive in the global economy. Downward pressure on male wages forces women into the workforce to guarantee family survival. While women's employment often creates new opportunities for women, these women tend to be employed in casual, insecure, and low-paid positions with few labor rights. Feminists have also argued that women's role in the private sphere means that they are increasingly responsible for assuming tasks of social reproduction as the result of cutbacks in state welfare services. However, not all women are affected in the same way by globalization, and globalization may open up new gaps between women both nationally and globally. The effects of globalization vary by production sector, region, class, race, ethnicity, marital status, and location in the global economy (Antrobus et al. 2002, 3; see also Macdonald 1999).

Early feminist evaluations of free trade focused on the negative impact of the CUFTA and the recession of the late 1980s and early 1990s for women in the manufacturing sector. Many of the sectors most threatened by lowered tariffs had large numbers of women workers, particularly immigrant women and women of color. For example, according to Cohen, women accounted for 75 percent of the labor force in the clothing industry. In the first 3 years of the CUFTA, women's employment in manufacturing decreased by over 11 percent or 66,400 jobs (Cohen 1994, 109). Similarly, Daniel Schwanen notes that in both manufacturing and services, the industries that were less sensitive to changes in trade rules because of already low tariff barriers had the lowest proportion of female employees, while vulnerable sectors had the highest proportion of female employees (Schwanen 2001, 174).

Nevertheless, recent evaluations show that in general, globalization and economic restructuring have not increased the gap between male and female earnings as feminist trade critics might have expected. In fact, Heisz, Jackson, and Picot argue that one of the most notable distributional inequalities resulting from changes in the Canadian labor market has been the decline in earnings for young men, while the gap between male and female earnings has been narrowing, although women still earn less than men:

> The ratio of annual earnings of women to men working full-year full-time rose from 58.4 percent in 1967 to 72.5 percent in 1997 . . . Drolet (2000) found that in 1997 the raw hourly wage ratio of women to men was 80 percent, but increased to 89 percent after controlling for a host of human-capital, productivity-related, and industrial and occupational characteristics.
>
> And over the 1990s, women's aggregate earnings increased much more quickly than men's. The weekly earnings of female full-time workers increased significantly more in the 1990s than in the 1980s, rising 13 percent between 1989 and 2000. (Heisz, Jackson, and Picot 2001, 260)

Similarly, Statistics Canada figures show that the gap in total income between the sexes is narrowing. In 1997, the total income equality index was 0.58, meaning that women received about 58 percent as much income as men, compared with an index of 0.49 in 1986. Because the income tax system is at least partially progressive, Canadian women pay less tax than men. Therefore, the after-tax income index stood at 0.63, up from 0.52 in 1986 (Clark 2001, 3–4). In 1998, lone-parent families and families headed by a senior received more in transfers than they paid in taxes (Status of Women 2001, 15). The Statistics Canada report states that gender differences in income and earnings may in part be attributed to women's concentration in part-time work and low-paying occupations, women's overrepresentation as single parents, and women's overrepresentation among seniors who have less income than younger people. The report also shows a decline in the gap between men and women's total workload, including both paid and unpaid labor, with women still working about 15 minutes more per day than men (Clark 2000, 3–4). Because of cultural, political, and institutional changes in Canada in preceding years, more women entered traditionally male-dominated and gender-neutral fields between 1981 and 1998. The numbers of women pursuing postsecondary education have increased dramatically, leading to concerns about educational achievements of boys and young men. In 1981, 37 percent of both women and men in the age group 20 to 29 were postsecondary graduates, while in 1996, 51 percent of women were postsecondary graduates compared to 42 percent of men. In 1997, 58 percent of all university graduates were women (Status of Women 2001, 19). Statistics Canada also shows that while both male and female university graduates were less likely to work in high-level jobs in 1998 than in 1986, the gap between women's and men's return on a university education had narrowed during this period (Clark 2001, 8).

Based on data from the late 1980s, Michael Baker and Nicole Fortin (2000) find a much stronger link between "female wages" and the gender composition of occupations in the United States than in Canada. They conclude that Canadian women benefit from higher levels of unionization (43 percent of women in "female jobs" were unionized in Canada versus 15 percent in the United States) and the existence of higher-wage levels in certain "public goods" occupations in Canada traditionally viewed as female such as educational services.

Important attitudinal differences exist between Canada and the United States that also affect gender inequalities. In his well-known study *Fire and Ice*, Michael Adams uses what he calls "patriarchy" as one of his main measures of the continued and growing divergence between the two countries. In 2000, only 18 percent of Canadians agreed with the statement that the father should be master in his own house, a decline from 26 percent in 1992. In contrast, 49 percent of Americans agreed with this statement in 2000, an increase from 42 percent in 1992. According to this data, the greater strength of traditional social values in the United States acts as an important obstacle for further social progress for American women, in contrast with Canadian women.

These figures provide some encouraging evidence about the success of Canadian women's struggles in achieving greater occupational and income equity within the Canadian economy (see Vickers et al. 1993). Nevertheless, aggregate statistics about the relative success of Canadian men and women tend to mask differences in occupational and earnings success among groups of Canadian women. As indicated above, recent Canadian census information shows increasing polarization within the Canadian population. Therefore, the gap between educated, middle- and upper-class women and poorer women is also growing. This apparent increasing equality between Canadian men and women hides worrisome trends among some sectors of Canadian women, particularly immigrant women, lone-parent women, and seniors.

As in other countries, Canadian women's labor force participation has increased in recent years, rising from 23 percent in 1953 to 58 percent in

1999. This rate is still lower than men's labor force participation rate of 71 percent in 1999. Increasing numbers of women with children under 3 are working, with the employment rate in this group going from 39 percent in 1981 to 56 percent in 1994. However, women's increased presence in the labor force predates the current phase of globalization, and appears to have leveled off since 1990. Women still participate in the labor force in a different way than men, with only 71 percent of women working full-time in 1998, compared to 90 percent of men (Status of Women 2001, 15). For recent immigrants, especially women, possessing higher levels of education is not correlated in the same ways with employment opportunities as it is for those born in Canada. Women with university degrees born in Canada had an employment rate of 86 percent, compared to 58 percent for recent immigrant women with university degrees.

As discussed above, levels of poverty have risen in Canada in recent years, and Canadian women are significantly more likely to live below the poverty line than Canadian men. In 1997, 18.3 percent of women were below Statistics Canada's LICO rate, compared with 14.3 percent for men, meaning women were 1.28 times more likely to live in poverty than men. In the period from 1993 to 1998, women were also more likely to stay in poverty longer than men, who were more likely to move in and out of poverty. In 1997, single mothers and senior women living alone are the groups most likely to live in poverty; with poverty rates of 57.1 percent for single mothers under the age of 65 with children under the age of 18, compared with 11.9 percent for couples with children and 10.9 percent for childless couples. Forty-nine percent of all unattached senior women and 93.3 percent of single mothers under the age of 25 lived in poverty (Status of Women 2001, 17–18). Thirty-seven percent of visible minority women are low income, compared with the 18.3 percent of all Canadian women who are low income (Canadian Research Institute 2002, 2).

Women have been particularly hard hit by the changes in systems of social transfers that occurred in Canada during the 1990s. While these changes were not a direct result of globalization or North American integration, they occurred in the context of the entrenchment of a neoliberal policy paradigm in which changes in domestic labor market and social policies were linked with issues of global competitiveness. The expansion of the Canadian welfare state from World War II until the mid-1970s was a victory for the Canadian women's movement (among other actors, especially unions), and also represented a substantial benefit for many Canadian women, even though it was based on a male wage-earner model that reinforced existing inequalities. Some restructuring of programs such as Unemployment Insurance (UI) dates back to 1975, but the main changes occurred in the 1990s. In particular, the 1995 federal budget both reduced expenditures on social transfers and restructured federal involvement in social policy. In this budget, the Canada Assistance Plan and the Established Programs Financing Act were replaced by the Canada Health and Social Transfer. Fiscal transfers to the provinces to cover social programs and education were dramatically reduced, and fewer strings were attached to how the provinces were able to spend this money. In response, the provinces have, to varying degrees, undertaken substantial policy reform in many areas, including reforms in education, health care and social assistance, privatization of many services, and the introduction of workfare programs (McKeen and Porter 2003, 115). Changes in UI (now known as "Employment Insurance") are particularly important for low-income women, since access to benefits has become more difficult to obtain for those working in the low-wage, contingent work sector, where women are traditionally overrepresented (p. 121). The elimination or reduction of state services also downloads responsibility onto the community and the family, increasing the pressures on women trying to juggle work and family responsibilities.

## Conclusion

This examination of the gendered impact of globalization in the Canadian case leads to some important conclusions. First, while many troubling tendencies exist, including polarization of income and growing poverty levels, the news is not as bad as it might be. The Canadian state has done a better job than the U.S. state in protecting its citizens from the dangers of a liberalized global marketplace. The Canadian welfare state remains remarkably more robust than that of the United States (or Mexico), despite predictions that Canadian standards would inexorably be driven downward by increased economic integration with the United States (Hoberg et al. 2002). As we have seen, Canadian women benefit disproportionately from this system of social protection. The Canadian experience demonstrates that states are not passive victims of globalization, but have varying degrees of capacity for resistance to globalizing pressures. Their capacity and political will to resist downward convergence is affected in part by the strength of social actors, including women's movements. As we see in the Canadian case, levels of unionization in traditionally female jobs also play an important role.

Second, while globalization is a gendered process, not all women are victims of globalization nor are most men beneficiaries. As we have seen, in Canada, recent years have witnessed a reduction of the gap between male and female earnings. This process results not primarily from an improvement of women's conditions, but rather from the decline in the prospects of male workers. According to Judy Fudge and Leah Vosko,

Throughout the 1980s, as the proportion of women in the labour force grew, employment standards deteriorated, wages dropped in real terms, and contingent work spread. The feminization of labour was matched by a feminization of employment norms: employment terms and conditions that historically have been associated with women, such as low pay, poor benefits, and part-time or temporary work. (2003, 198; see also Armstrong 1996; Fudge 1997; Vosko 2000)

These trends, they argue, intensified in the 1990s.

This analysis of the "feminization of employment norms" requires a shift of our understanding of gender and how it operates in the global economy. As Leslie Salzinger notes in her study of gender in Mexico's *maquila* factories, early feminist analysts of the new international division of labor adopted a commonsense essentialist understanding of gender:

> In arguing that capital is dependent on its access to women, they confused cause with consequence. Docile and dexterous women are produced in production relations, they do not autonomously enable them. On maquila shop floors, it is the insistent invocation of femininity, rather than its consistent enactment, which is most striking. Assuming gender's essential rigidity makes this process impossible to perceive. These analysts' failure to interrogate the illusion of gendered fixity thus impeded their capacity to recognize the ongoing and variegated constitution of feminine and masculine subjectivities within production relations. In turn, this led them to misunderstand the mechanisms through which gender plays a crucial role in global production. (2003, 15)

Similarly, the Canadian case confirms the flexibility of gender norms. More people, both male and female, have slipped into the category of contingent work relations traditionally associated with women's employment status. At the same time, growing polarization of the population and the restructuring of social programs mean that some Canadian women are enjoying unprecedented levels of affluence, while others are struggling to survive on the margins of the economy.

In this context, business groups and right wing think tanks after September 11 have suggested that Canada's leading international priority should be deepening integration with the United States. The record of economic integration to date has been decidedly mixed, and Canadian businesses and governments have failed to enact measures that would guarantee that more Canadians, including women, have access to the benefits associated with globalization. At the very least, greater public debate is needed on Canada's economic future. Given the decline of the organization that historically acted as the main voice for women in national-level policy, NAC, Canadian women must find new ways to guarantee that their voices are heard in future discussions on Canada's position in the continental and global economies.

## Notes

1. Foster and Dillon (2003, 87) report that manufacturing productivity in Canada stood at 83 percent of the U.S. level in the year before NAFTA was implemented, and dropped to 65 percent by 2000. They claim that the productivity gap is largely attributed to the dominance of foreign MNCs in the Canadian economy, since foreign corporations invest much less than domestic firms in industrial research and development.

2. Heisz, Jackson and Picot (2001, 256) also note that the drop in the real federal minimum wage over the 1980s and a continued decline in unionization help explain the increase of inequality in earnings in the United States.
3. There is a considerable debate in Canada about how to measure poverty. The most commonly accepted measurement is Statistics Canada's LICOs that represents "the level at which people spend so great a proportion of their income on basic necessities such as food and rent that they are living under straightened circumstances" (Canadian Research Institute 2002, 1).

# CHAPTER 7

# The Gendered Impact of Globalization on the United States

### JANE BAYES

## The United States as Global Hegemon

The impact of globalization in particular nations depends heavily on the status of each country in the global economy. In the early twenty-first century, the United States is the global hegemon economically, politically, and militarily. Although the United States faces increasing economic competition from Europe, Japan, and China, its status vis-à-vis other countries in North and South America and in other regions of the globe is one of unchallenged dominance. This gives the United States many advantages in comparison with other nation-states. Whereas other debtor countries must conform to structural adjustment policies imposed by the International Monetary Fund (IMF) and the World Bank to secure the refinancing of loans, the United States relies on the strength of its economy in the world to attract investors to its bonds and financial instruments. It does not have to answer to the dictates of the International Monetary Fund or the World Bank.

In many ways, globalization has strengthened the position of the United States and of a small group of corporate elites in the United States, while making segments of the middle and working classes less secure economically and less powerful politically (APSA 2004; Bartells et al. 2004; Schlozman et al. 2004). Although some scholars have argued that globalization has eroded and will continue to diminish the power of nation-states, including the United States (Ohmae 1995), others argue that globalization has not reduced the power of the nation-state. On the contrary, globalization has redirected the attention of the nation-state toward the business of attracting international capital and away from servicing its nonbusiness, domestic constituencies (Strange 1996). The demise of face-to-face political parties, the dramatic influence of mass media on elections, the huge influence of money in conducting campaigns and winning elections, the merging of most radio and major television stations with three or four major corporate conglomerates (e.g., Disney, General Electric, Time Warner, Clear Channel) has meant that monied corporate interests have come to have a much more pervasive influence on elections, governmental regulations, and the passage of legislation than has previously been the case in the United States. Recognizing that public opinion can be shaped by a concerted effort to promote a neoliberal ideology through independently funded research institutes, radio talk shows, targeted direct mail, political advertisements on television and radio, and other modes of financed persuasion, neoliberal political strategists have capitalized on the new media-driven form of politics to promote policies and political candidates that will promote the neoliberal agenda of free trade, free flow of financial capital, privatization, deregulation, corporate growth, and U.S. global military dominance.

Paradoxically at the same time that globalization has enhanced the position of the United States in the global economy, it has increased the interdependence of the United States with other parts of the world with regard to trade and investment. This is particularly true of Canada and Mexico, both of whom are extremely important trading partners for the United States. However, this is an asymmetric interdependence. Mexico and Canada have 52 percent and 46 percent, respectively, of their gross domestic product tied to trade mostly with the United States. In contrast only 13 percent of the U.S. gross domestic product depends on trade (Standing Committee 2002, 53). The size of the U.S. economy means that U.S. governmental actions to protect or enhance business opportunities for special (often local) interests in the United States such as timber or steel, or particular agricultural products, can have devastating impacts on major industries in Canada or Mexico. For example, opening Mexican agriculture to U.S. foreign investment has improved the profits of U.S. agricultural corporations while undercutting small scale Mexican corn farmers, forcing them off the land and into a migratory work force eager to find work in Mexico City or in the United States. Timber interests are a small and regionally specific part of the U.S. economy. Yet U.S. efforts to protect its timber interests with tariffs have an enormous impact on the entire Canadian economy as timber is a major Canadian export.

Globalization has had differential impacts on specific regions within the United States. Manufacturing industries requiring unskilled or semi-skilled blue collar labor such as textiles, electronics, automobiles, and even steel have moved their factories off shore to utilize cheaper sources of labor and to escape the environmental laws of the United States. This has caused local economies such as those in Detroit, the South, and much of the Midwest to decline, while centers of high technology such as those in Boston or Silicon Valley prospered in the 1970s through the 1990s. Proponents of economic restructuring have argued that the United States could not compete with the cheap labor of the world, but it could surpass others with its technologically trained labor force (Reich 1992). More recently, however, high technology centers in the United States have also been experiencing stiff international competition from offshore high-tech areas in India, Ireland, and even Mexico. Those corporations which have not chosen to relocate abroad have downsized their labor forces and outsourced much of their operations in an attempt to economize and remain competitive. By "outsourcing," a company contracts with another firm for a basic service such as janitorial work or computer programming, then does not have to pay full-time wages or benefits to permanent employees. To further reduce costs, some corporations have "flexibilized" their labor forces, converting stable full-time jobs with benefits to part-time, temporary jobs without benefits. As a consequence, many workers are faced with unstable employment at low wages without benefits. This aspect of globalization has contributed to a decline in male wages since 1970. To compensate for the loss in family income, many women have entered the waged-labor market.

Another consequence of its hegemony in the world economy in an age of instant communications is that U.S. economic and political ideas as well as popular culture are actively exported and consumed in other parts of the world. Corporations operating abroad become "cultural ambassadors," disseminating their marketing and advertising strategies, language, and way of doing business globally. U.S. movies, music, and television programming pervade the world's airwaves projecting U.S. culture, lifestyles, gender roles, and neoliberal economic and political ideas. Some countries accept this cultural invasion or "soft power" and selectively incorporate parts of it. Others find the influence of the United States to be imperious, offensive, immoral, even depraved. Resenting the power and privilege that global hegemony confers, many nations chafe against the United States' global military presence and/or the structural adjustment policies and other constraints imposed by international institutions, which they see as controlled by the United States and its neoliberal ideas.

## The Origins of Globalization in the
## United States Prior to 1970: Pax Americana

Many scholars begin their accounts of globalization in 1970, but the emergence of the United States as the global hegemon begins with events at the end of World War II. Insulated from the devastation caused by military combat in Europe and Asia, the United States emerged from the war with the strongest economy in the world and the only country with a functioning military organization. Just as Britain saw itself and was seen as the guarantor of world peace in the late nineteenth and early twentieth centuries ("Pax Britanica"), the United States assumed the role of guaranteeing peace in the period between 1945 and 1971 ("Pax Americana"). The United States was clearly the global hegemon during this period, but the world it confronted then was quite different from the one the United States faces in the early twenty-first century. Europe was decimated as was Japan and

Russia. U.S. foreign policy was focused on rebuilding the war-torn world through the American occupation in Japan, and the Marshall Plan, which provided money to rebuild European countries and economies. The Bretton Woods Agreement, signed in 1944, between the United States, Britain, and other western allies tied the world economy to an international "gold standard," which fixed the value of the U.S. dollar at US$35 per ounce of gold, and calibrated all other currencies in relation to the dollar. Designed to encourage world trade by eliminating the uncertainty of large fluctuations in the value of currencies, the gold standard also gave the dollar a large and critical role in international finance. Possessing the world's largest supply of gold and the world's strongest economy, the United States became the "lender of last resort," pledging to use its financial resources to guarantee global economic stability.

Constructing Soviet communism as a major threat, U.S. military and foreign policy sought to extend U.S. influence as it waged the "Cold War." Seeking to expand its sphere of influence by fostering capitalist development in Western Europe, Latin America, Africa, and Southeast Asia, the United States encouraged U.S. corporations to invest abroad during the 1950s and 1960s. "Friendly governments" such as South Korea, Taiwan, Brazil, and Argentina, many of which were run by military dictators, sought to attract U.S. foreign investment by offering low wages, no taxes, political stability enforced by military rule, and tight controls upon union activity. Within the United States, Congress passed tax laws and imposed tariffs that supported, if not encouraged, foreign investment by U.S. corporations. For example, Congress changed the U.S. Tax Code to permit U.S. corporations to deduct all their foreign income taxes from any taxes owed to the U.S. government, rather than deducting these foreign income taxes from revenues before paying taxes to the United States. By 1972, U.S. corporations paid an effective tax rate of only 5 percent on their foreign earnings, which totaled more than US$24 billion. In the 1960s, corporations used the U.S. Tax Code Item 806.30 to establish "export platforms" in foreign countries to take advantage of cheaper foreign labor and to avoid taxes. Under this provision, components manufactured in the United States could be shipped for assembly to plants in Mexico and other nations in the global South, then reimported back to the United States. Duty was paid only on the "value added" to the product, not on the total value of the assembled product (Bluestone and Harrison 1982, 126–127). In 1971, the government created the Overseas Private Investment Corporation (OPIC) as a self-sustaining U.S. government development agency whose mission was to mobilize and facilitate the participation of U.S. private capital and skills in the economic and social development of less developed countries and areas, and in countries in transition from nonmarket to market economies. To encourage corporations to make these investments, OPIC provided "political risk insurance" to corporations, direct loans and loan guarantees, and encouraged loans from private capital by backing them with OPIC government funds. Other government agencies, which had been established in the 1930s during the New Deal to encourage job creation by promoting exports, also transformed their missions in the 1950s and 1960s, providing funds to help U.S. corporations transfer equipment to subsidiaries in foreign countries (Export Import Bank) and to promote the sale of agricultural products abroad (Commodity Credit Corporation).

These policies—aided by technological developments that made global communications much cheaper, faster, and more available (telephones, fax, airlines)—set the stage for what became known as the "deindustrialization" of the U.S. economy in the 1970s and 1980s, and created the conditions for "the globalization era," beginning in 1971 (see Cairncross 1997).

## The End of Pax Americana and
## the Current Era of Globalization—1971 to the Present

During the 1950s and 1960s, the U.S. economy prospered, but it was not alone. Japan and Europe, in part because of help from U.S. corporations, and in part because of well-planned, state-driven economic policies, began to challenge the U.S. corporate hegemony in automobiles, steel, textiles, rubber, electronics, and footwear (Bluestone and Harrison 1982). During the 1960s, the U.S. share of world trade dropped by 16 percent. In the 1970s, it declined by another 23 percent (p. 140). In 1959, 111 of 156 of the world's largest multinational corporations were based in the United States; by 1976, this figure had dropped to 68 of the largest 156 (p. 142). In trying to support a foreign war in Vietnam and a "Great Society" at home, the United States was spending more money than it had. International lenders, especially France, began to demand gold rather than hold U.S. dollars. Because its debts were larger than its gold holdings, in 1971 the United States under President Nixon, decided to abandon the gold standard, ending the era of "Pax Americana." In the early 1970s, the U.S. economy was in a recession. The rate of return on investment for nonfinancial corporations dropped from 15.5 percent in the mid-1960s to 9.7 percent by 1978 (p. 147). The economic problems associated with increasing global competition were further exacerbated by rising energy costs.

In 1973, the Organization of Petroleum Exporting Countries (OPEC) led by Saudi Arabia raised the price of oil four times, and then five times creating another pressure on corporate profits and initiating a new era in world debt. Countries that needed to import oil to keep their economies functioning had to borrow money to cover the dramatically increasing oil costs. International banks (many based in the United States) and international banking institutions, such as the International Monetary Fund and the World Bank, became the mediators of this "debt crisis." Taking advantage of the desperate situation of borrowing nations, the banks imposed usurious interest rates for loans. In addition, the international banking institutions began to impose their own "conditionalities" on loans. Countries were required to conform to International Monetary Fund or World Bank rules and conditions, if they expected to receive future loans. These conditionalities came to be known as "structural adjustment policies," which countries had to adopt to qualify for loans. Structural adjustment policies typically required "debt reduction," privatization of state-owned industries, and national budgeting priorities that would guarantee that debts, and the interest on those debts, be repaid prior to any spending on social programs.

The response of many U.S. corporate managers to the squeeze on profits from the increased price of oil and the recession was to reduce costs by moving their plants either to regions of the United States where labor was nonunionized or to a nation abroad which provided even "cheaper" labor. Other responses included corporate "downsizing" (a reduction in employees), "outsourcing" (subcontracting out labor that had formerly been performed within the corporation), and merging into conglomerates. The closing of manufacturing plants in the Northeast, the Midwest, and the South became quite widespread, as did the trimming of salaried workers from firms that did not move abroad.

Bluestone and Harrison estimate that 38 million jobs were lost during the 1970s, the decade of deindustrialization. Many of these losses involved high-paying, unionized, blue-collar jobs in the basic industries of steel, automobiles, chemicals, and tires. New jobs were created as well, but these were not in the same industries, not in the same locations, and often involved the service sector, which was largely nonunionized. Newly created positions often required quite different skills, which put them beyond the reach of laid-off industrial workers. Job displacement has continued since the 1970s. In the mid-1980s, the federal government began to collect data on job displacement due to plant closings or layoffs. These data show that from 1985 to 1990, 4.3 million tenured workers lost their jobs. Between 1991 and 1993, a time of recession, 4.6 million persons permanently lost their employment. And between 1993 and 1996, 4.2 million more persons were put out of work (Ryscavage 1999, 74).

The end of the "Pax Americana" era also gave rise to changes in economic ideology and economic policies. Developed in reaction against the Keynesian economic policies that dominated the post–World War II era to that point, the neoliberal economic ideas of economists at the University of Chicago began to help shape economic policies, known as the "Washington Consensus." Within the neoliberal framework, "big government" was cast as a problem in need of fixing; and the market was construed as the appropriate regulator of the economy wherever possible. The role of the government was to promote policies that help the market function more efficiently. The "public interest" was defined as synonymous with the good of the market (Strange 1996).

## Gendered Consequences of Globalization
## in the United States

The gendered effects of globalization in the United States involve six major trends. *The first of these is the feminization of the labor force.* As U.S. corporations have moved their manufacturing operations offshore to utilize cheaper labor, male wages have declined in the United States and increasing numbers of women have entered the labor market (largely in service occupations) to help supplement declining family incomes. Women's growing labor-force participation has had consequences for the distribution of income within the country, for the structure of the family, for the distribution of power within the household, for the education of some women, and for the need for childcare.

*A second major trend involves changes in family structure.* The "traditional nuclear family," understood to include a married heterosexual couple living with their children, is no longer the modal family form in the United States. The number of married couples living with children has declined, as the numbers of single-parent households, unmarried adults sharing accommodations, and single adults living alone have increased. Women have had fewer children during this period and fertility rates for U.S. women, except for those of Hispanic origin, have fallen below replacement rate.

*A third major change involves an ideological shift with regard to the role of the state in regulating the economy and in supplying social services.* Neoliberalism has triumphed over Keynesian economics, producing important changes in monetary and fiscal policies, as well as a retreat from notions of welfare entitlements, a retreat that has particularly affected poor women and their children.

*A fourth major gendered consequence of globalization in the United States has been a decline in the strength of unions coinciding with the feminization of union membership.* The export of traditionally male-dominant, unionized manufacturing jobs in the automobile, steel, and manufacturing sectors has caused union membership to fall dramatically in the United States from a high of 35 percent of the work force in the early 1950s to 13 percent of the work force today. Unions have responded by organizing workers in industries, mostly the construction and the service sector, which are less likely to be moved because their business must be conducted in the United States. In an effort to unionize the largely female, low-waged service sector, unions have increasingly included women among their ranks, and some women have assumed important leadership positions within these unions.

*A fifth gendered consequence of globalization has been increased flows of immigration.* Immigration affects both men and women, but somewhat differently. Economic migrants enter into and help consolidate gender-segregated work forces. Within the United States, male migrants, especially from Mexico and Central America, provide a mobile agricultural labor force, while also participating in skilled trades such as construction and landscaping services. Women migrants tend to be concentrated in the provision of domestic labor and childcare in affluent households, house-keeping services in hotels, nursing services in hospitals and nursing homes. The movement of peoples across borders has important social and economic implications for both the sending and receiving societies.

*A sixth gendered consequence of globalization has been increasing inequality between the rich and the poor.* In the United States, these inequalities are gendered and raced, impacting women of particular racial and ethnic groups differently from men of particular racial and ethnic groups.

Each of these trends will be examined in greater depth in the remaining sections of the chapter.

### Feminization of the Labor Force

The participation of women in the waged-labor force was not a new phenomenon in 1970; however, during the 1960s and 1970s women entered the waged-labor force at an increasing rate. This rate leveled off in the 1990s with 59.9 percent of adult women working outside the home. From 2000 to 2002, women's workforce participation declined slightly to 56.3 percent (Bureau of Labor Statistics 2004; *Economic Report of the President* 2004) (see figure 7.1). Although "working-class" women have been part of the paid labor force since the 1830s and African American women worked in agriculture and domestic labor throughout the nineteenth and twentieth centuries, during World War II, many white, married women entered the waged-labor market as a part of the war effort, thereby increasing the participation rate of adult women in the labor force from 27.6 percent in 1940 to 36.1 percent in 1945 (Hartmann 1982, 21). In 1948, the waged-workforce participation rate for women was 33 percent, as some married women returned to full-time home making after the war. By 1971, women's labor-force participation had increased to 43.4 percent, reflecting rising educational levels for women, the impact of feminism, as well as the effects of declining male wages. As noted earlier, the restructuring or "deindustrialization" of U.S. manufacturing in the 1970s in response to global economic conditions motivated many more women to seek waged employment. Plant closures, especially in the Northeast, the Midwest, the South, and also all over the nation, combined with corporate downsizing and outsourcing caused increasing unemployment among men, while also contributing to declining male wages. Many men with high school educations, who lost their high-paying, unionized manufacturing jobs, were forced to take lower-paying employment if they were able to find work at all. To maintain family incomes, many women went to work. In 1980, the female participation rate was 51.5 percent. By 1990, it had grown to 57.5 percent, an increase of about 7 percent every 10 years (see figure 7.1). The ages at which women worked also changed. In 1950, the highest rate of workforce participation (43 percent) was among women between the ages of 16 and 24. Some women dropped out of the labor force during childbearing years, as a consequence, the labor-force participation rate for women aged 24–65 ranged between 34 and 39 percent. By 1998, however, women were working in the waged-labor force throughout their lifetimes with labor force participation rates of between 50 and 80 percent (Fullerton 2000) (see figure 7.2).

This change has had multiple consequences. More women are independent financially from their husbands or at least have some income that

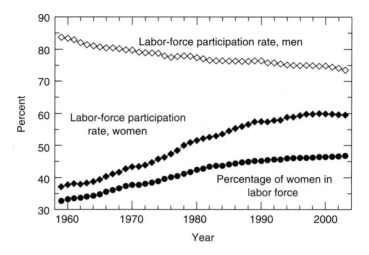

**Figure 7.1**  Labor-force participation rates for men and women and percentage women in the labor force 1959–2003

*Source*: *Economic Report of the President 2004*, Table B–39. Washington, DC: Government Printing Office. See http://www.gpoaccess.gov/eop/Bureau of Labor Statistics 2004 "Women in the Labor Force"; *A Databook 2004*. Washington, DC: U.S. Department of Labor.

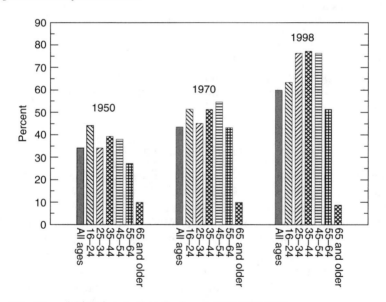

**Figure 7.2**  Women's labor-force participation by age: 1950, 1970, 1998

*Source*: Fullerton 1999. "Labor Force Participation: 75 Years of Change, 1950–1998 and 1998–2025." Table 1. *Monthly Labor Review*. December 4.

they can control. This does not mean that women are equal to men finan-cially. Women continue to earn less than men. Despite the passage of the Equal Pay Act of 1963, women earned only 63 percent of what men earned in 1970. By 2003, women on average earned only 77 percent of what men

Earnings in 2001 dollars

**Figure 7.3** Median earnings of full-time, year-round workers 15-years old and over by sex: 1960–2001

Source: U.S. Census Bureau, Historical Income Tables—People. Table P–38. Current Population Survey, Annual Demographic Supplements accessed at www.census.gov/hhes/income/histinc/p38.htm on March 29, 2005.

earned. Much of the apparent improvement in the ratio of women's to men's wages was not due to women earning more, but was due to the fact that men were earning less in 2003 than they did in 1970 (see figure 7.3).

## *Family Structure has Changed*

While the causal connections are a matter of speculation, family structure in the United States has changed dramatically during the three decades associated with increasing globalization. As figure 7.4 shows, between 1970 and 2000, the number of married-couple households with children declined from 40.3 to 24.1 percent of U.S. families (Fields and Casper 2001, 3). One reason for this is that young people are waiting longer to get married, if they get married at all. Higher divorce rates have also led to more single-parent families and to more single individuals living alone. For married heterosexual couples, the model of the "male breadwinner, female stay-at-home-mother/housekeeper" has declined. Among married couples with children, the proportion of wives working in full-time jobs rose from 17 percent to 39 percent over these three decades. For those couples without children, the percentage of working wives rose from 42 to 60 percent (McNeil 1998, 3 and 6). From 1969 to 1996, the percentage of single-parent households with children increased from 6 to 31 percent of families; while single-person households increased from 17 to 25 percent. In 1970, single-parent households headed by men constituted only 1 percent of all households; while

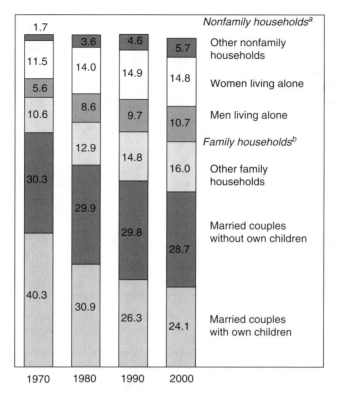

**Figure 7.4**    Households by type 1970, 1980, 1990, 2000 (percentage distribution)

*Notes*:

[a] A nonfamily household can be a person living alone or with nonrelatives.

[b] A family household has at least two members related by blood, marriage, or adoption.

*Source*:  U.S. Census Bureau. Current Population Survey, March supplements: 1970–2000 from Fields and Casper 2001.

single-parent households headed by women constituted 5 percent of U.S. families. By 2000, male-headed single-parent households grew to compose 5 percent of all households, while female-headed single-parent households grew to 26 percent of all households (Fields and Casper 2000).

Increasing percentages of women in the waged-labor force have changed expectations about lifelong career patterns for men and women in the United States. Both young women and young men expect women to go to school, get an education, and work in addition to caring for families. Women aged 25–34 years old in 2000 are very different from their counterparts of twenty-five years ago. Table 7.1 compares some demographic characteristics of those in the 25–34 age cohort in 1975 and in 2000. With regard to education, 30 percent of these women had completed four years of college in 2000, up from 18 percent in 1975. By comparison, only 29 percent of men in this age group had completed four years of college in 2000. Marriage and childbearing rates were much lower for the 24–35-year-old women in 2000. In 1975, 76 percent of women in this age group had children, and only 11 percent of the women had never been married.

**Table 7.1** Comparison of women and men aged 15–34: 1975 and 2000

| Characteristic | Women | | Men | |
| --- | --- | --- | --- | --- |
| | *1975* | *2000* | *1975* | *2000* |
| Population (in thousands) | 15,315 | 19,188 | 14,366 | 18,310 |
| *Race and Hispanic origin* | | | | |
| White | 86.6 | 79 | 88.7 | 81.6 |
| Black | 11.3 | 14.9 | 9.3 | 12.4 |
| Hispanic origin | 5.4 | 14.6 | 5.1 | 15.4 |
| *Education* | | | | |
| Some highschool or less | 20.2 | 10.9 | 17.9 | 13 |
| 4 years highschool | 45.9 | 28.9 | 36.9 | 32.4 |
| Some college | 16.3 | 30.3 | 19.6 | 25.9 |
| 4 years college | 17.6 | 29.9 | 25.6 | 28.7 |
| *Marital status* | | | | |
| Married spouse present | 76.3 | 57 | 74.6 | 49.5 |
| Never married | 10.8 | 30.2 | 17.1 | 41 |
| Divorced or separated | 12.3 | 12.4 | 8.1 | 9.3 |
| Others | 13.6 | 13.2 | 9.3 | 9.6 |

*Source*: Data from Current Population Survey, taken from DiNatale and Boraas 2002.

In 2000, only 60 percent of the 24–35-year-old women had children, and 30 percent had never been married. Between 1975 and 2000, the labor-force participation rate for women in this age group who had children under the age of 18, increased from 50 percent to 70 percent. For women with children under 3 years of age, the labor-force participation rate increased from 33 percent to 63 percent during the same period (DiNatale and Boraas 2002, 4–6). Despite the increased participation of mothers in the labor force, the labor-force participation rates of men with children remain somewhat larger than the labor-force participation rates of women with children.

With regard to occupations, women in the 24–35 age group in 2000 had increased their representation among executives, administrators, and managers (6 percent) and as professionals (2 percent), reflecting their higher educational levels. The percentage of men in these occupations increased only slightly (1.5 percent) between 1983 and 2000. Sales, service, and administrative support occupations continued to be strong for women with less education. While some men of the same age cohort were also in these occupations, they were more likely to be in manufacturing, repair, or working as machine operators than women (DiNatale and Boraas 2002, 6).

Fertility rates are another area of change. In the United States, as in other parts of the world, women are having fewer children. Women ending their childbearing years in 2002 had an average of 1.9 children compared to an average of 3.1 children for women in the same age group (40–44 years) in 1976. Race, ethnicity, and foreign-born status are correlated with differing fertility rates among women. In 2002, 15 percent of the women of childbearing age in the United States were foreign born. In 2001, they had a fertility rate of 71 births per 1,000 women compared to a birth rate of 60 births per 1,000 for women born in the United States. Hispanic women (both native and foreign born) had the highest birth rates in 2002 with 82 births per 1,000 women of childbearing age. Of these, native Hispanic women had 78 births per 1,000, while foreign-born Hispanic women had 86 births per 1,000. Non-Hispanic foreign-born women and non-Hispanic women born in the United States had similar birth rates of 57 births and 58 births per 1,000 respectively (Downs 2003, 3–5).

### Shift in Ideology from Keynesianism to Neoliberalism

In response to the devastating depression that followed the stock market crash of 1929, the "New Deal" in U.S. economic and social-welfare policy was premised upon a fundamental Keynesian consensus which recognized that the state should play a critical role in moderating the excesses of the market and in providing social welfare for the most disadvantaged members of the population. According to Keynesianism, monetary and fiscal policies should be used to stimulate or dampen the economy and provide a security net for those the market leaves behind. The state should also have a role in regulating industry to protect the environment and in providing for health, education, and social welfare. In the 1930s, Congress passed the Social Security Act, establishing contributory schemes to cover unemployment insurance, worker's compensation, and old age pensions for those employed full-time in most sectors of the waged-labor force. From the outset, the social security provision was raced and gendered. The two occupations in which African American workers were concentrated, agricultural labor and domestic service, were excluded from social security coverage at the insistence of members of Congress from southern states. Women's unwaged labor in the home was also excluded from the provisions of the act, making married women's access to benefits dependent upon the contributions of their husbands. Aid to Families with Dependent Children (AFDC), the primary "welfare" policy in the United States from the 1930s until 1996, was originally designed to provide benefits to widows who had no way to support their dependent children. Medicare, which provides health care coverage for people during their retirement years, was conceived in 1935, although not passed by Congress until 1965.

The exclusion of women's domestic labor from social security provision created a two-tiered social policy system tied to gender. While men had access to benefits on the basis of their status as workers, married women were constructed in state policies as "dependents" whose primary access to benefits was mediated by their husbands. Even women who worked in the waged-labor force throughout their lives had to choose at the time of retirement either to accept a pension tied to their wages or to receive a higher spousal pension calculated on the basis of their husband's lifetime earnings. By awarding "wives" the same benefit level, whether they had worked for wages outside the home or whether they had devoted their lives to unwaged labor in the home, the state effectively penalized married working women. Their lifelong contributions to social security were cancelled. For this reason, some feminist scholars have argued that the U.S. welfare state recognized women primarily as mothers, neglecting their roles as workers (Fraser and Gordon 1997; Gordon 1994). Although African American women, working-class women, and some women professionals spent most of their adult years in the waged-labor force, state policy treated men as if they were the exclusive wage earners for a family.

In additional to social-welfare provisions, Keynesian economic policies preserved antitrust laws, first initiated in 1890, to keep corporate entities from becoming too large and powerful and to keep any one firm from dominating the market. In the 1970s as international competition from state-sponsored corporations in Germany and Japan increased, the U.S. government altered its antitrust policies to allow corporate mergers, regardless of corporation size or their control of the market, as long as the merging corporations could show that their mergers did not raise prices for consumers. With the election of Ronald Reagan in 1980, the U.S. government began to repudiate Keynesian economic policies. Neoliberal economic policies were adopted that encouraged or required privatization, deregulation, free trade, tax cuts for the wealthy, supply-side economics, freer capital mobility, and restrictions on union activity. According to neoliberals, the state should act as a "handmaiden" to the market, ensuring a stable money supply, and fostering economic growth by devising tax policies attractive to corporations, reducing or eliminating any barriers to trade, eliminating any regulatory barriers to production, and in general, reducing the size and functions of the state (the public) in favor of the market (the private). To maximize the competitive position of U.S. corporations, neoliberals have sought to undermine, weaken, and eliminate unions, as President Ronald Reagan did when he opposed the air traffic control operators strike in the early 1980s. They have also sought to eliminate or weaken environmental controls, which they claim drive up production costs. They have also sought to "privatize" various government functions, such as prison guards and military operations, by contracting out these government services to private corporations, such as Wackenhut (prisons) or Halliburton (military support services and infrastructure).

Castigating social-welfare policies for promoting "dependency," neoliberals have also insisted that individuals, not the state, should be responsible for their own social and economic well-being. Indeed, neoliberals argued that "government hand-outs" undermined the work ethic and interfered with the operations of the market, which relied upon economic incentives to motivate and reward hard work, while penalizing the "lazy" who refused to work. Ignoring "structural problems" like high levels of unemployment caused by deindustrialization, neoliberals claimed that ample work was available for all who wanted it and attributed lack of work to the willful refusal of the poor to work. In keeping with long-standing policies in the United States that failed to recognize child rearing and domestic labor in the home as "work," neoliberals launched a trenchant attack on "welfare recipients," who, in 1990, included 4 million women heads-of-household and their 10 million children under the age of 18.

Neoliberal doctrines have had a particularly negative impact on poor women. After 15 years of demonizing the poor, neoliberals succeeded in abolishing "welfare entitlements" in 1996. Welfare "reform" was institutionalized with the passage of the Personal Responsibility and Work Opportunity Reconciliation Act (PRWORA) by the Republican-dominated 103rd Congress and was signed into law by a Democrat, President Bill Clinton. To foster "personal responsibility" PRWORA abolished AFDC, the welfare program that provided a "safety-net" for poor women and their children, and replaced it with Temporary Assistance for Needy Families (TANF). In contrast to the idea of a citizen's "entitlement" to social provision in difficult economic times, TANF sets a lifetime limit of 5 years for federal welfare assistance, regardless of the circumstances of the recipient. In addition, TANF imposes a mandatory work requirement as a condition for the receipt of benefits. While receiving this assistance, recipients are required to perform 30 hours of labor per week. While some states allow educational programs, such as vocational classes or college courses, to fulfill mandatory work requirements, it is far more typical for "workfare" jobs to involve menial tasks such as street cleaning, floor mopping, or leaf raking, tasks that do not enhance the "marketable skills" of the TANF recipient. Failure to perform this work results in termination of benefits. Although the primary recipients of TANF are single mothers who have young children, workfare requirements are mandatory and no provision is made for publicly provided childcare during work assignments. Thus TANF creates a very different relation between the state and poor women. The neoliberal state now seeks to transform mothers of young children into waged workers. Similar to structural adjustment policies promoted by the World Bank that construe employment in the formal sector as the primary means of "empowering women," TANF casts employment as mothers' best route to self-sufficiency, without addressing the pressing question of childcare provision. While AFDC embodied the principle of state responsibility for impoverished families, PRWORA makes it clear that childbearing and childrearing are private matters. Parents, including single mothers, should expect to work in the waged-labor force to support their families on their own.

TANF is a "block grant" program that funnels federal funds to state governments. State governments then devise their own rules and regulations for implementing the program. Consequently, poor women in some states have very different opportunities and constraints than those in other states. Despite considerable variation among the states in the implementation of TANF, most states have defined program "success" in terms of cutting the welfare case load. Between 1996 and 2000, the number of welfare recipients was cut in half. The women who have left welfare typically find work in unstable low-wage jobs, paying only slightly more than the federal minimum wage of US$5.15 per hour, far less than is needed to support their children. A woman who works full time at a minimum wage job earns US$10,800 per year, which is several thousand dollars less than the federal poverty line for a family of three and far less than a "living wage" in any metropolitan area in the United States. Mothers of young children who work in minimum-wage jobs are unable to afford childcare in licensed centers in the private sector. They often rely on extended family members (often grand-mothers, relatives, older children) or on friends and neighbors to care for their children. In response to this double bind, some women have been organizing to press local governments to provide publicly funded childcare programs. Los Angeles County, for example, recently recognized this need and instituted a limited childcare program. Women's groups hailed this as an important victory, for it signals public recognition of the importance of "care work," traditionally performed by unwaged women in the home, and pro-vides public funding for some women to engage in childcare as waged labor. This critical intervention by Los Angeles County, however, is at great odds with neoliberal policies, which continue to dominate public policy at the federal level and within most states in the United States at the outset of the twenty-first century.

## Union Membership

Union membership was at its peak in the United States in 1953 when 35 percent of the workforce belonged to a union. Reflecting the composition of the labor force, unions in the 1950s and 1960s were largely male domi-nated (with the exception of the International Ladies Garment Workers Union founded in 1900) and in traditional manufacturing industries, steel, automobiles, rubber, chemicals. The union movement in the United States was extremely important in pressing for worker safety, for higher wages, and for better living conditions, all of which increase labor costs, and, according to neoliberals, interfere with the ability of U.S. corporations to compete in a global market. Globalization undercuts unions as the traditional manufac-turing industries move abroad to take advantage of cheaper, nonunionized labor. By 1980, 20.1 percent of the labor force was unionized, a figure that has fallen to 12.9 percent in 2003. As women have joined the waged-labor force, unions, although weakened by deindustrialization, have begun to have larger percentages of women members. In 2003, men were still more likely to be union members than women, but the gender difference in union membership was quite small: 14.3 percent of male workers were union members, compared to 11.4 percent of women workers. In part, this convergence reflects the movement of union organizing away from pri-vate industry and toward the public sector, away from manufacturing and toward service occupations. Women tend to be employed in the public sector and in service occupations. Union membership in the public sector was four times the union membership in the private sector in 2003 (U.S. Department of Labor 2004).

## Immigration

The history of the United States is a history of immigration. The first non-indigenous settlers in what later became U.S. territory were the Spaniards and Mexicans who settled in Santa Fe, New Mexico in the sixteenth century. In the seventeenth, eighteenth, and nineteenth centuries, large numbers of immigrants came to the United States. Some came involuntarily as was the case with enslaved peoples from Africa. Others came voluntarily to settle in the "new world," first from Northern Europe, then from England, France, and Germany, and beginning in the 1840s from Ireland. After 1848, Japanese and Chinese laborers were brought to the West Coast to work on the railroads and in mines, until the Chinese Exclusion Act of 1882 put an end to this flow of migrants. In the late nineteenth century, large numbers of immigrants from Southern and Eastern Europe came to the United States. In the early twentieth century, increasingly hostile, anti-immigrant sentiments were circulated by white, Protestants who perceived immigrants as threats to the purity of "the civilized Christian race" (Newman 1999). In response, Congress began to limit European immigration, establishing a Literacy Act in 1917, and passing an Emergency Quota Act in 1921 that imposed immigration quotas based on nationality or country of origin. The National Origins Act of 1924 and the Immigration and Nationality Act of 1952 extended this quota system, which remained in effect until the Immigration and Nationality Act of 1965 eliminated all quotas based on national origin, race, or ancestry. With the passage of this new law, total immigration increased and shifted from Europe to Latin America. The percentage of immigrants from Europe declined from 74.5 percent to 15.3 percent between 1960 and 2000, while the percentage of immigrants from Latin America increased from 9.3 to 51 percent (Mosisa 2002, 4). Of those immigrants whom the U.S. Census Bureau was able to count in 2000, the largest number of foreign born were from Mexico. This does not include the undocumented migrants, who avoid and will not respond to a census survey. Experts agree that "legal immigration" from Mexico is only a fraction of the immigrant flow. Even with this acknowledgement of under-counting, census data suggest that the foreign-born population from Mexico currently living in the United States is 7.8 million, almost seven times that of any other foreign-born group (Mosisa 2002, 4). The next largest foreign-born group was from the Philippines, with immigrants from India, China, Cuba, El Salvador, Vietnam, South Korea, Canada, and the Dominican Republic being among the top ten (p. 4). Both documented and undocumented immigration to the United States increased dramatically after the 1965 Immigration and Nationality Act lifted immigration quotas. In 1960, the official figures suggest that foreign-born people constituted about 6.5 percent of the U.S. population. In 2000, foreign-born people constituted 13 percent of the population.

Although Mexicans currently constitute the largest immigrant group in the United States, to suggest that Mexican migration to the United States is a phenomenon of the late twentieth century would be to ignore the long and complex history of the movements of Mexicans across territories in the Southwest, which were later claimed by the United States. Mexicans were the first nonindigenous settlers in the "western territories" later annexed by United States. For centuries prior to the Louisiana Purchase in 1802, Mexicans were living in the territory that the United States "bought" from the French government. Beginning with settlements in what is now called "New Mexico," Mexicans formed a fan of settlement that ranged across territories that are now parts of California, Arizona, Colorado, and Texas, establishing communities and cultures that continue to survive today. To recruit agricultural labor, Congress created the "Bracero Program," which brought Mexican men to the United States on 18-month "guest-worker" contracts from 1942 to 1964. As implied by the concept of "guest-worker," Mexican workers were expected to return to Mexico after fulfilling their contracts. While many returned, many others did not.

The end of the Bracero Program did not end the stream of migrants to the United States. The long porous border between the United States and Mexico made it possible for many Mexicans, as well as many people from Central America, to come to the United States without official authorization. The difference in wages in the United States (US$5 an hour or more in the United States in 2000 compared to US$5 a day or less in Mexico) continues to persuade many Mexican men to brave the hazards and hardships of migrating North, whether they have proper documents or not. While some Mexican women have come North to join their husbands and a few have come on their own, the majority of migrants have been males, determined to earn money in the United States to support their families in Mexico. Only in the last 5–10 years have Mexican women begun to migrate in larger numbers, either with their husbands or independently (Cortes Jimenez 2004).

The North American Free Trade Agreement of 1994 is responsible for some of the surge of Mexican immigration. The negotiations leading to the passage of NAFTA allowed the importation of corn and beans from Canada and the United States to Mexico, as early as 1983. This was devastating to many of the 3 million Mexican corn producers (40 percent of all Mexicans working in agriculture were growing corn), as their small plots could not compete with the large-scale mechanized farming of the North. Monthly income for self-employed farmers fell from 2,000 pesos per month in 1991 to 200 pesos per month in 2003 (Women's Edge Coalition 2003). In addition, foreign direct investment by U.S. agricultural producers using capital-intensive fertilizers and machinery, took over some of the most fertile land in Guanajuato and elsewhere, driving small subsistence farmers off their land (Gonzalez 2001).

Comparing a variety of methods for estimating undocumented migration from Mexico including the number of border-patrol apprehensions along the U.S. southwestern border, estimates of unauthorized immigration from the Immigration and Naturalization Service and the Department of

Homeland Security, and nonrandom surveys of Mexican migrants taken at popular border crossing points, the Carnegie Endowment for International Peace reported in 2004 that all estimates show an increase in Mexican migration to the United States between 1990 and 2000. Some Mexican states such as Zacatecas and Guanajuato have a long tradition of sending migrants north to the United States. In the 1990s, states without such a tradition, such as Oaxaca, Guerrero, Puebla, Hildalgo, Veracruz, Morelos, and the state of Mexico, began to send significant numbers north. In contrast with previous years, only a minority of the Mexican migrants in the 1990s worked in agriculture either in Mexico or the United States. These migrants were less likely to have had a job in Mexico, less likely to have migrated before, and more likely to be undocumented (Audley et al. 2003, 49). They also moved to different destinations in the United States than they had prior to the 1990s. Instead of moving primarily to California, Texas, the Southwest, and selected areas in Michigan, and Pennsylvania, they began moving throughout the United States. The Mexican-born populations of Kentucky, Minnesota, North Carolina, and Arkansas, for example, increased over 1,000 percent between 1990 and 2000 (p. 49).

In education, the foreign-born in the United States tend to be divided into two disparate groups: those with relatively high levels of education and those with relatively low levels. The education of the U.S.-born population is more evenly distributed with larger numbers of high school graduates and those with some college. About 26 percent of both the foreign-born and U.S.-born populations have college degrees. The major difference between the two groups is among those with less than a high school diploma: 33 percent of foreign-born have no high school diploma compared to 13.5 percent of the U.S.-born population.

In comparison with native-born women, foreign-born women aged 16–24 were less likely to have completed high school and less likely to be in the labor force. The foreign-born women in this age group who had not graduated from high school were more than five times as likely to be married and more than twice as likely to have children. Among college graduates, both native-born and foreign-born were equally likely to have children (Mosisa 2002, 6).

*Inequalities in Income and Wealth*

Measuring income and wealth distribution can be a complex enterprise.[1] Nonetheless, U.S. Census data provides some insights into changes in the earnings of men and women over the past several decades. As mentioned above, median earnings of both men and women have gone up since 1979, with the difference between the two narrowing slightly by 2001 to the point that women's median earnings were 77 percent of men's. Both men and women's earnings have been and continue to be structured by race and ethnicity: median earnings of whites are greater than those of blacks and

Hispanics for both men and women (figure 7.5). In 2001, black men earned 75 percent of what white men earned, while Hispanic men earned 63 percent of what white men earned. Among women, black women earned 86 percent what white women earned, and Hispanic women earned 74 percent of what white women earned. While median earnings for white women are 77 percent of median earnings for white men, black women's median earnings are 64 percent and Latina's median earnings are 54 percent of white men's.

Figure 7.6 shows that since 1979, the changes in earnings for men have been strongly associated with years of education. The improvement of women's earnings over the same period is also associated with education but in a much more positive way, in that women's median wages have been improving for those with a high school diploma or more, while men's median wages have been going down for all those without a college degree (U.S. Bureau of Labor Statistics 2002, 4).

While median earnings and median incomes have been rising during the last third of the twentieth century even for the poorest category of single-parent families, the income distribution has been becoming more unequal. Figure 7.7 compares the change in family income by quintile for the period 1947–1970 and for 1970–2001. The top bar graph measuring change in income from 1947 to 1970 shows that all levels of the income distribution grew almost evenly, with the top 5 percent increasing slightly less than the other 80 percent of the population. In comparison, the period from 1970 to 2001 shows a positive income change for all quintiles, but a much higher percentage increase for those having the highest incomes.

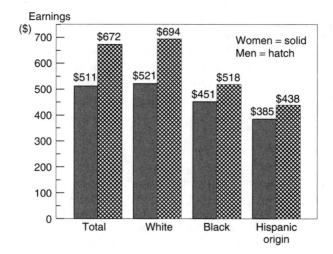

**Figure 7.5** Median weekly earnings of full-time workers by sex, race, and Hispanic origin, 2001 annual averages

*Source*: Bureau of Labor Statistics, 2002. "Highlights of Women's Earnings in 2001." Report 960. U.S. Department of Labor. Washington, DC: U.S. Government Printing Office. Chart 2.

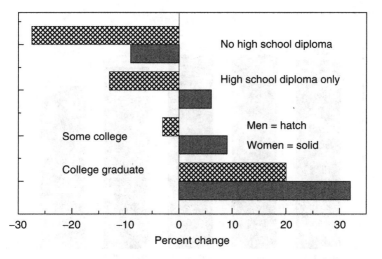

**Figure 7.6**   Percent change from 1979 to 2001 in median weekly earnings by educational attainment and sex

*Source*: Bureau of Labor Statistics. 2002. "Highlights of Women's Earnings in 2001." Report 960. U.S. Department of Labor. Washington, DC: U.S. Government Printing Office. Chart 3.

Another way to measure income inequality is to use the Gini Index that measures income inequality (0.0 means households have the same income; 1.0 means that one household has all the income, a situation of total inequality). The Gini Index went down from 1947 to 1967, falling from 0.376 to 0.348 (Ryscavage 1999, 54). After 1968, however, income inequality began to grow rather dramatically, with the Gini coeffficient rising from 0.340 to 0.409 for both men and women in 2001 (U.S. Census Bureau 2004a). For men during this period, the Gini coefficient rose from 0.314 in 1967 to 0.419 in 2001, an increase of 33.4 percent. For women, the Gini coefficient rose from 0.298 to 0.362 an increase of 21.5 percent (U.S. Census Bureau 2004a).

Looking at the changes in earnings of men and women by race and Hispanic origin from 1979 to 2001, a picture emerges with regard to the gender, race, and ethnic character of the income inequality distribution (see table 7.2). The wages for minority women did not keep pace with the wages for white, non-Hispanic women. In 1979, black women's wages were 91 percent of white, non-Hispanic women's wages, and Hispanic women's wages were 85 percent of white, non-Hispanic women's wages. In 2001, black women's wages were only 85 percent of white, non-Hispanic women's wages, while Hispanic women's wages were only 72 percent of white, non-Hispanic women's wages. The wages for white, non-Hispanic women rose 22 percent between 1979 and 2001; black women's wages rose 17 percent; and Hispanic women's wages rose only 8 percent during the same period. The picture for the income distribution for men is even more surprising. The wages for white, non-Hispanic men rose only 2 percent between

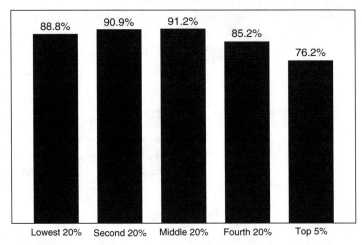

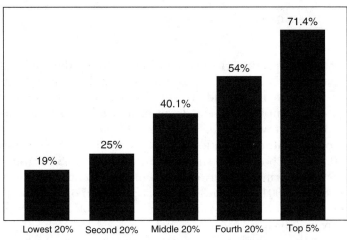

**Figure 7.7**   Change in family income for 1947–1970 and for 1970–2001 by income level

*Source*: U.S. Census Bureau, Historical Income Tables. Tables F–1. Income limits for each fifth and top 5 percent of families 1947–2001 in 2001 dollars. Upper limit of each quintile for four lowest fifths and lower limit for top 5 percent. Accessed at www.census.gov/hhes/income/histinc/f01.html on March 15, 2005.

1979 and 2001; wages for black men stayed the same; and wages for Hispanic men fell by 12 percent during this period. Overall, men earned more than women in every category in 1979. However, earnings by white, non-Hispanic women surpassed those of Hispanic men in 1990, and came to equal those of black men in 2001. Inequality among women increased during the period: the gap between white, non-Hispanic women and black women increased by 5 percent; while the gap between white, non-Hispanic women and Hispanic women increased by 13 percent. The same shift does

**Table 7.2**   Median weekly earning of full-time workers by sex, race, and Hispanic origin, selected years 1979–2001

| Year | White women | Black women | Hispanic women | White men | Black men | Hispanic men |
|------|-------------|-------------|----------------|-----------|-----------|--------------|
| 1979 | 418 | 384 | 357 | 678 | 517 | 499 |
| 1985 | 444 | 398 | 362 | 659 | 481 | 466 |
| 1990 | 466 | 407 | 367 | 651 | 476 | 419 |
| 1995 | 479 | 409 | 352 | 654 | 474 | 404 |
| 2000 | 514 | 440 | 374 | 687 | 517 | 426 |
| 2001 | 521 | 451 | 385 | 694 | 518 | 438 |

*Source*: Bureau of Labor Statistics, 2002. Table 14, 26–27.

not occur for men in all race and ethnic groups. Black men earned 76 percent of the median earnings of white, non-Hispanic in 1976, a figure that dropped by only 1.4 percent in 2001. Hispanic men, however, earned 73.5 percent of the earnings of non-Hispanic, white men in 1979, but only 63 percent of non-Hispanic, white men's earnings in 2001(Bureau of Labor Statistics 2002, 26–27).

Studies of changes in wealth, like those of changes in income distribution, show that the distribution of wealth in the United States was quite uneven in 1962. In that year, the top 1 percent of the population owned 33.5 percent all wealth; the top 10 percent owned 56.2 percent of the wealth; and the top 20 percent owned almost 82 percent of the total financial wealth. The bottom 40 percent, on the other hand, owned 0.3 percent of the total (Keister 2000, 64). Throughout the 1960s and 1970s, the wealth distribution remained unequal but stable. Beginning in 1979, however, wealth inequality began to rise, and by 1989, the top 1 percent owned 37.4 percent of the country's wealth. *Forbes* magazine's survey of the top 400 wealthiest individuals shows particular wealth concentration at the very top (Kennickell 2003, 3–5). The wealth of the vast majority of people in the United States—those below the top quintile—dropped from 18.7 percent of total wealth in 1983 to 16.4 percent in 1989. Throughout the 1980s, the rich became richer and the poor, poorer (Keister 2000, 65). Between 1998 and 2001, some improvement occurred in wealth distribution, as all groups either gained slightly or retained about the same proportion of the wealth distribution. The middle group of the population in the 1990s continued to hold about the same percentage of wealth throughout the decade, while the negative net worth of the bottom group declined slightly during the period (Kennickell 2003, 7–8). Looking at the entire 1989 to 2001 period, inequality in wealth increased as the bottom group lost net wealth rather than gaining it (pp. 7–8). The rich (especially those with a million dollars or more in net worth) continued to get wealthier, especially the very rich. From 1989 to 2002, the number of billionaires (in 2001 dollars) increased from 97 to 205. The wealth of the top 400 individuals increased from 1.5 percent of total wealth in 1989 to 2.2 percent of all wealth in 2001 (p. 3).

## Poverty

During the era of the "war on poverty," between 1959 and 1969 in the United States, poverty rates (percentage of all families living below the poverty level) went down from 18.5 percent of the population in 1959 to 9.7 percent in 1969. Throughout the 1970s, the poverty rate remained between 11 and 12 percent of the population. Poverty rates increased in the 1980s, rising to between 13 and 15 percent through 1997. Between 1997 and 2002, poverty rates hovered between 11 and 12.7 percent, increasing to 12.5 percent in 2002 (Proctor and Dalaker 2003). Single female heads-of-household increased in number between 1970 and 2002, increasing from 19.7 million to 40.5 million, but contrary to stereotypes, the percentage of women-headed households below the poverty line decreased from 38.1 percent in 1970 to 28.8 percent in 2002. Many associate poverty with single-parent, especially single mother households, but the significant increase in numbers of women-headed households since the 1970s has largely been among middle-class women. Thus the percentage of white, non-Hispanic female heads-of-household living in poverty decreased from 25 percent in 1973 to 20 percent in 2002; the percentage of black, single female heads-of-household in poverty went down from 56.5 percent in 1973 to 37.4 percent in 2002; and the percentage of Hispanic women single heads-of-household in poverty dropped from 57.4 percent in 1973 to 36.4 percent in 2002 (Proctor and Dalaker 2003, 22–27).

Overall, the median income of most people in the labor force in the United States increased between 1970 and 2002, with two notable exceptions: black men's earnings remained about the same; and Hispanic men's earnings decreased by 12 percent over the 1970–2001 period. White men's earnings increased by only 2 percent, while all women, especially white, non-Hispanic women, earned considerably more in 2002 than they had in 1970. Differences in earnings between men and women decreased, but persist, while salary differences among men of different races and ethnicities increased and salary differences among women of different races and ethnicities also increased. Wealth, while distributed extremely unevenly prior to 1970, became even more unequal during the 1970–2001 period, with the very wealthy increasing their wealth considerably, the middle remaining about the same, and the poor losing position with regard to overall wealth. People at the top of the income and wealth pyramid tended to be non-Hispanic, white, and male. White, non-Hispanic women improved their position considerably in terms of income, surpassing both black and Hispanic men. Although Hispanic women improved their median weekly wages over the period 1970–2002, their association with Hispanic men in Hispanic households means that for most, their household income decreased over the 30-year period. Relatively low levels of education in the Hispanic population, combined with the large flows of Hispanic immigrants from Mexico, are probably responsible for much of these income discrepancies for both Hispanic men and women. At the same time, Hispanic women with their higher fertility rates are largely responsible for the fact that the United States is able to maintain and replace its population, unlike Japan and many industrialized countries in Europe.

## Summary and Conclusions

This chapter has identified six areas in which globalization has had a gendered impact in the United States, changing the structure of the society in significant ways.

Women have joined the waged-labor force in significant numbers and most have improved their levels of education and levels of earnings as individuals, but not necessarily as households, because the earnings of men have declined. Some women have made some gains in traditionally male occupations, but most continue to be crowded into traditionally female occupations. Those women at the lower-income levels are disproportionately black and Hispanic. White, non-Hispanic women have gained the most of all groups using aggregate measures of median income.

Family structures have changed. Fertility rates have dropped for all but Hispanic families. Increased rates of divorce and childbearing out of wedlock have raised the percentage of single-headed households to 31 percent of all households. Of these, most are headed by women.

Neoliberal ideology has become securely entrenched in the society, culture, and government as evidenced by the 2004 electoral triumphs of President George W. Bush, although considerable opposition continues to exist in the society.

Union membership has declined, while at the same time union membership has become more feminized. Unions are an important component of the opposition to globalization.

Immigration, although not a new phenomenon, has had a dramatic gendered impact on the United States in the last 30 years. Mexican immigrants are the largest group of foreign-born living in the United States, outnumbering all other foreign-born living in the United States by eight to one. More Mexican men than women immigrate, but recently Mexican women have been immigrating in larger numbers. The fertility of migrants is responsible for keeping the U.S. population slightly above replacement rate.

Inequality in the distribution of income and wealth in the United States is growing. Aggregate statistics showing that median incomes have risen for almost all in the United States, except the lowest paid workers—many of whom are immigrants—mask the unequal distribution of these gains. The increasing inequality is dividing women and men by education, race, and ethnicity. Inequality among women existed in 1970, but that inequality has increased during the last 30 years, and is increasingly characterized by race and ethnic divisions.

A final consideration concerning globalization and its impact on the United States is that the gains accruing to the beneficiaries of globalization within the United States have often been at the expense of hardships, poverty, and exploitation imposed by United States and U.S.-led international institutions on peoples in other parts of the world. This chapter has surveyed a range of evidence suggesting that the inequitably distributed benefits to the United States from globalization stem from its hegemonic position in the global world order. Rather than passively suffering the effects of globalization, the neoliberal U.S. government actively promotes a globalizing agenda. The cheap foreign labor in offshore export zones and *maquiladoras*, much of it provided by women working under very poor working conditions (which contributes to U.S. corporate profitability) depends upon treaty agreements negotiated between the United States and other national governments. The takeover of Mexican agricultural land by U.S. capital-intensive, agricultural production, which contributed to the displacement of Mexican farmers, is the result of negotiations related to NAFTA. Immigrants' underpaid labor contributions to the U.S. economy are closely related to rules governing the admission of immigrants to the United States. In trade policy, the United States has consistently developed a "double standard," protecting many of its own industries such as steel, timber, and agricultural products with tariffs and quotas, while demanding that other countries engage in free trade, remove tariffs, and open their markets to U.S. goods and services. In economic and social policy, the neoliberal U.S. government has unleashed the market, while abandoning basic commitments to social provision created under the New Deal. This chapter has sketched the raced and gendered consequences of these neoliberal initiatives, demonstrating that the much acclaimed benefits of globalization for the corporate sector and for the rich are inseparable from increasing inequalities within the United States and across the globe.

## Note

1. Measuring the distribution of income or wealth is an extremely complicated affair, one that is replete with a variety of academic and political controversies. First is the question of whether to measure income or wealth. Earnings or income is not the same as net worth. Some argue that earnings should include the benefits that some receive and others do not. Still others believe that consumer and other debt should be a part of the measurement. Measuring changes in the distribution of income or wealth by noting the change in median income over the years will give an aggregate measure but says nothing about the changes in the distribution of wealth among the rich and the poor. Some divide the distribution into deciles or quintiles and note changes in the distribution by noting changes in the ratios between deciles or quintiles of the distribution. Statisticians have developed indexes as a means of ranking levels of inequality in a distribution. The Gini index, for example, creates an inequality scale ranging from 0 to 1, according to which 1.0 indicates complete inequality, and 0 complete equality. Some argue that whereas the major sources of wealth inequality at the beginning of the twentieth century involved stocks and bonds, in last part of the twentieth century, exorbitant multimillion dollar salaries handed out to corporate CEOs and NBA basketball players are the major sources of wealth creation. Piketty and Saez (2001) found that in 1916, the top 0.01 percent of tax returns showed that this group earned 70 percent of their income

from capital. In 1998 for this group, wages and salaries contributed 45 percent, business activities 33 percent and return on capital 22 percent. Others argue that the numbers of these "superwealthy" are so small as to be inconsequential when their salaries are lumped into the top quintile of all those who make over US$100,000 a year. For a good discussion of some of these problems, see Ryscavage (1999, 3–23). Another problem with this enterprise of measuring inequality in income or wealth is obtaining accurate data. The U.S. Census obtains data on earnings. Obtaining data on wealth is more difficult. Lisa Keister (2000) has devised a simulation model to attack this problem.

CHAPTER 8

# Future Prospects for Women, Globalization, and Democratization in North America

MARY HAWKESWORTH, LOIS HARDER,
AND JANE BAYES

Proponents of globalization assert that market liberalization will lead to increased democratization. According to this view, the economic forces fueling globalization will not only produce economic integration on the continent of North America, as trade, finance, and labor move freely across national borders, but will also contribute to increased personal autonomy and well-being. The individualism that informs capital market relations will spread with marketization, gradually eliminating ascription standards, which fix a person's place in the social order from birth on the basis of race, ethnicity, gender, class, and caste. Industrial production will provide increasing numbers of people with employment opportunities that enable them to break away from traditional modes of living and embrace notions of individual rights and self-reliance. Economic growth will lead to prosperity for all. The spread of the "achievement" standard will heighten individual aspirations and contribute to greater worker mobility as individuals move to seek better job prospects that will reward their hard work and talent. Moreover, growing notions of individual interest will foster the development of "civil society," that is, the growth of voluntary organizations, which seek to promote the interests of their members. As these interest groups and nongovernmental organizations proliferate, they will make increasing demands on political parties and the government for programs that will benefit their members. Representative government, competitive elections, norms of transparency and accountability, and voter mobilization—elements central to "democratization"—thus emerge as a result of forces put into play by globalization and marketization.

The World Bank publications not only subscribe to this scenario, but also link both economic development and women's empowerment to women's employment in the paid-labor force. In *Advancing Gender Equality* (2000), the World Bank suggests that women's employment in the formal sectors of the economy moves women out of patriarchal households, affording them independent incomes and new self-understandings as self-sufficient and self-reliant wage earners. Women's access to money, contributions to household income, and increasing self-confidence helps to shift gender power within households, producing more egalitarian relations between men and women. Empowerment within the workplace and within the household in turn gives women the confidence to move into the public sphere, mobilizing to press for governmental policies that will meet women's needs and interests, taking jobs in government agencies, and seeking electoral offices.

Extending this optimistic scenario to North America, then, one might predict that the continuing economic integration of Mexico, Canada, and the United States would foster political steps to merge into a regional union similar to that of the European Union. Borders would open to allow the free movement of workers, as well as the free movement of goods and capital. The governments of all three countries would work collectively to harmonize their laws and policies and to mitigate the disruption and social dislocation caused by globalization, extending expanded social benefits like those currently existing in Canada to all citizens of North America. Equipped with equal rights and equal benefits, Mexicans, Canadians, and U.S. citizens would forge a common identity as "North Americans" that would supersede their national identities. A common currency could be established for the three countries. Spanish, English, and French would coexist as official languages and citizens would develop bilingual and trilingual capacities. New transnational political institutions, comparable to the European Parliament and the European Commission, would be created to provide mechanisms for governance that accord equal representation to all three nations. Gender and racial equality provisions would ensure nondiscrimination across all policy domains. Expansion of the gender quotas devised within Mexico would contribute to equal participation of men and women in decision making in elective and appointive institutions. The three countries would become truly integrated economically, socially, and politically into the North American Community (NAC) or the North American Union (NAU).

How likely is this scenario? The analyses of gender, globalization, and democratization in Mexico, Canada, and the United States developed in the foregoing chapters suggest that the optimism of economic determinism fails fully to account for the complex economic, political, and interpersonal processes currently transforming North America. If the economic determinist model is too simplistic, are other forecasts available for the future prospects of gender, globalization, and democratization in North America? What effects will the shift from an industrial economy to a service economy have in North America? Will the demand for low-income labor in Canada and the United States combined with Mexicans' needs for livelihoods contribute to a more thorough-going regionalization of North America, generating open borders and the free movement of people without restriction?

Will regionalization give rise to new transnational structures and new political entities as has occurred in the European Union? How will differing birth rates among women in Mexico, Canada, and the United States affect long-term population trends? Will far higher birth rates among Latinas produce a "Mexicanization" of North America? Would greater *mestizaje* of nationalities and ethnicities reduce or heighten racism and xenophobia? How will the differing economic interests, social policies, and political priorities of the three nations of North America affect future transformations of the region? When disagreements are rife, whose national interests will prevail? How will the desire of the Mexican government to open the borders mesh with the new security concerns of the United States in the aftermath of September 11 bombings of the Pentagon and World Trade Towers? Will the Mexican government continue to support open borders? What will happen to the 5.5 million undocumented Mexicans who are already living in the United States? How will Canadian concerns with cultural autonomy withstand U.S. cultural hegemony? Will markedly different systems of social policy converge, erasing powerful traditions and constraints within a developing nation grappling with structural adjustment policies, a social welfare state, and a neoliberal state? The following sections will explore a range of economic and political factors that interact with globalization to suggest quite different scenarios for the future of North America.

## Globalization and the Prospects for
## Economic Integration

Neoliberal proponents of free trade have argued that free flows of finance, goods, and labor will generate growth and prosperity for all. Aggregate statistics support this claim for the United States: even the poorest 20 percent of the population in the United States have higher incomes than they did 35 years ago (See chapter 7, figure 7.7). The very rich have become much wealthier in all three countries. Many of the poor and middle-class in Canada and Mexico, however, have lost ground and are not better off economically than they were in 1970. The middle class in the United States has also suffered severe dislocations as corporations have downsized, moved production abroad, and flexibilized the labor force.

As the foregoing chapters have made clear, the effects of globalization vary within and across nations. Rather than the confident prediction of increased prosperity and democratization for all, inequalities have been exacerbated within and between Mexico, Canada, and the United States. Freer flows of capital, resources, and commodities have not been matched by a freer flow of labor. In addition, the economic transformations over the last ten years have been markedly asymmetrical. Freer flows of finance and trade among Mexico, Canada, and the United States have been conditioned by basic asymmetries in size and economic power among the three countries. Flows of finance and trade have contributed to a further integration of the three economies with one another, but in ways that are increasingly dominated by U.S. corporations.

The basic asymmetries that characterize the three countries have not been changed by globalization. The GDP of the U.S. economy (US$11 trillion) is approximately 12 times the GDP of either Canada (US$957 billion) or Mexico (US$941 billion). While the economies of Canada and Mexico are roughly comparable in GDP, Mexico has three times the population of Canada and a little more than a third of the population of the United States. The per capita income of Mexico is one-third that of Canada and a quarter of the per capita income of the United States. The United States has by far the largest and most robust economy and the largest number of people. The U.S. economy is also the least dependent on exports. In 1970, Canadian exports accounted for 21 percent of the Canadian GDP and Mexican exports were 10 percent of Mexican GDP. In contrast, U.S. exports were only 7 percent of GDP in the 1980s. By 2000, exports for Canada and Mexico had risen to 46 percent and 45 percent of GDP respectively, while U.S. exports were only 13 percent of GDP. The United States and Canada are each other's largest trade partners, but the asymmetry is such that 87 percent of Canada's exports go to the United States, while only 22 percent of the U.S. exports go to Canada. For the United States, only one-third of its trade is with Canada and Mexico. As Laura Macdonald points out in chapter 6, globalization for Canada means increased trade and financial flows with the United States, yet much of this increased flow is within firm investment and trade. In Mexico, foreign direct investment has generated a dual economy, one multinational and the other domestic. Although employment is slightly higher in Mexico's domestic manufacturing economy, profits and growth are much more robust in the multinational economy where foreign capital uses domestic Mexican labor to produce exports to be consumed mostly in the United States. Trade between Mexico and Canada has increased slightly, but overall is insignificant compared with both countries' trade with the United States. Less than 1 percent of Canada's exports go to Mexico and 3.6 percent of Canada's imports come from Mexico. While the Canadian economy and the Mexican economy are becoming more integrated with that of the United States, they are not becoming more integrated with each other. Nor is the U.S. economy becoming equally integrated with either the economy of Mexico or Canada.

Assessments of the success of the 1989 Canadian–U.S. Free Trade Agreement (CUFTA) and the 1994 North American Free Trade Agreement (NAFTA) are mixed with respect to their impact on Canada and Mexico. The governments of Canada and Mexico view these agreements as success stories. Productivity has increased in all three countries and many, who recognize the disappointing results in job creation and in wages over the last ten years, argue that long term prospects are much brighter. Others are less enthusiastic, noting that the agreements tie both Canada and Mexico more firmly to the performance of the U.S. economy rather than fostering increased competitiveness, employment, or per capita growth for either country independently. Job creation and changes in prevailing wage rates have been disappointing. In Canada, job loss due to cuts in Canadian tariffs was most dramatic in industries exposed to import competition. The increase in job creation that was expected in export-oriented industries did not materialize. Wages in Canada grew only slightly between 1989 and 2002. In Mexico, real wages have declined since 1980, primarily due to the debt crises of 1982 and 1994. Despite the boom period of the late 1990s, Mexican wages were lower in 2000 than they were in 1993. The loss of employment in Mexican agriculture—a loss of 1.3 million jobs—has not been offset by sufficient employment in manufacturing—a gain of 500,000 jobs, a situation that has increased the pressure on Mexicans to migrate to the United States.

Because the U.S. domestic economy is so large and much less dependent on trade than the economies of Canada and Mexico, globalization has not been as dramatically disruptive in the United States as it has been in Mexico or even in Canada. Two-thirds of U.S. trade is with countries other than Mexico or Canada. The U.S. economy has been influenced more by multi-lateral tariff reductions negotiated through the General Agreement on Tariffs and Trade (GATT) than by North American agreements. Estimates of NAFTA's impact on the United States suggest that the net job gain was slightly positive or remained the same. However, this does not mean that disruption did not occur or that wages remained the same. Over half a million U.S. workers lost their jobs due to NAFTA; half of these losses were due to the relocation to Mexico of production facilities primarily in the apparel, electronics, automobile, and prefabricated metal industries (Polaski 2003, 8). U.S. wages have fallen as the gap between skilled and low waged, flexible work grows.

"Prosperity for all" does not adequately convey the asymmetrical effects of globalization within and across the three nations of North America. Neoliberal trade theory would attribute some of these inequitable economic developments to the initial stages of adjustment, suggesting that wages in Canada and Mexico should rise after this initial period. This theory, however, does not take into account the continuing movement of production facilities to China or to other countries in Latin America where wage rates are even lower than in Mexico. In the past five years, global corporations have already begun to relocate their production facilities in China and Central America. *Maquiladora* employment in Mexico peaked in 2001. Thus neoliberal predictions of "prosperity around the corner" also seem suspect.

Neoliberal discussions suggest that "the laws of supply and demand" should govern labor as well as finance, trade, and raw materials. According to this theory, then, economic integration should enable labor to move as freely as capital, natural resources, and commodities. This has not been the case in North America. Again asymmetries characterize border crossings among these three states. For more than a century, Canada and the United

States have boasted the "longest undefended border" in the world. But open borders, for purposes of tourism, are not the same as "borderlessness" for economic migrants. Work permits are still required for Canadians seeking employment in the United States and for U.S. citizens seeking work in Canada and these government-issued permits are far more accessible to professionals with high levels of education than to low-income or unemployed workers in either nation. Racism and ethnocentrism have contributed to very different border relations between Mexico and the United States and between Mexico and Canada. Work permits are also required for Mexicans who seek employment north of the border, but these permits are far harder to come by and are subject to far more restrictions than any notion of "free movement of labor" would suggest. Even during the Bracero Program, when the United States was actively recruiting Mexican workers to redress labor shortages, the work permits allowed only temporary residence in the United States and required Mexican workers to return home after 18 months. Such "guest worker" programs entrench inequality, precluding individuals from responding freely to market demand and preventing them from benefiting fully from their hard work and talent. They also structure a situation in which economic migrants, who are desperately in need of work to support themselves and their families, are criminalized and subject to deportation. While the Mexican government prizes the economic contributions of migrants and has been seeking policy changes to facilitate the free flow of workers across the northern border, the United States maintains stringent border patrols and actively deports "illegal aliens" found within its territory.

Increasingly concerned with "homeland security" in the aftermath of the September 11 bombings, the United States has imposed further restrictions on the movement of peoples across its borders. Asymmetries structure these border arrangements as well. Canadians who wish to move fairly freely across the U.S. border have been offered a "fast track." If Canadians are willing to submit to "retinal scans" and finger printing and have this personal data included in a new transnational data base that allows instant security identifications, they are allowed to cross the border at will. While some Mexicans living in towns adjacent to the border have been offered the same option, sections of the U.S.–Mexican border have been sealed off, official border patrols have been increased, and new "vigilante patrols" (armed U.S. citizens who "police" stretches of the border) have surfaced in Texas, Arizona, and New Mexico. While these new mechanisms make border crossing more expensive and far more dangerous, they have not diminished growing economic migration by Mexicans to the United States.

Despite the heightened dangers created by "securitization" of the U.S. southern border, multiple factors fuel Mexican migration to the United States. As Laura Gonzalez documents in chapter 5, economic exigencies created by globalization such as increasing poverty, the displacement of agricultural labor by mechanization within multinational agribusiness, and more recently, the displacement of factory workers by the closure of *maquiladoras* makes economic migration essential for livelihood. The demand for Mexican workers in the United States also makes migration north a rational course of action. Moreover, the strong historical social, familial, and political ties connecting Mexicans in Mexico with Mexicans in the United States encourages and supports continuing migration. The growing importance of remittances from Mexican workers in the United States for the sustenance and welfare of Mexican families and for the overall Mexican economy makes it a near certainty that economic migration will continue to increase. Indeed, some demographers predict that the higher birth rates of Mexican Americans, in combination with growing migration rates of Mexicans to the United States, make it likely that Mexican Americans will constitute 25 percent of the U.S. population by 2050, creating a voting bloc with the potential to transform dramatically the ethnic distribution of power and the public and foreign policies of the United States.

Increasing levels of economic migration from Mexico combined with increasing levels of securitization by the United States suggest several possible scenarios for North America that differ significantly from the optimism of the economic determinist model. Deindustrialization and the shift to a service economy could further exacerbate inequalities, as economic migrants from Mexico are recruited to provide low-income labor in construction, restaurants, hotels, and homes. The U.S. government's refusal to grant work permits, permanent residence status, or opportunities to become citizens to the economic migrants from Mexico could heighten the vulnerabilities of undocumented workers while increasing the power of unscrupulous employers to exploit these vulnerabilities. As U.S. and multinational corporations move their production facilities off North American shores to countries with lower wage rates, high levels of unemployment in Mexico, Canada, and the United States could continue to grow. Polarization between the affluent who are benefiting from globalization and the poor could become more pronounced, contributing to punitive policies that further dehumanize the poor. Poverty among the growing numbers of poor within all three nations could generate unrest, growing racism and xenophobia, political instability, and violence. Trade in illegal drugs and human trafficking could increase. Xenophobia and nativism could heighten nationalism and threaten transnational ties among the three states. The borders could become increasingly militarized and violent.

How likely is this scenario? The theory of relative deprivation, which was advanced as an alternative to the economic determinism of modernization theory, suggests that growing inequalities, especially in contexts where the poor live in close proximity to the rich, who openly exploit the vulnerabilities of the poor, can produce quite incendiary results. Poverty, dehumanization, and desperation can fuel political violence, as the history of revolutions clearly attests. Precisely this combination of factors fueled the Zapatista uprisings in Chiapas in 1994. Some historical precedents, then, suggest that violence and political upheaval could be as likely a consequence of the growing inequalities and polarization of classes under globalization as democratization. The evidence of growing inequalities presented in this book calls the inevitable "prosperity" assumptions of neoliberalism into question. While the relative deprivation hypothesis remains a subject of contestation, countenancing such a possibility, however remote, can provide a helpful antidote to the excessive optimism of economic determinist models. Examination of the experiences of other nations in Latin American reveals that other scenarios are also possible. Since 1998 in Venezuela, Chile, Ecuador, Brazil, Argentina, Bolivia, Panama, and Uruguay, political elites and some governments have turned to the left or center-left in reaction to neoliberal policies. That could happen in North America as well.

## Globalization and Future Directions for Social Policy

The chapters in this book have demonstrated that neoliberalism is influencing social policies and economic policies in all three states. One might argue that neoliberalism has tended to make the social policies of Canada and the United States more like those of Mexico by decreasing state support for welfare, health, and unemployment. In the United States, federal welfare programs were cut considerably in the year 1996, social security is currently under attack, and medicare programs promise to be the next neoliberal target. In Mexico, where food aid and other distributions from the state have historically been tied to support of the ruling political party, the remittances provided by the earnings of migrants working in the United States and Canada provide an alternative to public provision, a privatized safety-net for poor Mexicans. Canada has resisted these tendencies, however, continuing to retain state support for health and other safety net provisions, although levels of support have been somewhat reduced. Given the ascendance of neoliberalism in the early twenty-first century, should we expect a convergence of social policies within North America? And if so, which social policies will prevail? Asymmetries in power among the three nations of North America influence the likely transformations in social policy, just as they influenced economic policies.

To date, the primary thrust of neoliberal social policy developments in North America has been to encourage everyone to join the waged-labor force, while also protecting some of the most vulnerable members of society from globalization's worst effects. These developments differ in each of the North American countries as a result of the prevailing political dynamics and social-policy traditions. In Mexico, antipoverty initiatives with an emphasis on human capital are a key social policy focus. In exchange for agreeing to send children to school and to have regular visits to local health clinics (primarily rural), Mexicans living in extreme poverty have gained access to nutritional and income supports as well as health services and education (Harder and Taylor 2005). Nonetheless, these initiatives are highly politicized as their targets are not simply poor people, but poor people whose political support is valued by the governing parties at the federal, state, and municipal levels and whose potential for political disruption is deemed to be high (Harder and Taylor 2005). In Canada, despite a relatively robust tradition of state support for health, education, welfare and other social services, neoliberalism has done much to undermine the scope and reach of such social programs. Decentralization and reduced federal funding have weakened the capacity of social programs to articulate a common, national identity. Universal income-support programs have largely been replaced by targeted programs in an effort to deliver the greatest good to those most in need, and the private provision of social support—whether through the market, voluntary organizations, or the family—are strongly encouraged. Low-income, working parents have been a focus of recent policy innovations. In the United States, where demands for state-funded health and welfare programs have historically made little headway, in part because many workers had generous employee benefit packages, the flexibilization of labor markets (i.e., outsourcing, downsizing, part-time employment) and the reduction in employee-benefit plans require an increasing number of Americans to rely on their own earnings and savings to provide for their social well-being in periods of economic dislocation and unemployment. Welfare recipients have lost their entitlement to public support, are limited to five years eligibility, and are compelled to work in return for the receipt of Temporary Assistance for Needy Families (TANF). At the same time, the working poor raise increasingly important social-policy issues. Full-time work at minimum wage fails to provide an escape from poverty. Indeed, full-time work in a minimum wage job fails to provide an income adequate to support a family. As Mary Hawkesworth notes in chapter 4, a woman with two children who works 40 hours per week at minimum wage, earns several thousand dollars less than the federal poverty level for a family of three. Despite recurrent lobbying to increase the incomes of low-waged workers, the U.S. Congress has not increased the minimum wage during the past ten years.

Overwhelmingly, recent neoliberal social-policy initiatives are focused on promoting and supporting the participation of North Americans in the paid-labor force. Social reproduction, that is, the activities involved with childcare, education, health, and care taking for the ill and elderly, which was one important focus of postwar social policy in Canada and to a lesser degree in the United States, has receded from the public agenda. In gendered terms, women are being integrated into wage earning in the same way as men, but the caring work that they provided as social workers and government employees in social welfare, in redistributive agencies, and in the home is no longer deemed a subject worthy of much state attention. Yet the need for social reproduction—including care for the young, the sick, and the elderly and domestic maintenance—has not disappeared. To date, women have attempted to accommodate the increased demands on their time by doing double duty—working for a wage and performing unwaged "care work" at home—but the costs of bearing the additional workload include increased stress, declining health, and strained relationships. Recent state initiatives that respond to the "work-family balance" crisis emphasize private solutions. The Canadian caregiver leave program, through which individual workers can receive paid leave to care for a dying family member by drawing on their Employment Insurance contributions, illustrates this response.

Another example of "private solutions" for the care of children and the elderly is the growing employment of migrant workers as nannies, elder-care providers, and nurses. Yet neoliberal states fail to recognize and provide programs to support migrant workers. Despite the central role of Mexican and multinational migrants in performing vital functions for the economy and for the sustenance of the families of affluent and middle-class Canadian and U.S. citizens, recognition of their contributions through access to social benefits is actively denied. Moreover, in Mexico, where poor women never had access to even minimal levels of welfare or other public support, structural adjustment policies pressure women to supplement their subsistence activities with increased participation in the formal and informal economies. Yet, no provision is made for childcare or elder care. In rural areas, where men have migrated north in search of wages, women must stretch their days to meet the demands of triple and quadruple shifts, engaging in subsistence farming, formal and informal employment to earn some income, community governance activities, and family and household maintenance. The notion that women's labor is infinitely expandable is fast approaching the limits of human endurance and exhaustion.

While neoliberal social policies cutback social welfare provision and pose large challenges for care-work within families, various forces are resisting neoliberalism's privatizing impulse. In Canada, new public investment in childcare is being proposed at the same time that the privatization of health care is debated. In the United States, the G. W. Bush administration faces considerable opposition to its proposals for the partial privatization of social security (old age pensions). Such resistance suggests some hope. While neoliberals' relentless claims of "unsustainability," derisions of "dependency," and advocacy for private alternatives undermine support for a robust state involvement in providing a safety net for individuals in all three nations, differences in national traditions, economic resources, and political commitments continue to produce profound differences in social policy in these states.

Over the past 30 years, some feminists have been critical of state welfare policies and social policies that have reinforced traditional gender roles and responsibilities, assigning caregiving to women while exempting men from these responsibilities. Their goal, however, was to pressure states to provide benefits free of the taint of gender domination and subordination. The state's contemporary retreat from social provision is not an encouraging development for gender equality and does not begin to address feminist concerns about traditional relations of domination. Indeed, the increasing incorporation of women within the labor market and the growing reliance on women's expanded work in the realm of social reproduction render the goal of gender equality even further from reach. The increasing "outsourcing" of reproductive labor, that is, the reliance of affluent women upon low-income migrant laborers, often undocumented, for childcare, elder care, and domestic labor within the home usually for very low wages, heightens rather than mitigates inequalities among women in all three nations of North America.

## Globalization and the Prospects for Democratization Within and Across States

Feminist conceptions of democracy expand the conception of politics to encompass relations of domination and subordination in public and private spheres. To assess the prospects of democratization from a feminist perspective, it is important to expand the framework of analysis beyond questions concerning the rule of law, competitive elections, and democratic elitism. Within a feminist frame, democratization encompasses issues of bodily integrity, reproductive freedom, equitable divisions of labor within the household and workplace, as well as gender parity in the public sphere. Is globalization fostering the "thicker" democracies that feminists envision? Is globalization supporting "policy learning" that enables states to learn about the innovative gender policies of other polities and incorporate them into their own legal and constitutional frameworks? When questions of gender and democratization are the focal points of analysis, some of the traditional asymmetries within North America cease to play the same formative roles.

According to several political indicators, Mexico and Canada have far more gender democracy than does the United States. As Patricia Begné notes in chapter 2, since the introduction of a "quota system" that precludes any gender from holding more than 70 percent of the seats in the legislature, women in Mexico have gained important ground in public office, holding 23 percent of the seats in the federal Chamber of Deputies. By contrast, Canadian women hold 21 percent of the seats in the federal Parliament and U.S. women hold 14 percent of the seats in the House of Representatives. Thus Mexico is ranked twenty-seventh in the world in terms of women in public office, while Canada is ranked thirty-first and the United States is ranked only fifty-seventh among the 190 nations. Despite the impressive demonstration that party quotas succeed in increasing women in elective and appointive offices, neither Canada nor the United States seems likely to follow Mexico's lead. In terms of feminist public policies, such as reproductive freedom, paid maternity leave, paid family leave, protection from violence against women, equitable employment policies, guarantees against pregnancy discrimination, access to health care, social-welfare benefits, Canada has been ranked the best in the world, while the United States and Mexico lag behind (Weldon 2002). Despite evidence of the important policy achievements produced by the "women's state machinery" in Canada, neither Mexico, nor the United States is replicating Canadian innovations. Indeed, as Lois Harder points out in chapter 3, even Canada has taken steps in recent years to dismantle the women's policy making apparatus that has secured such impressive benefits for women.

Beyond the issue of women's equal participation in governance, asymmetries structure women's rights to physical integrity and reproductive freedom in the three nations of North America. While abortion is legal in Canada and the United States, women's access to these medical services is not equal in both nations. In the United States, abortion rights have been under attack from Christian fundamentalists for three decades, and as a result, 88 percent of the counties in the United States provide no abortion services. In addition, federal Medicaid benefits and many private insurance plans do not cover abortion services, hence significant financial barriers preclude many low-income women's access to the medical procedure. In Mexico, abortion is illegal under most circumstances. Although several states allow an exception in cases of rape, even this limited access is not secure. For example, in 2000, the *panista* state government intervened to prevent a 15-year-old rape victim from receiving an abortion, although the young woman was entitled to an abortion under state law (Rodríquez 2003, 194).

Women in all three nations confront problems of rape and domestic violence. The incidence of violence against women in each nation is a subject of contestation. In Mexico, no official statistics are kept on violence against women. In the United States and Canada, governmental agencies acknowledge that official statistics are unreliable because acquaintance rape and violence inflicted by intimates are markedly underreported. Conservative estimates indicate that one in three women in the United States is raped (Koss et al, 1987; Koss 1992a, b, 1993) and one in five is battered by a partner (Collins 1999; Heise et al, 1999; Kelly 2003). Feminist activists in all three nations report that acquaintance rape and violence by intimates far exceeds violence inflicted by strangers. None of the states have devised successful means to prevent, reduce, or resolve problems pertaining to violence against women even when perpetrated by intimates. Thus feminist activists suggest that women's fundamental rights to physical integrity and bodily security have not been guaranteed by any of these democratic nations.

As problems of domestic violence suggest, democracy in the family remains an elusive goal, even as families are undergoing major transformations as Jane Bayes points out in chapter 7. Recent and rapid changes to family formation present some women with opportunities to reconfigure their lives. In all three North American countries, women's increased labor-force participation has provided wives with greater control over the family income. Access to reliable birth control has provided women with some measure of control over their fertility. Liberalized divorce laws have made it possible for both men and women to leave unhappy and unfulfilling marriages.

In the United States, single-parent families now outnumber two-parent families. However, flexibilization of labor markets and the inability of a single wage to support a family have made many single-parent families economically unsustainable. Single mothers, in particular, suffer from high rates of poverty, a situation exacerbated by the gendered wage gap and inadequate childcare provision. The state's response to this development has been to pursue fathers as a private source of support. When paid, the resulting income can substantially improve women's economic well-being, but forcing an unwilling father to provide support may increase the risk of harm or exploitation to women and their children.

Family formations are changing in all three nations even when divorce is not an issue. The prevalence of economic migration in Mexico means that families often live apart, remittances are shared throughout an extended family and grandparents are mobilized in the care of children. In all three countries, remarriage and the subsequent establishment of step- or blended families are increasingly common. In addition, more couples, both opposite and same sex, are eschewing marriage, choosing instead to live in common-law relationships. Same-sex marriage and the ability of same-sex partners to adopt children are now possible in Canada; one state in the United States (Massachusetts) has also recognized same-sex marriage, and many U.S. states allow adoption of children by same-sex couples. This pluralization of family forms is likely to continue, leading governments either to develop legislation recognizing the benefits and obligations of family members in these new settings, as is happening in Canada in the context of common-law relationships and same-sex unions, and in Mexico with regard to migrant family members; or to resist these developments as in U.S. marriage promotion initiatives and the efforts of some U.S. states to tighten divorce laws. Regardless of how families are configured and even if women gain power within their families, the increased instability of family finances and the polarization of incomes may ultimately diminish the social relevance of women's increased personal economic power.

Over the past three decades, feminist activists in many nations have sought to use international conventions and international organizations to pressure their national governments to enhance women's rights and women's roles in governance. In North America, women's success in such endeavors has varied markedly across the three states. Canada and Mexico have ratified the Convention to Eliminate All Forms of Discrimination Against Women (CEDAW); the United States has not. Mexican women's rights activists mobilized in the 1970s to use the occasion of the UN First World Conference on Women, which was held in Mexico City, to pressure the government to enhance women's constitutional and political rights. Although all three nations have sent delegations to the four World Conferences on Women and all have submitted documents to the UN Commission on the Status of Women to report on "progress" in achieving the gender-equality goals established in the Beijing Platform for Action, asymmetries among the states profoundly affect women's rights activists' abilities to use these international processes productively within their national contexts. Seeking to use the expertise of members of the UN Commission on the Status of Women and the international monitoring process itself as means to promote change, Mexico's reports for the Beijing-Plus-Five and Beijing-Plus-Ten meetings at the United Nations provide detailed information on the progress that Mexican women have made, the challenges they face, and the issues that require government action. By contrast, Canadian feminists report frustration that the Canadian government has used the Beijing Platform's mandate for "gender mainstreaming" (i.e., the incorporation of gender equity concerns in all governmental operations) as a justification for eliminating cabinet rank of the Minister Responsible for Women's Issues and for cutting the resources of Status of Women Canada, the government agency that had been created to address women's needs and interests. Although the United States lags behind Mexico and Canada in efforts to redress the historic underrepresentation of women in political decision making, both the Clinton and the G. W. Bush Administrations chose not to address the continuing inequities that circumscribe women's lives in the United States in their reports to the UN Commission on the Status of Women. Instead they emphasized U.S. foreign policies designed to improve the prospects for women in other nations, primarily in the global South.

## Conclusion

When gender is used as a category of analysis and women's as well as men's lives are considered in the assessment of the effects of globalization, facile predictions of inevitable democratization are difficult to sustain. As this book has demonstrated, women remain far from the goal of parity in governance and far from the attainment of equal power in public and private sectors, despite nearly 200 years of feminist mobilization to attain these ends.

Beyond the evidence of continuing underrepresentation of women in decision-making, the effects of globalization upon women are uneven, varying significantly within and across nations. Globalization has increased inequalities among women. As the data concerning class polarization in all three nations demonstrates, some women are flourishing, while others are losing ground. Non-Hispanic white women in the United States have increased their incomes considerably in the last thirty years relative to other women and men. Indeed between 1970 and 2001 in the United States, globalization has improved the incomes of even the bottom 20 percent of the population by 19 percent (although only by 3 percent between 1979 and 2001). Those in higher income brackets have increased their incomes even more during this period (see chapter 7, figure 7.7). In Mexico and Canada, the aggregate picture is less clear. Canadian wages were only slightly higher in 2002 in constant dollars than they were in 1989 (Polaski 2004, 30). Among Mexicans in the last ten years, the top 10 percent of households have increased their share of the national income, while 90 percent have either remained the same or lost position with regard to income share. Real wages for most Mexicans are lower than they were ten years ago (Polaski 2003, 33). Yet some experts argue that without globalization, specifically without NAFTA, Mexico might well be much worse off than it is now (Papademetriou 2003, 53).

Contrary to neoliberal rhetoric concerning the "shrinking of the state," poor women's lives in the United States have been increasingly regulated as changes in welfare laws subject women to mandatory work requirements, as well as restrictions upon their privacy, reproductive choices, and bodily integrity. In all three countries, "empowerment" strategies that focus on women's involvement with the formal sector, while ignoring the growing crisis in childcare, health care, and safety-net programs, condemn women, especially poor and low-income women, to triple and quadruple shifts as they continue to provide subsistence labor and unwaged labor in the home, while engaging in informal and formal sectors to generate cash income as well as contributing to voluntary associations to address community needs.

Although the majority of Mexican women may have lost ground economically in the last ten years, they have paradoxically experienced a greater gain with regard to representation in political office than either Canadian or U.S. women. Another important positive change has been the increase in education for women in Mexico. Women now outnumber men in Mexican educational institutions at all levels. Mexican women who migrate to the United States and Canada also experience increased opportunities for political participation in grassroots community activities and in transnational organizations that operate across national borders. Indeed as Mexico experiments with new organizations like *Consejo Consultivo de Instituto de Mexicanos en el Exterior* (CCIME or the Consultative Council), Mexican men and women living in the United States and Canada have new political opportunities to influence policy formation affecting Mexicans at home and abroad.

Elite women in all three nations have benefited and continue to benefit from new economic opportunities and increasing levels of affluence. Class polarization within and across these three states, however, raises significant challenges to the concept of equal citizenship and equality before the law. While women's rights activists continue to work within Canada, Mexico, and the United States and in transnational coalitions to transform relations of domination and subordination and to enhance gender democracy, they face challenges posed by growing inequalities. The "thicker" democracy that feminists envision include forms of governance that are inclusive of all women and men regardless of class, race, ethnicity, or sexuality. As this review of women's economic and political struggles in the three countries of North America shows, in complicated and very specific ways, the changes associated with globalization and democratization have not yet realized this democratic vision. By making the gaps between feminist democratic ideals and present social, economic, and political practices visible, *Women, Democracy, and Globalization in North America* seeks to map the terrain on which future struggles for economic justice and inclusive democracy must take place.

# REFERENCES

Abele, F. 1997. "Understanding What Happened Here: The Political Economy of Indigenous Peoples." In *Understanding Canada: Building on the New Canadian Political Economy*, ed. W. Clement. Montreal and Kingston: McGill-Queen's University Press. 118–140.

Abu-Laban, Yasmeen and Christina Gabriel. 2002. *Selling Diversity: Immigration, Multiculturalism, Employment Equity and Globalization*. Peterborough: Broadview Press.

Adams, Michael. "Fire and Ice: The Myth of Converging Values," accessed at www.ppforum.ca/ow/Micheal_Adams_Presentation.pdf on August 24, 2004.

Alba, Francisco. 1982. *The Population of Mexico: Trends, Issues, and Politics*. Trans. Marjory Mattingly Urquidi. New Brunswick: Transaction Books.

Albers, Patricia and Beatrice Medicine. 1983. *The Hidden Half: Studies of Plains Indian Women*. Washington, DC: University Press of America.

Alexander, Bobby C. 2004. "The Role of a Mexican Pentecostal Church and Its U.S. Congregations in Transnational Migration." Presented at the Joint Session of the Latina/o Religion, Culture, and Society Group and the Evangelical Theology Group of the American Academy of Religion in San Antonio, Texas, November 22.

Anderson, Kristi. 1996. *After Suffrage: Women and Partisan Politics Before the New Deal*. Chicago: University of Chicago Press.

Antrobus, Peggy et al. 2002. "Editorial," *Women, Globalization and International Trade*, special issue of *Canadian Woman Studies* 21/22(4/1): 3.

APSA. 2004. "Task Force on Inequality and American Democracy." American Political Science Association. Accessed at www.apsanet.org on August 17, 2004.

Apter Klinghoffer, Judith and Lois Elkis. 1992. "The 'Petticoat Electors:' Women's Suffrage in New Jersey, 1776–1807." *Journal of the Early Republic* 12(2): 159–193.

Armstrong, Pat, 1996 "The Feminization of the Labour Force: Harmonizing Down in a Global Economy." In *Rethinking Restructuring: Gender and Change in Canada*, ed. Isabella Bakker. Toronto: University of Toronto Press. 29–54.

Audley, John J. 2003. "Introduction." *NAFTA's Promise and Reality: Lessons from Mexico for the Hemisphere*. Washington, DC: Carnegie Endowment for International Peace.

Audley, John J., Demetrios G. Papademetriou, Sandra Polaski, and Scott Vaughan. 2003. *NAFTA's Promise and Reality: Lessons from Mexico for the Hemisphere*. Washington, DC: Carnegie Endowment for International Peace.

Babb, Sarah. 2001. *Managing Mexico: Economists from Nationalism to Neoliberalism*. Princeton, NJ: Princeton University Press.

Baker, Michael and Nicole Fortin. 2000. "The Gender Composition and Wages: Why is Canada Different from the United States?" Ottawa: Statistics Canada Catalogue No. 11F0019MIE00140.

Banting, Keith, Andrew Sharpe, and France St-Hilaire. 2001. "The Longest Decade: Introduction and Overview." *The Review of Economic Performance and Social Progress: Canada in the 1990s* June 1: 1–20. Accessed at http://www.csls.ca/repsp/repsp1.asp.on August 17, 2004.

Bartels, Larry, Hugh Heclo, Rodney Hero, and Lawrence R. Jacobs. 2004. "Inequality and American Governance." American Political Science Association Task Force on Inequality and American Democracy. Washington, DC: APSA. http://www.apsanet.org/Inequality/researchreviews.cfm.

Bashevkin, Sylvia. 1985. *Toeing the Lines*. Toronto: University of Toronto Press.

Battle, Ken and Sherri Torjman. 1996. "Desperately Seeking Substance: A Commentary on the Social Security Review." In *Remaking Canadian Social Policy: Social Security in the Late 1990s*, ed. Jane Pulkingham and Gordon Ternowetsky. Halifax: Fernwood. 52–66.

Bayes, Jane H. and Nayereh Tohidi, eds. 2001. *Globalization, Gender, and Religion: The Politics of Women's Rights in Catholic and Muslim Contexts*. New York: Palgrave.

Begné, Patricia. 2004. *Mujeres*. Guanajuato, MX: Instituto de la Mujer Guanajuatense.

Bennett, Vivienne. 1998. "Everyday Struggles: Women in Urban Popular Movements and Territorially Based Protests in Mexico." In *Women's Participation in Mexican Political Life*, ed. Victoria E. Rodríguez. Boulder: Westview Press. 131–145.

Benoit, Celia. 2000. *Women, Work and Social Rights: Canada in Historical and Comparative Perspective*. Scarborough: Prentice Hall Allyn and Bacon Canada.

Bluestone, Barry and Bennett Harrison. 1982. *The Deindustrialization of America: Plant Closing, Community Abandonment, and the Dismantling of Basic Industry*. New York: Basic Books, Inc.

Bourne, Paula. 1993. "Women, Law and the Justice System." In *Canadian Women's Issues: Twenty-Five Years of Women's Activism in English Canada vol. 1: Strong Voices*, ed. Ruth Roach Pierson, M. Griffin Cohen, P. Bourne, and P. Masters. Toronto: James Lorimer & Company. 321–348.

Brown, Jennifer. 2001. "Partial Truths: A Closer Look at Fur Trade Marriage." In *From Rupert's Land to Canada*, ed. Theodore Binnema, Gerhard Ens, and R. C. Macleod. Edmonton: University of Alberta Press. 59–80.

Bruhn, Kathleen. 2003. "Whores and Lesbians: Political Activism, Party Strategies, and Gender Quotas in Mexico." *Electoral Studies* 22(1): 101–119.

Buhle, Mary Jo and Paul Buhle. 1978. *The Concise History of Woman Suffrage: Selections from the Classic Work of Stanton, Anthony, Gage and Harper*. Urbana: University of Illinois Press.

Bullock, Charles and Patricia Lee Findley Hays. 1977. "Recruitment of Women for Congress." In *Portrait of Marginality: The Political Behavior of American Women*. ed. Marianne Githens and Jewel Prestage. New York: McKay. 210–220.

Bureau of Labor Statistics. 2002. "Highlights of Women's Earnings in 2001." Report 960. U.S. Department of Labor. Washington, DC: U.S. Government Printing Office.

——— 2004. *Women in the Labor Force: A Databook 2004*. U.S. Department of Labor. Washington, DC: U.S. Government Printing Office.

Burt, Sandra and Sonya Lynn Hardman. 2001. "The Case of Disappearing Targets: the Liberals and Gender Equality." In *Power in Transition: How Ottawa Spends 2001–2002*, ed. Leslie Pal. Toronto: Oxford University Press. 201–222.

Butterfield, L. H. 1963. *The Adams Papers, Adams Family Correspondence*, Series II. Cambridge, MA: Harvard University Press.

Cairncross, Francis. 1997. *The Death of Distance: How the Communication Revolution Will Change Our Lives*. Cambridge, MA: Harvard Business School.

Canadian Council on Social Development. 2003. "Census shows growing polarization of income in Canada." Press release, May 16. Accessed at www.ccsd.ca/pr/2003/censusincome.htm on August 17, 2004.

Canadian Labor Congress. 2003. "Submission in response to Finance Canada's EI Premium Rate-Setting Mechanism Consultation." June. Accessed at www.fin.gc.ca/consultresp/eiratesResp_2e.html on October 12, 2004.

Canadian Research Institute for the Advancement of Women (CRIAW). 2002. "Factsheet Women and Poverty." March. Accessed at www.criaw-icref.ca/indexFrame_e.htm on August 12, 2004.

Cano, Gabriela. 1991. "Las feministas en campaña." *Debate Feminista* 2(4): 269–294.

Castells, Manuel. 1996. *The Rise of the Network Society*. Oxford: Blackwell Publishers.

Cavanaugh, Cathy. 2005. "Out of the West: History, Memory and the 'Persons' Case, 1919–2000." In *Forging Alberta's Constitutional Framework*, ed. Richard Connors and John Law. Edmonton: University of Alberta Press.

Chappell, Louise. 2002. *Gendering Government: Feminist Engagement with the State in Australia and Canada*. Vancouver: University of British Columbia Press.

Chatman Catt, Carrie and Nettie Rogers Shuler. [1926] 1969. *Woman Suffrage and Politics: The Inner Story of the Suffrage Movement*. Seattle: University of Washington Press.

Chen J. A., Hicks W. W., Johnson S. R., and Rodriquez R. C. 1990. "Economic Development, Contraception and Fertility Decline in Mexico." *Journal of Development Studies* 26(17).

Clark, Warren. 2001. "Economic Gender Equality Indicators 2000." Statistics Canada. Ottawa: Government of Canada. Accessed at www.swc-cfc.gc.ca/pubs/egei2000/egei2000_e.pdf on August 13, 2004.

Cleverdon, C. L. 1974. *The Woman Suffrage Movement in Canada.* 2nd ed. Toronto: University of Toronto Press.

Cohen, Jean and Andrew Arato. 1992. *Civil Society and Political Theory.* Cambridge, MA: MIT Press.

Cohen, Marjorie Griffin. 1994. "The Implications of Economic Restructuring for Women: The Canadian Situation." In The Strategic Silence: Gender and Economic Policy.

Cohen, Marjorie Griffin, Laurell Ritchie, Michele Swenarchuk, and Leah Vosko 2002. "Globalization: Some Implications and Strategies for Women." *Canadian Woman Studies* 21/22(4/1): 6–14.

Collins, Karen Scott, Cathy Schoen, Susan Joseph et al. 1999. Health Concerns Across a Woman's Lifespan: The Commonwealth Fund Survey of Women's Health. New York: The Commonwealth Fund. May. Accessed at www.cmwf.org/publications-show.htm/doc_1d=221554.

Committee on Elimination of Discrimination Against Women. 1998. "Progress Made in Advancement of Mexican Women, but Changes not yet 'Radical', Anti-Discrimination Committee Told." Press Release WOM/1020, January 30. Accessed at www.scienceblog.com/community/older/archives/L/1998/A/un980079.html on January 23, 2005.

——— 2002. "Mexican Women Still Face Discrimination, Despite Significant Steps, Committee Told; Exceptional Session Concludes Consideration of First Country Report." 569th and 570th Meeting. Press Release WOM/1352, July 8. Accessed at www.un.org/News/Press/docs/2002/wom1352. doc.htm on January 23, 2005.

CONAPO. 2005. Consejo Nacional de Población. Accessed at www.conapo.gob.mx/mig_int/series/05.htm on January 13, 2005.

Connors, Richard and John Law, eds. 2005. Forging Alberta's Constitutional Framework. Edmonton: University of Alberta Press.

Consejo Nacional Para La Cultura y las Artes. 2001. "Los Rostros Anónimos de la Revolución Mexicana; Las Mujeres que no Dejaron Huella." April 19. Accessed at www.cnca.gob.mx/cnca/nuevo/2001/diarias/abr/190401/veterana.html on September 10, 2004.

Cook, Ramsey and Wendy Mitchinson, eds. 1976. *The Proper Sphere: Woman's Place in Canadian Society.* Toronto: Oxford University Press.

Cortes Jimenez, Adriana. 2004. Interview, June. Uriangato, Mexico.

Cosmes, Francisco. 1979. *Historia General de Mexico.* Mexico, DF: Fondo de Cultura Economica.

Cross, D. Suzanne. 1977. "The Neglected Majority: The Changing Role of Women in 19th Century Montreal." In *The Neglected Majority: Essays in Canadian Women's History*, ed. Susan Mann Trofimenkoff and Alison Prentice. Toronto: McClelland and Stewart. 66–86.

Dahlerup, Drude and Lenita Freidenvall. 2003. "Quotas as a 'Fast Track' to Equal Representation for Women." Paper presented at the Nineteenth International Political Science Association Meeting, June 29–July 4; Durban, South Africa.

de la Cour, Lykke and Rose Sheinin. 1991. "The Ontario Medical College for Women, 1883–1906: Lessons from Gender-Separatism in Medical Education." In *Re-Thinking Canada: The Promise of Women's History*, 2nd ed. Ed. Veronica Strong Boag and Anita Clair Fellman. Toronto: Copp Clark Pitman. 206–214.

Department of Foreign Affairs and International Trade (DFAIT), 2003. "NAFTA@10: A Preliminary Report." Ottawa: Government of Canada. Accessed at http://www.dfait-maeci.gc.ca/eet/research/nafta/nafta-en.asp#lined on August 17, 2004.

Department of International Trade. 2003a. "Canada and the North American Free Trade Agreement." Ottawa: Government of Canada. October. Accessed at www.dfait-maeci.gc.ca/nafta-alena/menu-en.asp on August 17, 2004.

Department of International Trade. 2003b. "NAFTA: A Decade of Strengthening a Dynamic Relationship." Ottawa: Government of Canada. June. Accessed at www.dfait-maeci.gc.ca/nafta-alena/nafta10-en.asp on August 16, 2004.

Diamond, Larry. 1993. "The Globalization of Democracy." In *Global Transformations and the Third World*, ed. Robert O. Slater, Barry M. Schutz, and Steven R. Dorr. Boulder, CO: Lynn Reinner.

*Diario de Debates del Congreso Constituyente 1916–1917.* 1990. Mexico D.F.: Congreso de Unión.

*Diario de Debates.* 1967. Guanajuato, Mexico: Congreso del Estado de Guanajuato.

*Diario Official Tomo* DC XXI. 2005. Mexico City: Mexican Federal Government.

DiNatale, Marisa and Stephanie Boraas. 2002. "The Labor Force Experience of Women from 'Generation X'." *Monthly Labor Review.* 125 (March): 3–15.

Dobrowolsky, Alexandra. 2000. *The Politics of Pragmatism: Women, Representation and Constitutionalism in Canada.* Toronto: Oxford University Press.

Downs, Barbara. 2003. "Fertility of American Women: June 2002." Current Population Reports P20–548. U.S. Census, U.S. Department of Commerce.

Dresser, Denise. 1993. "Exporting Conflict: Transboundary Consequences of Mexican Politics." In *The California–Mexico Connection*, ed. Abraham Lowenthal and Katrina Burgess. Stanford, CA: Stanford University Press.

Driscoll, Heather Rollason. 2001. " 'A Most Important Chain of Connection': Marriage in the Hudson's Bay Company." In *From Rupert's Land to Canada*, ed. Theodore Binnema, Gerhard Ens, and R. C. Macleod. Edmonton: University of Alberta Press. 81–107.

Drolet, Marie. 2000. "The Persistent Gap: New Evidence on the Canadian Gender Wage Gap." Analytical Studies Branch Research Paper Series, Statistics Canada Catalogue #11F0019MPE, 157. Ottawa: Statistics Canada.

Durand, Jorge, Nolan Malone, Alfred Buch, and Douglas S. Massey. 2002. *Beyond Smoke and Mirrors: Mexican Immigration in an Era of Economic Integration.* New York: Russell Sage Foundation.

Durst, Douglas, ed. 1999. *Canada's National Child Benefit: Phoenix or Fizzle?* Halifax: Fernwood.

Duerst-Lahti, Georgia. 1989. "The Government's Role in Building the Women's Movement," *Political Science Quarterly* 104(2): 249–268.

Duverger, Maurice. 1955. *The Political Role of Women.* Paris: UNESCO.

*Economic Report of the President.* 2004. Washington DC: U.S. Government.

Edwards, Rebecca. 1997. *Angels in the Machinery: Gender in American Party Politics from the Civil War to the Progressive Era.* New York: Oxford University Press.

Eisenberg, Avigail. 1998. "Domination and Political Representation in Canada." In *Painting the Maple: Essays on Race, Gender and the Construction of Canada*, ed. Veronica Strong Boag, S. Grace, A. Eisenberg, and J. Anderson. Vancouver: UBC Press. 37–52.

Eisenstein, Hester. 1996. *Inside Agitators: Australian Femocrats and the State.* Sydney: Allen and Unwin.

Erie, Steven, Martin Rein, and Barbara Wiget. 1983. "Women and the Reagan Revolution: Thermidor for the Social Welfare Economy." In *Families, Politics and Public Policy*, ed. Irene Diamond and Mary Shanley. New York: Longman. 94–119.

Etienne, Mona and Eleanor Leacock. 1980. *Women and Colonization: Anthropological Perspectives.* New York: Praeger.

Evans, Peter. 1998. "The Eclipse of the State? Reflections on Stateness in an Era of Globalization." *World Politics* 50(1): 62–87.

Evans, Sara. 1979. *Personal Politics: The Roots of Women's Liberation in the Civil Rights Movement and the New Left.* New York: Vintage.

——— 1997. *Born for Liberty: A History of Women in America.* New York: Free Press.

Faludi, Susan. 1991. *Backlash: The Undeclared War Against American Women.* New York: Crown.

Fernandez-Kelly, Patricia. 1983. *For We are Sold, I and My People.* Albany: State University of New York Press.

——— 1991. *A Collaborative Study of Women in the Garment and Electronics Industry: Final Report.* New York: Center for Latin American Studies, New York University. Printing Office. Accessed at www.gpoaccess.gov/eop/ on July 24, 2004.

Fields, Jason and Lynne M. Casper. 2001. *America's Families and Living Arrangements.* Current Population Reports, U.S. Census Bureau, U.S. Department of Commerce. Washington, DC: June.

Fitzgerald, David. 2000. "Negotiating Extra-Territorial Citizenship: Mexican Migration and the Transnational Politics of Community." Monograph Series 2. La Jolla, CA: Center for Comparative Immigration Studies, University of California, San Diego.

Flammang, Janet. 1997. *Women's Political Voice.* Philadelphia: Temple University Press.

Flexner, Eleanor. 1975. *Century of Struggle: The Woman Rights Movement in the United States.* Cambridge, MA: Belknap Press of Harvard University Press.

Flores, Juan Carlos. 2000. *Análisis Jurídico de la Mujer en Mexico.* Guanajuato, Gto. Mexico: Universidad de Guanajuato.

Foppa, Alaíde. 1975. "Imagen y Realidad de la Mujer." Editorial SEP: 240. Mexico D.F.: Secretaria de Educacion Publica.

Foster, John W. and John Dillon. 2003. "NAFTA in Canada: The Era of a Supra-Constitution." In *Lessons from NAFTA: The High Cost of "Free Trade,"* ed. Karen Hansen-Kuhn and Steve Hellinger. Ottawa: Canadian Centre for Policy Alternatives. 83–115.

Foulché-Delbosc, Isabel. 1977. "Women of Three Rivers: 1651–1663." In *The Neglected Majority: Essays in Canadian Women's History,* ed. Susan Mann Trofimenkoff and Alison Prentice. Toronto: McClelland and Stewart. 14–26.

Fowlkes, Diane. 1984. "Ambitious Political Women: Countersocialization and Political Party Context." *Women and Politics* 4(Winter): 5–32.

Franceschet, Susan and Laura Macdonald. 2004. "Hard Times for Citizenship: Women's Movement in Chile and Mexico." *Citizenship Studies.* 8(1) (March): 3–23.

Fraser, Nancy and Linda Gordon. 1997. "Genealogy of Dependency: Tracing a Keyword in the U.S. Welfare State." In *Justice Interruptus,* ed. Nancy Fraser. New York: Routledge.

Freedom House. 2005. Accessed at http://www.freedomhouse.org/ratings/index.htm on January 13, 2005.

Freeman, Jo. 1975. *The Politics of Women's Liberation.* New York: David Mckay Company.

———— 2000. *A Room at a Time: How Women Entered Party Politics.* Lanham, MD: Rowman and Littlefield.

Fudge, Judy. 1997. *Precarious Work and Families.* Working Paper for the Centre for Research on Work and Family. Toronto: York University.

———— 2002. "From Segregation to Privatization: Equality, the Law and Women Public Servants 1908–2001." In *Privatization, Law and the Challenge to Feminism,* ed. Brenda Cossman and Judy Fudge. Toronto: University of Toronto Press. Hanover, NH: University of New England Press. 86–127.

Fudge, Judy and Leah Vosko. 2003. "Gendered Paradoxes and the Rise of Contingent Work: Towards a Tranformative Feminist Political Economy of the Labour Market." In *Changing Canada: Political Economy as Transformation,* ed. Wallace Clement and Leah Vosko. Montreal and Kingston: McGill-Queen's University Press. 183–209.

Fullerton, Howard N. Jr. 2000. "Labor Force Participation: 75 years of change 1950–1998 and 1998–2025." *Monthly Labor Review,* December 4.

Gabriel, Christina and Laura Macdonald. 2004. "Of Borders and Business: Canadian Corporate Proposals for North American 'Deep Integration.'" *Studies in Political Economy* 74 (Fall): 79–100.

Garcia, Alma. 1997. *Chicana Feminist Thought.* New York: Routledge.

Giddens, Anthony. 1990. *The Consequences of Modernity.* Cambridge, UK: Polity Press.

Giddings, Paula. 1984. *When and Where I Enter: The Impact of Black Women on Race and Sex in America.* New York: William Morrow.

Gilroy, Paul. 1992. *The Black Atlantic: Modernity and Double Consciousness.* Cambridge, MA: Harvard University Press.

Glantz, Margo. 2000. *Sor Juana: la Comparación y la Hipérbole.* Mexico: CONACULTA, Sello Bermejo.

Gonzalez, Laura. 1992. *Respuesta Campesina a la Revolución Verde en el Bajío.* Mexico D.F.: Universidad Iberoamericana.

———— 2001. "Mexico/US Migration and Gender Relations: The Guanajuatese Community in Mexico and the United States." In *Gender, Globalization, and Democratization,* ed. Rita Mae Kelly, Jane H. Bayes, Mary Hawkesworth, and Brigitte Young. Boulder, CO: Rowman and Littlefield.

Gordon, Linda. 1994. *Pitied But Not Entitled: Single Mothers and the History of Welfare.* Cambridge, MA: Harvard University Press.

Gray White, Deborah. 1999. *Too Heavy a Load: Black Women in Defense of Themselves, 1894–1994.* New York: W. W. Norton.

Greenberg, Cheryl., ed. 1998. "SNCC Women and the Stirrings of Feminism." *A Circle of Trust: Remembering SNCC.* New Brunswick: Rutgers University Press.

Hacker, Andrew. 1992. *Two Nations: Black and White, Separate, Hostile, and Unequal.* New York: Scribners.

Hamilton, Alexander, James Madison, and John Jay. 1961. *The Federalist Papers.* Introduction by Clinton Rossiter. New York: New American Library.

Harder, Lois. 2003. "Whither the Social Citizen." In *Reinventing Canada: Politics of the 21st Century,* ed. Janine Brodie and Linda Trimble. Toronto: Prentice Hall. 175–188.

Harder, Lois and Marcus Taylor. 2005. "Ragged Cruelty? Social Policy Transformation in North America." In *North American Politics: Globalization and Culture,* ed. Yasmeen Abu-Laban, François Rocher, and Rhadda Jappan. Peterborough, Ontario: Broadview Press.

Harding, Sandra. 1986. *The Science Question in Feminism.* Ithaca, NY: Cornell University Press.

Hardt, Michael and Antonio Negri. 2000. *Empire.* Cambridge, MA: Harvard University Press.

Hartmann, Susan M. 1982. *The Home Front and Beyond: American Women in the 1940s*. Boston: Twayne Publishers.

Hawkesworth, Mary. 1997. "Confounding Gender." *Signs* 22(3): 649–686.

Heise, L., M. Ellsberg, and L. Gottemoeller. 1999. *Ending Violence Against Women*. Population Reports, Series L, No. 11. Ottowa: Government of Canada.

Heisz, Andrew, Andrew Jackson, and Garnett Picot. 2001. "Distributional Outcomes in Canada in the 1990s." *The Review of Economic Performance and Social Progress*: 1–20. Accessed at www.csls.ca/repsp/repsp1.asp.on August 17, 2004.

Held, David, Anthony McGrew, David Goldblatt, and Jonathan Perraton. 1999. *Global Transformations: Politics, Economics and Culture*. Stanford: Stanford University Press.

Heredia, Carlos. 2000. "The Mexican Economy: Six Years into NAFTA." Speech given at forum organized by the Development GSP and the Economic Policy Institute, Mayflower Hotel, January 20 Washington, DC. Accessed at www.development gap.org/heredia_nafta.html on January 17, 2005.

Hirst, Paul and Graham Thompson. 1999. *Globalization in Question: The International Economy and the Possibilities of Governance*, 2nd. ed. Oxford: Polity Press.

Hoberg, George, Keith Banting, and Richard Simeon. 2002. "The Scope for Domestic Choice: Policy Autonomy in a Globalized World." In *Capacity for Choice: Canada in a New North America*, ed. George Hoberg. Toronto: University of Toronto Press. 252–299.

Hoff Summers, Christine. 1994. *Who Stole Feminism?* New York: Touchstone/Simon & Shuster.

Hole, Judith and Ellen Levine. 1971. *Rebirth of Feminism*. New York: Quadrangle Books.

Hoover, Kenneth and R. Plant. 1989. *Conservative Capitalism in Great Britain and the United States: A Critical Appraisal*. New York and London: Routledge.

Huntington, Samuel. 1991. *The Third Wave: Democratization in the Late Twentieth Century*. Norman, OK: University of Oklahoma Press.

Ikeda, Satoshi. 2004. "Zonal Structure and the Trajectories of Canada, Mexico, Australia, and Norway under Neo-Liberal Globalisation." In *Governing Under Stress: Middle Powers and the Challenge of Globalization*, ed. Marjorie Griffin Cohen and Stephen Clarkson. New York: Zed Books. 263–290.

Innis, Harold. 1977. *The Fur Trade in Canada: An Introduction to Canadian Economic History*. revised ed. Toronto: University of Toronto Press.

Instituto de los Mexicanos en el Exterior (IME). 2004. "Remesas." *Lazos*. Boletín 15. Mexico, DF: August 19.

Isaak, Robert A. 2005. *The Globalization Gap: How the Rich Get Richer and the Poor Get Left Further Behind*. Upper Saddle River, NJ: Financial Times, Prentice Hall.

Jackson, Andrew. 1999. "The Free Trade Agreement—a decade later." *Studies in Political Economy* 58 (Spring): 141–160.

James, Paul. 2004. "The Matrix of Global Enchantment." In *Rethinking Globalism*, ed. Manfred Steger. Lanham, MD: Rowman and Littlefield. 27–38.

Jenson, Jane and S. Phillips. 1996. "Regime Shift: New Citizenship Practices in Canada." *International Journal of Canadian Studies* 14: 115–145.

Johnson, Chalmers. 2004. *The Sorrows of Empire: Militarism, Secrecy and the End of the Republic*. New York: Henry Holt and Company.

Katzenstein, Mary Fainsod. 1998. *Faithful and Fearless: Moving Feminist Protest inside the Church and the Military*. Princeton, NJ: Princeton University Press.

Keister, Lisa A. 2000. *Wealth in America: Trends in Wealth Inequality*. Cambridge: Cambridge University Press.

Kelly, Kristin. 2005. *Domestic Violence and the Politics of Privacy*. Ithaca, NY: Cornell University Press.

Kelly, Rita Mae, Jane Bayes, Mary Hawkesworth, and Brigitte Young. 2001. *Gender, Democratization and Globalization*. Lanham, MD: Rowman and Littlefield.

Kelly, Rita Mae, Mary Guy, Jane Bayes, Georgia Duerst Lahti, Mary Hale, Cathy Johnson, Amal Kawar, and Jean Stanley. 1991. "Public Managers in the States: A Comparison of Career Advancement by Sex." *Public Administration Review* 51(5): 402–412.

Kennickell, Arthur B. 2003. "A Rolling Tide: Changes in the Distribution of Wealth in the U.S., 1989–2001." Washington DC: Federal Reserve Board, September. Accessed at www.federalreserve.gov/pubs/oss/oss2/papers/concentration.20 01.10.pdf

Kerber, Linda. 1980. *Women of the Republic: Intellect and Ideology in Revolutionary America*. Chapel Hill: University of North Carolina Press.

Keyssar, Alexander. 2000. *The Right to Vote: The Contested History of Democracy in the United States.* New York: Basic Books.

Koss, Mary. 1992a. "The Measurement of Rape Victimization in Crime Surveys." *Criminal Justice and Behavior* 23(1): 55–69.

——— 1992b. "The Underdetection of Rape: Methodological Choices Influence Incidence Estimates." *Journal of Social Issues* 48(1): 61–65.

——— 1993. "Detecting the Scope of Rape: A Review of Prevalence Research Methods." *Journal of Interpersonal Violence* 8(2): 198–222.

Koss, Mary, Mary Harvey, and James Butcher. 1987. *The Rape Victim.* New York: Viking, Penguin.

Lakatos, Imre. 1970. "Falsification and the Methodology of Scientific Research Programmes." In *Criticism and the Growth of Knowledge*, ed. Imre Lakatos and Alan Musgrave. Cambridge, United Kingdom: Cambridge University Press.

Lee, Marica. 1976. "Why Few Women Hold Public Office: Democracy and Sexual Roles." *Political Science Quarterly* 91: 297–314.

——— 1977. "Toward Understanding Why Few Women Hold Public Office: Factors Affecting the Participation of Women in Local Politics." In *Portrait of Marginality: The Political Behavior of American Women*, ed. Marianne Githens and Jewel Prestage. New York: McKay. 118–138.

Macdonald, Laura. 1999. "Trade with a Female Face: Women and the New International Trade Agenda." In *Trade and the New Social Agenda*, ed. Annie Taylor and Caroline Thomas. London: Routledge. 53–71.

——— 2003. "Gender and Canadian Trade Policy: Women's Strategies for Access and Transformation." In *Feminist Perspectives on Canadian Foreign Policy*, ed. Claire Turenne Sjolander, Deborah Stienstra, and Heather A. Smith, Toronto: Oxford University Press.

Martin, Marguerite. 1991. *Social Protest in an Urban Barrio: A Study of the Chicano Movement, 1966–1974.* Lanham, MD: University Press of America.

McKeen, Wendy and Ann Porter. 2003. "Politics and Transformation: Welfare State Restructuring in Canada." In *Changing Canada: Political Economy as Transformation*, ed. Wallace Clement and Leah F. Vosko. Montreal and Kingston: McGill-Queens University Press. 109–134.

McKinley, James C. 2005. "Lawmakers in Mexico Approve Absentee Voting for Migrants." *New York Times.* A, 4.

McNeil, John. 1998. *Changes in Median Household Income 1969–1996.* Current Population Reports Special Studies P 23-196. U.S. Census. U.S. Department of Commerce. Washington, DC: U.S. Government Printing Office. July.

Miller, Francesca. 1991. *Latin American Women and the Search for Social Justice.* Hanover, NH: University of New England Press.

Ministry of Finance and Public Credit of Mexico Hacienda 2000 "Foreign Direct Investment in Mexico." Mexico's Bimonthly Economic News No. 14. June 13. Accessed on January 18, 2005 at www.shep.gob.mx/english/docs/mben/mben1400.html.

Mora, Miguel. 1985. *La igualdad jurídica del varón y la mujer.* Mexico City: Consejo Nacional de Población.

Morgan, Jennifer. 2004. *Laboring Women: Gender and Reproduction in the Making of New World Slavery.* Philadelphia: University of Pennsylvania Press.

Morton, Ward. 1962. *Woman Suffrage in Mexico.* Gainesville: University of Florida Press.

Mosisa, Abraham T. 2002. "The Role of Foreign-Born Workers in the U.S. Economy." *Monthly Labor Review* May: 3–14.

Newman, Louise. 1999. *White Women's Rights.* New York: Oxford University Press.

Niethammer, Carolyn. 1977. *Daughters of the Earth: The Lives and Legends of American Indian Women.* New York: Collier Books.

Noël, Jan. 1991. "New France: Les Femmes Favorisées." *In Re-thinking Canada: The Promise of Women's History.* 2nd ed. Ed. by V. Strong-Boag and A. C. Fellman. Toronto: Copp Clark Pitman Ltd. 28–50.

Ohmae, Kenichi. 1995. *The End of the Nation State: The Rise of Regional Economics.* New York: The Free Press.

Orloff, Ann. 1996. "Gender in the Welfare State." *Annual Review of Sociology* 22: 51–78.

Papademetriou, Demetrios G. 2003. "The Shifting Expectations of Free Trade and Migration." In *NAFTA's Promise and Reality: Lessons from Mexico for the Hemisphere*, ed. John Audley, Sandra Polaski, Demetrious G. Papademetriou, and Scott Vaughan. Washington, DC: Carnergie Endowment for

International Peace. 39–59. Accessed at www.carnergieendownment.org/pdf/File/NAFTA_Report_ChapterTwo.Pdf on August 7, 2005.

Pardo, Mary. 1998. *Mexican American Women Activists*. Philadelphia: Temple University Press.

Pateman, Carole. 1989. *The Disorder of Women: Democracy, Feminism, and Political Theory*. Oxford: Polity Press.

Perez, Emma. 1999. *The Decolonial Imaginary: Writing Chicanas into History*. Bloomington, IN: University of Indiana Press.

Picard, Alberto Arroyo. 2003. "Introduction." In *Lessons from NAFTA: The High Cost of "Free Trade,"* eds. Karen Hansen-Kuhn and Steve Hellinger. Ottawa, UN, Canada: Canadian Centre for Policy Alternatives.

Polaski, Sandra. 2003. "Jobs, Wages, and Household Income." *NAFTA's Promise and Reality: Lessons from Mexico for the Hemisphere*, eds. John Audley, Sandra Polaski, Demetrious G. Papademetriou, and Scott Vaughan. Washington, DC: Carnergie Endowment for International Peace. 11–21. Accessed at www.carnergieendownment.org/pdf/File/NAFTA_Report_Chapter Two.pdf on August 7, 2005.

Prentice, Alison, Paula Bourne, G. Cuthbert Brandt, B. Light, W. Mitchinson, and N. Black. 1988. *Canadian Women: A History*. Toronto: Harcourt, Brace, Jovanovich Press.

Prince, Michael J. 1999. "From Health and Welfare to Stealth and Farewell: Federal Social Policy, 1980–2000." In *How Ottawa Spends 1999–2000: Shape Shifting: Canadian Governance Toward the 21st Century*, ed. Leslie Pal. Toronto: Oxford University Press. 151–196.

———— 2004. Le Petit Vision, Les Grands Decisions: Chrétien's Paradoxical Record in Social Policy. *Special Issue of the Review of Constitutional Studies: The Chretien Legacy*, ed. Steve Patten and Lois Harder. 9(12): 199–219. Princeton, NJ: Princeton University Press.

Piketty, Thomas and Emmanuel Saez 2001. "Income Inequality in the United States 1913–1998." Working Paper No. w8467. Cambridge: NBER. Available at http://emlab.berkeley.edu/users/saez/w8467.pdf or www.nber.org.

Proctor, Bernadette D. and Joseph Dalaker. 2002. "Poverty in the United States: 2002." Current Population Reports. US Census Bureau. U.S. Department of Commerce. September. Table A–1. 22–27.

Rai, Shirin. 2002. *Gender and the Political Economy of Development*. Cambridge, UK: Polity Press.

Ramos Escandón, Carmen. 1993. *Mujeres y Revolución, 1910–1917*. Mexico City: INAH.

———— 1994. "Women's Movements, Feminism, and Mexican Politics." In *The Women's Movement in Latin America*. 2nd ed. Ed. Jane Jaquette. Boulder, CO: Westview Press.

———— 1998. "Women and Power in Mexico: The Forgotten Heritage, 1880–1954." In *Women's Participation in Mexican Political Life*, ed. Vitoria Rodriquez. Boulder, CO: Westview Press. 87–102.

Reich, Robert. 1992. *The Work of Nations*. New York: Vintage.

Reitz, Jeffrey. 2002. "Immigration and Canadian Nation-building in the Transition to a Knowledge. Economy." June. Accessed at http://www.utoronto.ca/ethnicstudies/Reitz_June2002.pdf on August 18, 2004.

Richardson, Marilyn. 1987. *Maria Stewart, America's First Black Woman Political Writer*. Bloomington: Indiana University Press.

Robertson, Roland. 1992. *Globalization*. London: Sage.

Rodríguez, Victoria E. 2003. *Women in Contemporary Mexican Politics*. Austin, TX: University of Texas Press.

Rule, Wilma and Joseph Zimmerman. 1994. *Electoral Systems in Comparative Perspective: Their Impact on Women and Minorities*. Westport, CT: Greenwood Press.

Ryscavage, Paul. 1999. *Income Inequality in America*. Armonk, NY: M.E. Sharpe.

Salzinger, Leslie. 2003. *Genders in Production: Making Workers in Mexico's Global Factories*. Berkeley: University of California Press.

Sanbonmatsu, Kira. 2002. *Democrats/Republicans and the Politics of Women's Place*. Ann Arbor: University of Michigan Press.

Sandler, Bernice. 1973. "A Little Help from Our Government: WEAL and Contract Compliance." In *Academic Women on the Move*. ed. Alice Rossi and Anne Calderwood. New York: Russell Sage.

Schlozman, Kay L., Benjamin I. Page, Sidney Verba, and Morris Fiorina. 2004. "Inequalities of Political Voice." American Political Science Association Task Force on Inequality and American Democracy. Washington DC: APSA. Accessed at http://www.apsanet.org/Inequality/researchreviews.cfm.

Schwanen, Daniel. 2001. "Trade Liberalization and Inequality in Canada in the 1990s." *The Review of Economic Performance and Social Progress*. 1: 161–182. Accessed at http://www.csls.ca/repsp/repsp1.asp. on August 17, 2004.

Scott, Joan. 1986. "Gender: A Useful Category for Historical Analysis." *American Historical Review* 91: 1053–1075.

Shoemaker, Nancy. 1995. *Negotiators of Change: Historical Perspectives on Native American Women*. New York: Routledge.

Siltanen, Janet. 1994. *Locating Gender: Occupational Segregation, Wages and Domestic Responsibilities*. London: UCL Press.

Silva, Luz de Lourdes. 1989. "Las mujeres en la élite política de Mexico, 1954–1984." In *Trabajo, poder y sexualidad*, ed. Orlandina de Oliveira. Mexico City: El Colegio de Mexico.

Smart, Carol. 1992. "The Woman of Legal Discourse." *Social Legal Studies* 1(1): 29–44.

Standing Committee on Foreign Affairs and International Trade (SCFAIT). 2002. *Partners in North America: Advancing Canada's Relations with the United States and Mexico*. Ottawa: Parliament of Canada. December.

Stasiulis, Daiva. 1997. "The Political Economy of Race, Ethnicity and Migration." In *Understanding Canada: Building on the New Canadian Political Economy*, ed. Wallace Clement. Montreal and Kingston: McGill-Queen's University. 141–171.

Statistics Canada. 2003. "Women in Canada: Work Chapter Updates." Ottawa: Government of Canada.

Status of Women, Canada, Federal/Provincial/Territorial Ministers Responsible for the Status of Women. 2001. "Women's Economic Independence and Security: A Federal/Provincial/Territorial Strategic Framework." Ottawa: Government of Canada.

Status of Women, Canada. *2003–2004 Estimates: A Report on Plans and Priorities*. Accessed at www.tbs-sct.gc.ca/est-pre/20032004/SWC-CFC/SWC-CFCr34e_asp# on October 24, 2004.

Stetson, Dorothy and Amy Mazur. 1995. *Comparative State Feminism*. Newbury Park, CA: Sage.

Strange, Susan. 1996. *The Retreat of the State: The Diffusion of Power in the World Economy*. Cambridge: Cambridge University Press.

Strong-Boag, V. 1977. "Setting the Stage: National Organization and the Women's Movement in the Late 19th Century." In *The Neglected Majority: Essays in Canadian Women's History*, ed. S. Mann Trofimenkoff and A. Prentice. Toronto: McClelland and Stewart. 87–103.

——— 1991. " 'Ever a Crusader': Nellie McClung, First-Wave Feminist." In *Rethinking Canada: The Promise of Women's History* 2nd ed. Ed. Veronica Strong-Boag and Anita Clair Fellman. Toronto: Copp Clark Pitman. 308–321.

Sulzenko, Andrei. 2003. "Economics of North American Integration: A Canadian Perspective." *Horizons* (Policy Research Initiative). 6(3): 35–40.

Trimble, Linda and Jane Arscott. 2003. *Still Counting: Women in Politics Across Canada*. Peterborough, ON: Broadview Press.

Todd, Emmanuel. 2002. *After the Empire: The Breakdown of the American Order*. New York: Columbia University Press.

UN Committee on the Elimination of Discrimination Against Women Report. 2005. United Nations: CEDAW/C/2005/OP.8 Mexico. 32nd Session. January 10–28. Accessed at www.un.org/womenwatch/daw/cedaw/cedaw32/Mexico%20findings%20and%20recommendations%2032nd%20session%20%20English-%20CEDAW-C-2005-OP.8-MEXICO.pdf on February 8, 2005.

U.S. Bureau of Labor Statistics. 2002. "Highlights of Women's Earnings in 2001" Report 960, U.S. Department of Labor, Washington, DC: Accessed at www.b/s.gov/cps/cpswom 2001.pdf on 28 July 2005.

U.S. Bureau of Labor Statistics. 2004. *Women in the Labor Force: A Databook*. Washington, DC: Bureau of Labor Statistics.

U.S. Census Bureau. 2002. "Poverty in the United States: 2001." Washington, DC: U.S. Department of Commerce, Economics, and Statistics Administration.

U.S. Census Bureau. 2004a. "Historical Income Tables Income Equality." Table IE-1, IE-2, and IE-6. Washington, DC: Department of Commerce. Accessed at www.census.gov/hhes/income/histinc/ieq.html on March 7, 2005.

U.S. Census Bureau. 2004b. "Historical Income Tables—People." Table P-38. Washington, DC: Department of Commerce. Accessed at www. census.gov/hhes/income/histinc/P38.html on April 6, 2005.

U.S. Department of Labor. 2004. "Union Members in 2003." Technical Information. News Release, January 21. USDL 4–53. Accessed at www.bls.gov/news.release/union2nr0.html.

van Kirk, Sylvia. 1991. "The Role of Native Women in the Fur Trade Society of Western Canada, 1670–1830." In *Rethinking Canada: The Promise of Women's History* 2nd ed. Ed. Veronica Strong-Boag and Anita Clair Fellman. Toronto: Copp Clark Pitman. 73–80.

Vickers, Jill, Pauline Rankin, and Christine Appelle. 1993. *Politics As If Women Mattered: A Political Analysis of the National Action Committee on the Status of Women.* Toronto: University of Toronto Press,

Vosko, Leah. 2000. *Temporary Work: The Gendered Rise of a Precarious Employment Relationship.* Toronto: University of Toronto Press.

Washington Times. 1998. "Some Insight Into Long-Term Capital." October 1. Accessed at www. freerepublic.com/forum/a3614368c6bb7.htm on January 7, 2005.

Weldon, S. Laurel. 2002. *Protest, Policy, and the Problem of Violence Against Women: A Cross National Comparison.* Pittsburgh, PA: University of Pittsburgh Press.

White, E. Frances. 2001. "Black Feminist Interventions." *Dark Continent of Our Bodies.* Philadelphia: Temple University Press.

Women's Edge Coalition. 2003. "NAFTA and FTAA's Impacts on Mexico's Agricultural Sector." November 18. Accessed at www.womensedge.org on August 18, 2004.

World Bank. 2000. *Advancing Gender Equality: World Bank Action Since Beijing.* Accessed at http://siteresources.worldbank.org/INTGENDER/Resources/fullrpt.pdf on March 3, 2005.

Young, Brigitte. 2001. "Globalization and Gender: A European Perspective." In *Gender, Globalization and Democratization,* ed. Rita Mae Kelly, Jane H. Bayes, Mary E. Hawkesworth, and Brigitte Young. Boulder, CO: Rowman and Littlefield.

Young, Lisa. 2003. "Can Feminists Transform Party Politics? The Canadian Experience." In *Women and Electoral Politics in Canada,* ed. Manon Tremblay and Linda Trimble. Toronto: Oxford. 76–90.

# NOTES ON AUTHORS

**Jane Bayes** is Professor of Political Science and Director of the Institute of Gender, Globalization, and Democracy at California State University, Northridge. She is also the Director of the International Social Science Council's Research Programme on Gender, Globalization, and Democratization (ISSC-GGD). Her teaching and research interests are in the areas of women and politics, political economy, and globalization and gender. She is an author in and editor or co-editor of *Globalization, Gender, and Religion; The Politics of Implementing Women's Rights in Catholic and Muslim Contexts* (Palgrave 2001); *Gender, Globalization and Democratization* (Rowman and Littlefield 2001). *Women and Public Administration: International Perspectives* (Hayworth Press 1991) and *Comparable Worth, Pay Equity and Public Policy* (Greenwood Press 1998). Her other books include *Minority Politics and Ideologies in the United States,* and *Ideologies and Interest Group Politics* (both Chandler and Sharp 1982).

**Patricia Begné** is Professor of Law in the School of Law at the University of Guanajuato in Mexico, where she has taught since 1980. She has also practiced law and serves as a consultant to law firms in the United States. She was a Fulbright Scholar at Pennsylvania State University in Spring 2000, and has been a visiting professor or guest lecturer at several law schools in the United States. Her publications include: *MujereS* (2004); *Women and Law in the State of Guanajuato* (2003); *University Women Facing the 21st Century* (1998); *The Mexican Woman: Her Legal Situation* (1990); and *Guide to Women's Rights* (1987).

**Laura Gonzalez** is a Research Scientist at the School of Social Sciences, University of Texas at Dallas and the Executive Director and Founder of the Oak Cliff Center for Community Studies (www.oakcliffccs. org). She is an expert on Mexican immigration to the United States, author of the Repuesta Campesina a la Revolución Verde en el Bajío (Universidad Iberamerica 1992) as well as other scholarly articles and papers about Mexican migration and editor of *Memorias del Primer Coloquio Internacional sobre Migración Mexicana a Estados Unidos, a book published by the State of Guanajuato in 1996.* In 2002 she was elected Consejera of the Consejo Consultivo del Instituto de los Mexicanos en el Exterior (CCIME) representing Mexicans living in the United States to the government in Mexico, for the period 2003–2005.

**Lois Harder** is Associate Professor of Political Science at the University of Alberta. She has published extensively on the politics of gender in her home province, including a book: *State of Struggle: Feminism and Politics in Alberta.* Other research has included several articles on the use of the Canadian tax system to deliver social policy. Her most recent project focuses on the gendered dimensions of welfare reform initiatives in Canada and the United States. Her teaching interests include Canadian political economy, social policy, feminism, and globalization.

**Mary Hawkesworth** is Professor of Women's and Gender Studies at Rutgers University. Her teaching and research interests include feminist theory, women and politics, contemporary political philosophy, philosophy of science, and social policy. Hawkesworth is the author of *Globalization and Feminist Activism* (Rowman and Littlefield, 2006); *Feminist Inquiry: From Political Conviction to Methodological Innovation* (Rutgers University Press, 2006); *Beyond Oppression: Feminist Theory and Political Strategy* (New York: Continuum Press, 1990); and *Theoretical Issues in Policy Analysis* (Albany: State University of New York Press, 1988); editor of *The Encyclopedia of Government and Politics* (London: Routledge, 1992; 2nd Revised Edition, 2003); and *Feminism and Public Policy* (*Policy Sciences* 27(2–3), 1994); and co-editor of *Gender, Globalization and Democratization* (Rowman and Littlefield, 2001). Her articles have appeared in leading journals including the *American Political Science Review, Political Theory, Signs, Hypatia, Women and Politics, Journal of Women's History, NWSA Journal, International Journal of Women's Studies, and the Women's Studies International Forum.* She has served on the Editorial Boards of *Signs: Journal of Women in Culture and Society, Women and Politics* and the *International Feminist Journal of Politics.* She is serving as the Editor of *Signs: Journal of Women in Culture and Society,* 2005–2010.

**Laura Macdonald** is Professor in the Department of Political Science and the Institute of Political Economy at Carleton University, and the Director of the Centre on North American Politics and Society. She is the author of *Supporting Civil Society: The Political Impact of Non-Governmental Assistance to central America* (Macmillan/St. Martin's 1997). She has published numerous articles in journals and edited collections on such issues as the role of nongovernmental organizations in development, global civil society, citizenship struggles in Latin America, Canadian development assistance and the political impact of the North American Free Trade Agreement (NAFTA) on human rights and democracy in the three member states. Her current research projects concern the impact of civil society in trade discussions in the Americas.

# INDEX

Page numbers in *italics* refer to figures and tables.